Postfoundationalist Themes in the Philosophy of Education

James D. Marshall

# Postfoundationalist Themes in the Philosophy of Education

## Festschrift for James D. Marshall

*Edited by*
**Paul Smeyers and Michael A. Peters**

**Blackwell**
Publishing

BLACKWELL PUBLISHING
350 Main Street, Malden, MA 02148-5020, USA
9600 Garsington Road, Oxford OX4 2DQ, UK
550 Swanston Street, Carlton, Victoria 3053, Australia

First published 2006 by Blackwell Publishing Ltd

*Library of Congress Cataloging-in-Publication Data has been applied for*

ISBN 1-4051-4536-6 (paperback)

A catalogue record for this title is available from the British Library.

Set in 10/13pt Plantin
by Graphicraft Limited, Hong Kong
Printed and bound in the United Kingdom
by TJ International, Padstow, Cornwall

The Publisher's policy is to use permanent paper from mills that operate a sustainable forestry policy, and which has been manufactured from pulp processed using acid-free and elementary chlorine-free practices. Furthermore, the publisher ensures that the text paper and cover board used have met acceptable environmental accreditation standards.

For further information on
Blackwell Publishing, visit our website:
www.blackwellpublishing.com

3/6/06

# Contents

INTRODUCTION

# Festschrift: Essays in honour of James D. Marshall

The concept of the *Festschrift* is well known in the academic world, English as well as German, as a volume of learned essays and other writings contributed by students, colleagues, admirers and old friends noting a special occasion and serving as a tribute to a noted scholar, often on their retirement. The word comes to us from the German as a combination of *Fest* meaning 'festival' and *Schrift* meaning 'writing'. In this case we are pleased to bring together a set of essays in honour of James D. Marshall, a well-known and respected philosopher of education, who has had a considerable impact both through his work and his personality on a range of scholars, many of whom were his students.

In this collection there are tributes to James D. Marshall, the person, in the form of interviews, testimonials, brief biographies by Paulo Ghiraldelli Jr., Michael A. Peters, Kevin Harris, and Colin Lankshear, and, appropriately, a comment by Denis Philips—one of Jim's oldest friends—on his marriage with Lynda Stone, an event that took place August 2005, with Denis officiating. We would like to take the opportunity to wish them a happy, productive and long relationship: Jim is presently writing a great deal on de Beauvoir; we hope that Lynda might contemplate writing something on Sartre! Denis Philips and Kevin Harris, as Australians, were part of the original Philosophy of Education Society of Australasia when it first began, and met Jim at the annual conferences. Colin Lankshear and Michael Peters were colleagues with Jim at the University of Auckland. In addition, Peters was a student of Marshall's completing his Ph.D. on the later Wittgenstein under his supervision.

The second part, titled 'The Scholarly Legacy' contains essays by Tina Besley, Nesta Devine, and F. Ruth Irwin, Bruce Haynes, Felicity Haynes, Bert Lambeir, Cris Mayo, Mark Olssen, Michael Peters, Robert Shaw, Paul Smeyers, Richard Smith and Nick Burbules, Paul Standish and Lynda Stone. (We let Lynda have the last word!) These scholars come from New Zealand, Australia, Belgium, the U.S., and the U.K

Jim has been active in the field of philosophy of education for three decades, both nationally and internationally. He has contributed in many areas of scholarship concerning education. Thus he has proved to be a long standing critic of the public education system of New Zealand which has, throughout its history, been involved in the testing and selection of the young for later professional and technocratic positions in life. The research, he argues, on which the measurement industry was based, was essentially psychological and, also, positivistic. He diagnoses recent reforms as moves towards what Lyotard termed 'performativity', i.e. the subsumption of what had been a very successful state education system to the demands of efficiency and the production of saleable *useful* 'knowledge'. And these are for him clearly signs that the knowledge economy and the knowledge society, along with moves towards globalisation, bear witness to yet another positivistic turn in the universal application of business technologies to all forms of institutions.

His intellectual fathers are surely Wittgenstein and Nietzsche. Starting from an interest in the relevance of the later Wittgenstein for various problems in philosophy of education, he broadened his perspective by including in his reflections particularly the French philosophers, heirs to the thoughts of that other genius. In the many international conferences he attended and where he presented his work, he became known as someone who usually sat quietly and listened to what others had to tell. He turned out not to be the kind of philosopher who abuses the opportunity to raise a question or make a comment, turning it into a lecture of what he thought to be important, but of which others could not see the relevance for the present discussion. When he intervened, he tried to develop further a point the speaker made, or drew attention to some literature that may be worthwhile to study in depth.

We hope that the contributions in this collection can be seen in the same vein.

MICHAEL A. PETERS & PAUL SMEYERS
*University of Glasgow; University of Leuven*

# 1

# Jim Marshall: Foucault and disciplining the self

A. C. (TINA) BESLEY

*University of Glasgow*

I lay the blame almost entirely at Professor James Marshall's door for my beginning to read Michel Foucault. As one of the supervisors for my PhD at the School of Education, University of Auckland, I am indebted to Jim for his support and encouragement, questions, comments and expertise in different areas. Jim's scholarship on Foucault, philosophy and education has been invaluable. He has helped me to clarify my thoughts and to explore certain themes concerning power and knowledge that radically called into question my then profession of school counselling as well as my own practice. It is not entirely correct to say that Jim provided my first brush with Foucault. That occurred in 1989, when I attended a course on narrative therapy at the Durham Centre, Christchurch. This was not only my introduction to Michael White and David Epston's narrative therapy but also to Foucault and to his concepts of the Panoptican and power/knowledge (White & Epston, 1990). However, it was almost ten years later that it started to make sense when Jim encouraged me to read *Discipline and Punish* (Foucault, 1977).

As a counsellor in a large urban secondary school, the next logical step seemed to be to read *Discipline and Punishment in New Zealand Education* (Marshall & Marshall, 1997), a book co-written by Jim and his son Dominique. This monograph visits the literature that had mostly appeared in journals, newspapers and books to provide a Foucauldian genealogy of approaches that New Zealand has adopted to both punishment and discipline. For New Zealand 'discipline' had long been almost synonymous with 'corporal punishment'—a physical assault on the body of the person—the abolition of which had engendered a hugely emotive and long-running debate especially during the 1970s. Although many co-educational schools had informally dropped the practice some years prior, corporal punishment was only officially outlawed from schools with the Education Act, 1989.

Marshall and Marshall point out that the literature on the effects of corporal punishment is seldom empirical, instead it is primarily anecdotal, and is a 'moral, almost religious, literature' (Marshall & Marshall, 1997, p. 10). They contend that it is only by considering the wider discourse about young people, behaviour, human nature, psychology, education and sociology that the legitimation of New Zealand's schooling practices can be found. Their working hypothesis looks 'towards the daily practices of discipline and punishment which the young experience' (Marshall &

Marshall, 1997, p. 11) to ascertain how these might be incompatible with legal and philosophical theories. In doing so they take a Foucauldian stance to examine 'the practices of punishment, of who gets punished, the form that it takes and how much they receive' to arrive at an understanding of 'the meaning and justification of punishment' (Marshall & Marshall, 1997, pp. 11–12).

From a theoretical point of view, Jim had explored Foucault's work in earlier papers (Marshall, 1987, 1989, 1990, 1995, 1996), but the final chapter of the monograph provides a brief overview and discussion of several Foucauldian notions, viz. power/knowledge, technologies of domination, technologies of the self, governmentality (Foucault's neologism for 'governmental rationality'). By harnessing the Foucauldian notions of disciplinary punishment taking both negative and positive forms whereby individuals become constituted to lead useful, practical and relatively docile lives, plus governmentality as a form of governing the self and others, it was argued that 'punishment has been used in New Zealand to shape up the young, even if it was unclear as to the kind of individual deemed desirable, and there was confusion over the most efficacious processes' (Marshall & Marshall, 1997, p. 129). The chapter explores what this power is and how it is exercised. It points out that in seeming to object to the intrusion of the state into peoples' lives Foucault appears to take a neoliberal stance. This intrusion is not so much what Foucault objects to, but to the underlying assumptions that have lead to certain procedures whereby 'because they have been constituted to think that they are free and autonomous, and that this very constitution has permitted the advance of power/knowledge and the subjugation of people as subjects to lead useful, docile and practical lives' (Marshall & Marshall, 1997, p. 137). It is the notion of autonomy that was central to Jim's earlier text, *Michel Foucault: Personal Autonomy and Education* (Marshall, 1996) that is discussed later.

In relation to punishment and governmentality in New Zealand, a Foucauldian analysis provides an account that is 'more fruitful and interesting, but which is neither so hopeful, nor as deterministic or as debilitating' as traditional liberal humanistic and Marxist inspired accounts (Marshall & Marshall, 1997, p. 138). It indicates that governmentality was operating in the nineteenth century when education was seen as a means of changing class and social differences in the production of good citizens through the development of physical, intellectual and moral capabilities. This was not just for the good of the individual, but also for the society as a whole in ways that were embedded in the human sciences. Capitalising on, rather than wasting human potential became evident in the late nineteenth century when dealing with delinquents who were seen to not only need improvement and/or control, but who could be included and made useful instead of being excluded from society. This was achieved through governmentality, through the human sciences, through learning more about the young person and individual differences and then applying selected interventions with the aim of cure, improvement or change. Rather than considering disciplinary punishment in terms of a simple binary of 'liberal humanists' versus 'bashers and floggers' that has seen the 'humane carers (or child savers)' victorious in state schools, it can be seen from a Foucauldian viewpoint as 'how to constitute a particular kind of individual'

(Marshall & Marshall, 1997, p. 139). Corporal punishment did not constitute the sort of individual that the state in the late twentieth century deemed appropriate because corporal punishment tended to exclude rather than include. Yet the replacement of corporal punishment by the 'the caring alternatives need to be interpreted as examples of strong disciplinary punishment and from Foucault's position as possessing strong manipulative potential' (Marshall & Marshall, 1997, p. 139).

It was within the realm of one of the caring alternatives that of guidance counselling— my former job and the main object of my thesis—and in applying Foucauldian notions to the profession that some of my subsequent work including a book is located (Besley, 2002a, 2002b, 2002c, 2002d). Without deliberately setting out to do so, to a certain extent this work follows on from Jim's. 'Disciplinary punishment and the alternatives—rational persuasion, counselling and a caring inclusive approach— run together (or hunt together) through the notion of governmentality' (Marshall & Marshall, 1997, p. 140). I have become particularly interested in understanding the philosophical thought that underpins the assumptions made in counselling and in how the major discourses of psychology and sociology construct notions of adolescence/youth (Besley, 2002a). In turn this has led me to examine how youth constitute themselves and negotiate living in the globalised postmodern era (Besley, 2003).

In *Individualism and Community: Education and Social Policy in the Postmodern Condition*, a book co-written with Michael Peters, the focus is also on the New Zealand context, in this instance, combining shared interests in politics, policy and philosophy (Peters & Marshall, 1996). This book pulls together and extends work that Michael and Jim had collaborated on throughout the 1980s and 1990s. It analyses political philosophy and social and educational policy as New Zealand changed from a welfare state, considered to be the social laboratory of the western world since the 1930s, to a neoliberal state—termed 'the New Zealand experiment' by Jane Kelsey—in the mid 1980s and which has persisted largely unchanged till today (Kelsey, 1995). Foucauldian understandings about power, bio-power, govern- mentality, autonomy and subjectivity are brought to bear in their analysis as they argue that:

> the relation between the individual and the community is of fundamental importance to social policy, not only as a basic philosophical assumption, but also in terms of its practical effects in the formulation, design and imple- mentation of programmes and policies. (Peters & Marshall, 1996, p. 2)

Starting from analysing the failure of social policy from 1984–1994, the book is subdivided into four sections that move from introducing the crisis in the welfare state under postmodernity, analysing communitarian approaches, neoliberal indi- vidualism, methodological responses and finally suggesting the postmodern 'way out' of the crisis. These 'solutions' include postmodernism's critique of reason and new social movements, liberalism, education and the critique of individualism, edu- cation and the politics of difference. The book concludes by pointing to the need for developing a critical social policy, which suggests eight theoretical components (see Peters & Marshall, 1996, pp. 208–211). What could be added to this list is a phenomenology of the body, the politics of identity, the philosophy of technology and constructions of youth, since so much of educational policy is directed at them. By demonstrating how education policy is intimately linked with state economic policy, the book emphasises that understanding the politico-economic context is vital for understanding and critiquing education policy.

Unlike Jim's other New Zealand oriented text, this book has become used extensively as a set text for courses on educational policy and philosophy, especially at post-graduate level. However after recently using this as a central text when co-teaching with Jim and Michael at a level 3 undergraduate course in educational policy and philosophy, it became apparent that their sophisticated analysis and the level of philosophical understandings required make the book rather too hard for undergraduates if they have no philosophical background. In light of this we are contemplating re-writing and up-dating the book.

Jim's work in the 1997 monograph builds on his major work on Foucault, *Michel Foucault: Personal Autonomy and Education* (Marshall, 1996). The introduction and first chapter of this work provide an overview that contextualises the work of Foucault by outlining something of who he was, despite his many masks, and of the 'intellectual climate(s) in France post World war II, and the ideas, works and thinkers against which, and against whom, he defined and elaborated his thought' (Marshall, 1996, p. 1). In this work that is of, about and for education—a field that had paid scant attention to Foucault until the mid-late 1990s—not only does Jim provide a clear and useful summary of the context in which Foucault was situated, but also he explores some key assumptions in liberal education and philosophy of education through a Foucauldian lens. Jim makes it clear that *the* aim of liberal education especially as per John Dewey & R. S. Peters is personal autonomy, so the central notions the book pursues are personal autonomy and power. In the process Jim provides both explanation and critique of many Foucauldian notions, viz. power/knowledge, punishment, technologies of domination, technologies of the self and governmentality.

Furthermore re-visiting liberal education is timely because of the attacks on it, and especially on 'autonomy' from neoliberal 'reforms' that began in many western capitalist democracies in the 1980s. Jim argues that personal autonomy has been replaced by the notion of the 'autonomous chooser ... whose choices have been structured through the manipulation of needs and interests by what I call bio-power' and that freedom *from* is the prime neoliberal emphasis (Marshall, 1996, p. 213). However, he also critiques the way liberal education's pursuit of personal autonomy and development of the mind masks the way governmentality, authority and power relations operate. What is rather surprising is that he does not discuss in any great extent the normalisation process that Foucault described in *Discipline and Punish* (1977) and the enormous effect this has in schools, in the rise of the 'psy' sciences and in constituting the self (Dreyfus, 2002; Foucault, 1977, 1988; Rose, 1989, 1998c). In fact one limitation of this book is that like Foucault himself, who states that he may have concentrated 'too much on the technology of domination and power', this book focuses perhaps rather too much on notions of disciplinarity and does not move sufficiently on to Foucault's later works (Foucault, 1988b, p. 19).

It engages more with *Discipline and Punish* than with Foucault's later writing and interviews, apart from those on the *Technologies of the Self*. In addressing the liberal notion of autonomy, Jim tends to look more at other writers in philosophy of education perhaps more than Foucault himself.

For Foucault both 'technologies of domination' and 'technologies of the self' produce effects that constitute the self. They define the individual and control their conduct (Marshall, 1996). These technologies are harnessed 'to make the individual a significant element for the state' through the exercise of a form of power—governmentality—in becoming useful, docile, practical citizens (Foucault, 1977, 1988c, 1991). Technologies of power, 'determine the conduct of individuals and submit them to certain ends or domination, an objectivizing of the subject' (Foucault, 1988b, p. 18). Foucault's earlier work emphasised the application of such technologies of domination through the political subjugation of 'docile bodies' in the grip of disciplinary powers and the way the self is produced by processes of objectification, classification and normalization in the human sciences (Foucault, 1977). Foucault himself defended the 'determinist' emphasis in *Discipline and Punish*, admitting that not enough was said about agency, so he re-defined power to include agency (see Rabinow, 1997). Technologies of the self, are ways the various 'operations on their own bodies and souls, thoughts, conduct, and way of being', that people make either by themselves or with the help of others, in order to transform themselves to reach a 'state of happiness, purity, wisdom, perfection, or immortality' (Foucault, 1988b, p. 18).

Governmentality emerges with the development of liberalism and is directed through the notion of policing, administration and the governance of individuals (Foucault, 1979, 1991). For Foucault governmentality means the complex of calculations, programs, policies, strategies, reflections and tactics that shape the conduct of individuals, 'the conduct of conduct' for acting upon the actions of others in order to achieve certain ends. Those ends are 'not just to control, subdue, discipline, normalize, or reform them, but also to make them more intelligent, wise, happy, virtuous, healthy, productive, docile, enterprising, fulfilled, self-esteeming, empowered, or whatever' (Rose, 1998, p. 12). Governmentality is not simply about control in its negative sense but also in its positive sense, in its contribution to the security of society. Foucault poses questions about the *how* of government—'how to govern oneself, how to be governed, how to govern others, by whom the people will accept being governed, how to become the best possible governor' (Foucault, 1991, p. 87). Self-government is connected with morality; governing the family is related to economy and ruling the state to politics. These aspects of governmentality and how they apply in education are not pursued in Jim's 1996 book.

Jim could perhaps be considered something of a Francophile, having spent sabbatical leave in France, the most recent in 2001 with his late wife Bridget—a steadying, supportive, loyal friend and wonderful hostess—but who was suffering dreadfully from a terminal heart condition at the time. Armed with a dictionary, Jim's ability to read and understand French allowed him to access texts at the Bibliothèque Nationale de France in Paris. His interests extend to not only Foucault, whose archives he researched in Paris at the Bibliothèque Saulchoir (these are now housed at Institut Mémoires de l'Edition Contemporaine, IMEC) but also to Simone de Beauvoir, Albert Camus and Henri Bergson all of whom he researched at the Bibliothèque Nationale. As those who know Jim personally will attest, his interest of course did not end with the philosophical but extended to French cuisine and red wine. The latter has at times been something of a curse that Jim has battled with as he has faced his personal demons over the years. Nevertheless as one of my PhD supervisors who has become a personal friend, I can vouch that Jim has a wonderful analytical mind and was instrumental in helping me to move further into philosophy of education, and to study Foucault. To end, I wish Jim all the very best for a well-deserved, long and happy retirement—those trout better beware, there are no more excuses—he has lots of time for fishing now!

# References

Besley, T. (2002a) *Counseling Youth: Foucault, Power and the Ethics of Subjectivity* (Westpoint, CT, & London, Praeger).

Besley, A. C. (Tina) (2002b) Fess Up or Else! Truth-telling, confession and care of the self in secondary schools, in: T., Kvernbekk & B. Nordtug (eds), *The Many Faces of Philosophy of Education: Traditions, Problems and Challenges*, Conference Proceedings, International Network of Philosophers of Education, 8th Biennial Conference, University of Oslo, Norway, 2002, pp. 26–36.

Besley, A. C. (Tina). (2002c) Foucault and the Turn to Narrative Therapy, *British Journal of Guidance & Counselling*, 30:2, pp. 125–143.

Besley, A. C. (Tina). (2002d) Social Education and Mental Hygiene: Foucault, discipline, technologies and the moral constitution of youth, *Educational Philosophy and Theory*, 34:4, pp. 419–434.

Besley, T. (2003) *Globalisation and Hybridisation: Youth in the Postmodern Condition.* Paper presented at Between Empires: Communication, Globalisation and Identity Conference, Auckland University of Technology, Auckland, New Zealand.

Dreyfus, H. (2002) *Heidegger and Foucault on the Subject, Agency and Practices*, Regents of University of California, Berkeley. accessed October 2002: <http://socrates.berkeley.edu/~hdreyfus/html/paper_heidandfoucault.html>

Foucault, M. (1977) *Discipline and Punish: The Birth of the Prison* (London, Penguin).

Foucault, M. (1988a) Truth, Power, Self: an interview with Michel Foucault, in: L. H. Martin, H. Gutman, & P. H. Hutton (eds) *Technologies of the Self: A seminar with Michel Foucault* (Amherst, University of Massachusetts Press) pp. 9–15.

Foucault, M. (1988b) Technologies of the Self, in: L. H. Martin, H. Gutman, & P. H. Hutton (eds) *Technologies of the Self: A seminar with Michel Foucault* (Amherst, University of Massachusetts Press) pp. 16–49.

Foucault, M. (1988c) The Political Technology of Individuals, in: L. H. Martin, H. Gutman, & P. H. Hutton (eds) *Technologies of the Self: A seminar with Michel Foucault* (Amherst, University of Massachusetts Press) pp. 145–162.

Foucault, M. (1997) The Ethics of the Concern for Self as a Practice of Freedom, trans. Robert Hurley and others, in: P. Rabinow (ed.) *Michel Foucault: Ethics, Subjectivity and Truth, The Essential Works of Michel Foucault 1954–1984*, Vol. 1 (London, The Penguin Press) pp. 281–301.

Kelsey, J. (1995) *The New Zealand Experiment: A world model for structural adjustment?* (Auckland, Auckland University Press, in assoc. with Bridget Williams Books).

Marshall, J. D. (1987) An Anti-foundational Approach to Authority and Discipline, *Discourse: the Australian Journal of Education*, 7:2.

Marshall, J. D. (1989) The Incompatibility of Punishment and Moral Education: a reply to Peter Hobson, *Journal of Moral Education*, 18:2.

Marshall, J. D. (1990) Asking Philosophical Questions about Education: Foucault on punishment, *Educational Philosophy and Theory*, 22:2.

Marshall, J. D. (1995) Wittgenstein and Foucault: Resolving philosophical puzzles, in P. Smeyers and J. D. Marshall (eds), *Philosophy and Education: Accepting Wittgenstein's Challenge* (Dordrecht, Kluwer).

Marshall, J. D. (1996) *Michel Foucault: Personal autonomy and education* (Dordrecht; Boston, Kluwer Academic Publishers).

Marshall, J. D. (1997) Michel Foucault: Problematising the individual and constituting 'the self', *Educational Philosophy and Theory*, 29:1, pp. 20–31. Special issue: Education and the constitution of self, M. Peters, J. Marshall & P. Fitzsimons (eds).

Marshall, J. D. & Marshall, D. (1997) *Discipline and Punishment in New Zealand Education* (Palmerston North, Dunmore Press).

Peters, M. A. & Marshall, J. D. (1996) *Individualism and Community: Education and social policy in the postmodern condition* (London, Falmer Press).

Rabinow, P. (1997) Afterword, in: P. Rabinow (ed.) trans. Robert Hurley and others, *Michel Foucault: Ethics, subjectivity and truth, the essential works of Michel Foucault 1954–1984*, Vol. 1 (London, The Penguin Press).

Rose, N. S. (1989) *Governing The Soul: The shaping of the private self* (London, Routledge).

Rose, N. S. (1998) *Inventing Our Selves: Psychology, power, and personhood* (Cambridge. Cambridge University Press).

White, M. & Epston, D. (1990) *Narrative Means to Therapeutic Ends* (New York, W.W. Norton).

## 2
# Autonomy, Agency and Education: He tangata, he tangata, he tangata

NESTA DEVINE & RUTH IRWIN

*University of Waikato; University of Glasgow*

The authors of this paper are equally responsible, and the alphabetic order of names should not be interpreted as a sign of seniority or greater contribution in the writing.

## He tangata, he tangata, he tangata

The Maori quotation, part of a *whakatoke*, with which we title this essay reflects the wonderfully confused society in which James Marshall and we ourselves have lived. The full proverb asks what is important? And the answer is: 'he tangata, he tangata, he tangata'. This answer is frequently used by liberals and neoliberals in Aotearoa New Zealand to mean 'a person, the individual, the disaggregated mass of individuals which are to be opposed to notions of collective, state, and '*raison d'état*', and to imply the autonomy of that person as an answer to all political and philosophical questions about the relation of government to persons, or indeed of government to businesses, which seem to have become surreptitiously persons. But the culture in which 'he tangata' has its place is a collective, not an individualistic one, and the phrase is more accurately translated 'the people, the people, the people'. So, in this very phrase we have the substance of this essay: when is a person a people?

## Unpacking Autonomy

The nature of the subject really opened up for debate in the west when Augustine wrote his *Confessions*. Since then, a self-reflective, autonomous, moral soul has dominated the western tradition's conceptualisation of individuals, and coloured our interaction with society. However the conceptual categories of the subject, the soul, and the individual, have undergone serious debate since Nietzsche announced that 'god is dead' and put forward, in the *Genealogy of Morals* a more empirical and phenomenological theory of subjectivity. In this paper we wish to examine the notions of autonomy and regulation and the ways these twin concepts have contributed to an increasingly confined means for human beings to exist with each other and in relation to the environment. Liberalism has been complicit, almost despite itself, in accentuating the individuality necessary for the governmentality of a modern population. That is, the discourse of personal autonomy, has legitimised even as it rejects, the categorisation and surveillance, the internalisation of norms, and the individualised vehicle for power relations that maintains the modern global 'machine'.

But it is worth noting here that our aims have not been to limit the notion of the individual or the human subject to something less than the liberal tradition would recognize, but to put those claims of genuine decision-making and agency onto a firmer footing: if the individual or the human subject is not—cannot be— both autonomous and free, then it is not to the advantage of human freedom or autonomy to claim that s/he is so by definition. The work of freedom can be better pursued by an honest appraisal of the degree to which it is possible for freedom of thought and action to happen than by a programmatic claim to a freedom which must be exercised in certain ways—in other words which is not free—or to an autonomy which is in fact the application of heteronomy.

Part of James Marshall's work which we have found interesting and productive is the work he has done on the nature of the individual and education. This question is of immediate importance to teachers, since the nature of their work involves constant interaction with individuals, and the nature of the pedagogy they use depends in large part on how they think these individuals are constructed. The question is of wider importance in the broader field of education since the purpose and nature of education depend to a large extent on what kind of person or individual we think we are and we are engaged with. That very notion 'what kind of person' in itself suggests an essential nature to personness, to the teacher and the pupil and hence to the relations between them which underlies much of the work done in educational theory and educational psychology during the twentieth century at least.

In the field of education we live and work in a context which is overwhelmingly dominated by liberal theories in the politics of pedagogy. This is not just a phenomenon without history: it is an instance of 'governmentality'. That is, governmentality is part of the assemblage of government. The notion of the free individual is essential to the functioning of liberal government and the idea is so pervasive that it has an important presence in education, despite the simultaneous popularity of mechanistic behaviourist theories.

The notion of the free and autonomous individual is also found specifically promulgated or examined in the education literature. Sometimes it is as an aim of education, sometimes it is as an *a priori* of education; assuming free will is the nature of the individual whom we teach. Not many contemporary philosophers have been prepared to defend the latter view, preferring in general the notion that the student- individual is as yet uncompleted and therefore not completely auto- nomous (e.g. R. S. Peters, 1983, p. 249), and the role of education is to develop the rationality which will achieve that autonomy. Yet paradoxically, Foucault describes the individual whom we encourage towards rational freedom through education is as deeply governed as s/he is free,

> The man described for us, whom we are invited to free, is already in himself the effect of a subjection much more profound than himself. A

'soul' inhabits him and brings him to existence, which is itself a factor in the mastery that power exercises over the body. The soul is the effect and instrument of a political anatomy; the soul is the prison of the body. (Foucault, 1977, p. 30)

Those writers (e.g. Glaser, 1992) who insist on 'choice' however, when it is choice on the part of the student, are promoting the idea that the student is always already an autonomous, rational being.

There are problems for the teacher in both accounts, that of the pre-rational student and the rational, autonomous, choice-making student. If the student is completely autonomous, there is little for a teacher to do except point to the books, demonstrate, and assess. This seems to be the conception that lies behind the New Zealand curriculum, and its subsequent regulatory mode which insists on the 'delivery' rather than the teaching of the curriculum. No pedagogic effort is required: just handing knowledge and skills over to a pre-prepared recipient. On the other hand, if the student is not yet autonomous, in the sense of being not yet rational, then the teacher has to inculcate rationality by treating the student as irrational, a difficult task indeed.

## Marshall and Lankshear

Jim Marshall and Colin Lankshear cleared the ground by a thorough examination of the concepts of autonomy and freedom. Both challenge the customary usage of the notion of autonomy, through looking at its historical and philosophical derivatives. Marshall doubts the logical possibility of autonomy, both historically and in contemporary society. Both start with the Greek view, unpacking the term into its component parts. Lankshear also investigates what actually occurs to people who, by accident and circumstance, are outside any human society and utterly autonomous and free.

## Marshall's Critique of Autonomy

Autonomy has conventionally implied freedom from authority. It is also a rational self-control or mastery of the self that prevents the subject becoming a 'slave' to their own passions (Marshall, 1996, p. 83). Marshall takes the problems of autonomy right back to the very concept, the construction of the word. In Greek 'auto' he argues means self, but 'nomos' means knowledge, law, rule, or standards and since knowledge and standards are socially constructed, nomos can never be the totally individualistic, solitary creation of one individual. That self can only exist in the context of the knowledge of its own society, and can therefore never be autonomous—or indeed free, since it will always reflect the bounds and conventions of its own history. This philological argument confirms an important critique that Marshall directs against common misconceptions in the social sciences and education; that the individual is ontologically separate, and has separate interests from society. It is not a question of agency versus structure, but the way they integrate and mutually inform one another.

## Lankshear's Autonomy

Lankshear argues that the Greek view of the free person was fourfold: First, the democratic character, who was distinguished by its degree of versatility and spontaneity (p. 80) but according to Plato lacked '*inner* order or restraint, as opposed to restraint or order imposed from without, e.g., by laws, sanctions etc.' (footnote p. 81); second, the free person who remains true to herself, that is, (in the context of Greek thought), a free person remains true to herself in the face of the control of her fate by the Gods or other immutable forces. (p. 82); third a person possessing characteristics considered appropriate for an individual of free legal status, that is, one who is the recipient of a 'liberal' education in the sense of an education fit for one who is free—*liber* in Latin; and finally, one who is free in virtue of her reason being the controlling influence in her life. This last definition, according to Lankshear, is the one which allows of a view of education as liberating, as setting a person free in the sense of promoting the escape from unreason. A person cares for her soul, he says (p. 86) through pursuit of truth: knowledge of good or virtue, and for Socrates as for Plato pursuit of knowledge of Good is exclusively a rational or intellectual affair. Reason alone can reveal knowledge of true virtue. ... In this pursuit, we preserve our real self, and hence our actions, purposes, and intentions, from contamination by passions, desires, urges and impulses. By failing to care for the soul one runs the risk that it may be overwhelmed by one's 'lower' self (Lankshear p. 86).

Lankshear argues that Kant takes up this idea, that freedom is intimately associated with rationality, since if one were not free to follow one's rational conclusions in action, one would not bother to do the thinking. External determination would imply 'cognitive suicide'(Lankshear, 1982, p. 92). But the rational person is not free to do as she likes, since that would be irrational: her conduct will follow universal moral and logical principles. But these will be prescribed to herself. In this way Kant (along with Rousseau) attempts to over-ride the bounds and fallibilities of contemporary norms and mores with an individuated nomos that derives from a universal rationality. Lankshear explains that she:

> acts or judges in accordance with a law (nomos) which she prescribes to herself (autos). It is her own self, identified with her reason, which constitutes the source of the action or belief which she arrives at by the exercise of pure reason—since it provides the sole grounds upon which her action or belief is determined. (Lankshear, p. 95)

The autonomous person, on this account, may refuse to do what is expedient, customary or regulatory, on the grounds that her logic leads her to an understanding of a universal law, moral in nature, which suggests that she should do otherwise. Lankshear goes on to discuss the contemporary educational renditions of 'autonomy'. In educational literature, he observes, it is possible to talk about the 'autonomy' of two year-olds, or to reserve autonomy as the goal towards which we educate adolescents, or, as Kohlberg does, to regard 'autonomy' in a moral sense as the ultimate condition of adulthood—the 'stage of universal ethical principle orientation' (Lankshear, p. 102).

However, Lankshear summons various writers (Piaget, Wittgenstein, Benn, Barrow) to argue that rationality is heteronomous to the self: that in a sense the person who is rational subjects their 'real' self to the government of a rationality which is outside of themselves, and is in fact part of the structure of laws, reasons etc. which are formed in a social context. It is:

> a precondition of traditional thought and action that one possess not only a set of criteria on the basis of which to make judgments, but also a conceptual scheme with which to grasp issues, alternatives, and the need for decision or judgment in the first place ... Does this not mean that *anyone's* rational nomos is inevitably derived from others, not only in the sense that she has to be initiated into an awareness of rational criteria, but more fundamentally, that her very appreciation of options and issues, perception of facts, and interpretation of data, are all conditioned by a conceptual framework which has been imposed on her by other people? (Lankshear, p. 107)

We have seen that the rational nomos is not sourced from the self, which would be the most authentic definition of autonomy. From the position that the nomos is socially produced arises the question of how it affects the autos. Lankshear postulates the autos as 'some organising, integrating factor which regulates, governs, or determines what she believes, prefers, decides upon and does'(Lankshear, p. 99).

The myth of the autonomous self is not put forward as free from the laws and rules of its society. As far as the liberal mythology goes, those who are totally outside the rule of social rules are in a condition of anomie or individualised anarchy. They are alienated, not autonomous. Moreover, autonomous persons can be distinguished from heteronomic persons in a way which valorizes autonomy over heteronomy. A heteronomic person follows laws defined by others, so the person merely obeys, without deciding to integrate, hierarchize or reflect upon the rules imposed from outside the self. It is the level and process of internalisation and regulations of social mores that differentiates the heteronomous from the autonomous person. In this sense, because the autonomous person has not simply accepted, but has in some sense internalised, adopted, become conscious, there is a possibility of escape from nomos, or at least from a particular reading of nomos.

Both Lankshear and Marshall draw attention to the emergence of self-legislation from normalised societal codes of practice. These two positions amount to a grand attack on the liberal notion of the free individual but they do not, as yet, give us a great deal to replace them.

Rationality itself has been divided into personal or subjective, and universal or objective. Personal self-interest can be defined as perfectly rational, a concept utilised by the 'realism' of neoliberals. Kant, on the other hand, advocates that universal principles should be adhered to by everyone, and that moral actions are decided in each particular situation autonomously. This rests upon the humanist assumption that the 'real self' is transcendent, and will over-ride immediate self-interest.

Kant introduced morality in connection with Reason as a self-governing principle. This is 'mature' or objective reason, which does not focus on self-interest, but on the interests of society. Like Rousseau, he was aiming at connecting the individual's will to societies'.

R. S. Peters (and others) use the Kantian notion that the subject is *not yet* mature, and that therefore the teacher is at liberty to treat the student as not yet rational. The recognition that nomos is contextualised in the norms and rhythms of society repositions maturity and learning as never finalised, complete, or universal. Rationality is an ongoing process as the autos integrates and rationalises the myriad ideas, events, contacts and phenomena they come across. There is no longer a patronising position of finalised rational authority for the teacher to hold. However the teacher is still as an authoritative contributor of knowledge and regulator of institutional and societal norms and regulations.

To treat students as already rational and autonomous, as Lankshear seems to suggest, is a very productive form of pedagogy perhaps because the students themselves find it so surprising. But the nature of schools and curriculum tend to make the effort self-defeating. Choices have to be offered within the context of prior (official) decisions and so may tend to triviality. However in the context of problems in which there are already highly articulated, (and genuine), conflicts between pressures present in students' own lives, there is a real opportunity to exercise a pedagogy based on respect for student autonomy. But it would be a mistake to regard that autonomy as extending too far: it is not an infinite but a bounded sense of being able to make choices only within a limited range of possibilities.

There are many student desires to which it might be difficult to accord the status of rationality. Rationalised 'choices' in the classroom tend to be trivial, (e.g. 'shall we do "Black Civil Rights", or "New Zealand Race Relations" first?') and need not be accorded the weight lent it by (neo)liberalism.

Marshall and Lankshear then, pulled apart the concept of 'autonomy', and found it untenable, as the self is always contaminated with the rules or principles that structure society and a personality separated and autonomous from the community is not meaningful in any real sense.

Hence the 'liberal' claim that personal autonomy is the aim of education is brought into jeopardy. Yet Marshall is not at all interested in substituting for the liberal self a totally deterministic self which can only exist as an automaton. This is the danger, not the promise. In developing understanding of effective and well-grounded pedagogic practice, it is necessary to find some other theoretic position which allows for choice, but does not impose either the whole overblown notion of already always existing individual freedom and rationality, or the notion of an immature rationality which can be developed by imposition.

## Neoliberal Individual

The critique of autonomy is extremely pertinent to the prevailing educational policies and pedagogic assumptions circulating in most nations since the 1970s and 80s. These ideas, under the broad heading 'neoliberalism' rely heavily on a version of the autonomous rational individual but the depth of that commitment to autonomy is mirrored by the depth of neoliberal commitment to the constraints of regulation and surveillance. The self of neo-classical economic theory, pervasive in the public choice and market literature depends on a notion of *homo economicus,* sometimes known as the rational utility maximizer,—always male, always self interested, always rational, if only in its ability to place the ranking of its desires in a cardinal order. This form of individual does not exist as an aim of education—or of anything else—but as a function of the market: it is only by the exercise of choice by this rational cipher that the market performs its catallactic role of perpetual social evolution both in its own historical position as the means of exchange and in a proposed political position as a model for human political conduct.

The individual of human capital theory has a slightly different role. In human capital theory it is the economy, rather than the market which has become the trope for society in general, and the individual is no longer a decision maker but a resource. Sometimes the resource of the individual is employed in its own interest, but is more often regarded, in Heidegger's term, as a standing reserve, a reserve of potentiality for the needs of 'the economy'. The chooser of human capital theory has to make vocational choices which fit in with a highly determined economistic prediction of the 'needs' of the economy. In this form of governmentality the account of the self is initially based on self interest (investment in the self for, presumably, deferred dividends) but is actually about a form of government interest in the self as resource for, equally deferred, dividends to the 'economy'. Neither of these forms of the self, in either public choice or human capital, has anything to do with any concept of *public* interest, since both depend upon a denial of the existence of any entity of a collective nature which might be called a public.

Marshall developed the notion of 'busno-power' (Marshall, 1994) to encapsulate the kind of thinking which lies behind these forms of the individual and the society into which they are interpolated. Busno-power is based on Foucault's notion of 'biopower', the form of governmentality which sought to control the bodies and procreativity of persons in the interests of a particular form and time of government, although busno-power has some significant differences:

> By busno-power we mean a form of power directed at individuals to turn
> them into autonomous choosers and consumers. (Marshall, 1994)

The focus is on the extraordinary sharing of vision and purpose between government and business in the late twentieth century:

> the exercise of busno-power there can be seen a merging of the economic,
> the social and the activity of Government. (Peters & Marshall, 1997)

The 'autonomous chooser' is the manifestation of busno-power in its human form. And of course there is an irony in the term because the autonomous chooser is not autonomous: s/he has to choose, cannot choose not to choose, because the whole market edifice would collapse if the choices were not made, or were made in irrational ways, or rather if the choices were made in accordance with a rationality which was not that of the market. Hence the compulsion which Peters and Marshall

(1997) detect in the role of the autonomous chooser: where liberty depends on the market, and the market depends on individual choices then refusal to choose is a refusal of liberty—and when the market is conceptually expanded to cover all forms of social institution including government then such a refusal amounts to treason. Yet behind both forms of neoliberal individual, that of public choice and that of human capital theory, lies a Kantian idea that rationality will lead to a form of universal moral value that will ultimately serve the good of the whole. Kant advocates that universal principles should be adhered to by everyone, and that moral actions are decided in each particular situation autonomously. This rests upon the humanist assumption that the 'real self' is transcendent, and will over-ride immediate self-interest. Kant introduces morality in connection with Reason as a self-governing principle. This is 'mature' or objective reason, which does not focus on self-interest, but on the interests of society. Like Rousseau he was aiming at connecting the individual's will to the will of society, and at least in terms of their writing, this remains the intent of the neoliberals: it is through the market in their opinion that the individual's *will*, in the material form of individual's choices or purchases will link together with the choices of others to create either the perfect market, or in the utopia of Perfect Unanimity, the ultimate form of governmentality (see for instance Hayek, 1988, or Buchanan & Tullock, 1968). If one takes Kant or even later enlightenment writers from a neoliberal point of view, the autonomous individual acting rationally acts in a way which is in accordance with universal laws.

But to Foucault, following Nietszche, universal law, as a moral code, masks (and marks) political interests. We are back into the limitations of a particular code of being, the code of conduct for a certain time and place, that is, governmentality. The relationship between rationality/rationalization and excesses of political power is evident. We should not need to wait for the bureaucracy of concentration camps, the gulag, prisons, or the revolutionary Terror to recognize the existence of such relationships. Nor should we wait for the exhaustion of the earth's resources. While neoliberal theory remains indifferent to the technological enframing that orders the 'choices' available, in terms of exploiting or storing every aspect of the earth as a commodity, a transaction, resource, an opportunity for consumption, the self that is constituted as an autonomous individual ends up suffocated rather than free.

## Escape from Nomos

Michel Foucault combines these issues of autonomy and heteronomy as he attempts a description, an analysis, of the cling-wrap impermeablity of the social order, and the drive to find some kind of escape, some kind of possibility for thinking outside the confines of existing thought. The first concept is that of governmentality, and the second that of 'technologies of the self'. 'Governmentality', as a concept is influenced by Althusser, Heidegger and Kant. 'Technologies of the self' has genealogical roots in early Greek thinking, through to romantic and late modern ideas about creating personhood.

Foucault's concept of governmentality owes much to Louis Althusser's use of 'ideology' as the pervasive nature of the social and political assumptions in which we are reared and have our existence, Heidegger's notion of 'enframing', and Kant's concept of universal laws. 'Governmentality' postulates an:

> ensemble formed by the institutions, procedures, analyses and reflections, the calculations and tactics that allow the exercise of this very specific albeit complex form of power, which has as its target population, as its principal form of knowledge political economy, and as its essential technical means apparatuses of security. (Foucault, 1991, p. 102)

Althusser, a mentor of Foucault, envisaged that individuals could be hauled into distinct forms of existence within ideological constraints by 'interpellation' and that institutions such as schools exist precisely to do this.

The concept of governmentality also owes a conceptual debt to Heidegger's *Gestell*; the technological enframing of every thing and every object into the governing paradigm of consumable 'standing reserve'. Technical enframing co-opts all aspects of being into a rationale of calculus and measurement, including the rational autonomous individual utility maximiser of neoliberalism who is the ultimate form of the modern ideal of *animal rationalis*. Finally, Foucault is critical of Kant's concept of 'Universal law', which, as moral code also contributes to a form of governmentality. Foucault argues that the morals that have become accepted as 'universal' are simply a mask for political interests. Transformation of the prevailing paradigm or world view is both subjective and communal at the same time.

'Technologies of the self' invokes a kind of agency which is missing from the accounts of ideology or governmentality. The second volume of *The History of Sexuality* examines various ways in which historically the issue of 'care of the self' has been addressed. Using Baudelaire and Seneca among others, Foucault interrogates ways in which one can exercise some kind of influence on the self one is becoming. The models of dress and writing he cites have their own pitfalls, but the substance of the idea is the search for a way of getting outside of existing governmentality, whether that governmentality be in the form of 'police', 'biopower', or the market liberalism of human capital theory. The inherent problem remains, that the self has only the tools of its own time (including its own past) and place (however imagined) with which to think itself out of that time and place. Foucault's schema for 'technologies of the self' is a process of conscientisation. It involves the honest appraisal of governmental techniques and an understanding (as far as we are able) to make these techniques visible to ourselves. It is a process of *parrhesia* that throws light on the ways we are each complicit in the ordering of the world that exacerbates the all-encompassment of the technological *Gestell*. Foucault, Heidegger and Nietzsche focus on *thinking, poetry and art* as the means to exceed the world of totalising calculation and rational control. As Heidegger points out, thinking the essence of technology is only possible when approached from the relation between humanity and Being. The relation of human beings to the environment (past, present and future) challenges the anthropocentric autonomy of the individualised, solipsist humanist subject. Neoliberal theories of the self are constituted by traditional and, we argue, particularly impoverished versions of humanity as the autonomous *animal rationalis*.

## Exceeding the Autonomous Individual

Marshall has been very important for bringing the conceptual framework of sub-jectivity to the attention of educators in order to show up the ways institutional frameworks compound or resist dominant forms of governmentality. With these aims in mind, Marshall has kept abreast of alternative ways of theorizing subjec-tivity, that exceeds the limited notion of the autonomous rational individual utility maximiser, but pays very close attention to maximising spaces available for the 'freedom' of agency and respect. In this section we attempt to summarise some of the more interesting avenues we know of which might bring us into larger spaces for agency.

There appear to be two main trends of escape from governmentality and the enframing *Gestell* of technology. The first is non-rationality: the excess of sensibility over self interest, the second is the phenomenological integration of bodily subjec-tivity in the immediate surroundings. Relating to this mutual absorption of subject and object is the maintenance of a nominalist 'distance' to reflect on the motives, practices and self understanding of human beings in relation to the tangled com-plexities of the environment.

The first mode, of exceeding the self absorption of autonomous individualism, does not limit itself to a manner in which the nomos affects the autos by universal moral law, or normative social conventions, or even in the phenomenological sense of environment affecting subjectivity. Escape from the autonomous rational indi-vidual utility maximiser is about the excess, the non-rational, the emotional, the hysterical, the unexplainable—exceeding the rules and norms that have hitherto rationalised our understanding of the surrounding events and structures within which we live. The second way of escaping governmentality is by integrating the body and mind, individual and environment, subject and object, and thus rejecting the presumptuous isolation of anthropocentric solipsism while retaining a notional nominalist distance within which to think. Thus when social rules or nomos are integrated into the self there is thinking space to accept, modify, alienate or find alternatives to the prevailing paradigm. This is a deeper, broader plateau of think-ing than 'rational choice.'

## Excess, or Supplement

The English conservative, Burke, along with the early twentieth century liberal, D. H. Lawrence, the neoliberal Hayek, and the feminist, Irigaray, all bring those characteristics of people which exceed reason into the equation. Autonomy, for Lawrence and Irigaray does not exclude emotions. Irigaray adds that rationality has 'fixed' a male dominant hierarchy, and that women's options for autonomy (as a kind of resistance) are through emotion, hysteria or insanity, to exceed it. Burke and Irigaray include the Sublime and the Beautiful—awe and sex—as key aspects of what it means to be human. Burke and Hayek argue that tradition (and hierarchy of class) is important, as reason cannot compute all variables, and besides, not everyone is capable of reasoning. This is part of Hayek's justification for valorization of the market, because human rationality is not sufficient in itself, to procure perpetual progress, but is so when the choices of individuals are meliorated, by processing through the mechanism of the market (Hayek, 1988).

## Reinvesting the Body

The harshly individuated subject proposed by Descartes has been undermined by a variety of philosophers since Nietzsche, and indeed, Kant. Nietzsche's phenomenological account of the subject integrated body and mind, self and surroundings. While trying to appreciate the manifold bombardment of impressions that impact and transform the body, the 'mind' is constrained to a lagging process that, after the fact, sorts and includes the new into already existing systems of order, sense and language.

In Nietzsche's wake, Merleau-Ponty reinvests the body into accounts of the self, Irigaray draws attention to the fluid excesses of the body that overflow the neat and tidy, regulated and encapsulated rhythms of 'society'. Deleuze and Guattari emphasise the 'becoming' rather than the being of the person, laying emphasis on the fluidity of that becoming and set lifehistories into a nomadic rather than a static frame.

## Nominalist Distance

Foucault has emphasised both the importance of the social to the body; in his account of 'discipline' and the agency we can apply to training ourselves to be something more than a governable, individuated, *animal rationalis*. In *Discipline and Punish* Foucault describes education and more particularly schooling as a government apparatus for disciplining children's bodies. Normalisation is a primary goal to curriculum and pedagogy. But his purpose is not to legitimise these processes. Bringing these techniques of the disciplines of governmentality out of the concealment of the familiar, subsumed in the smooth normalised, closed behaviours that concentrate on consumerism, is itself in some sense an emancipatory act. Foucault encourages people to resist being fitted as potential resource into the conditions of an alienated post-industrialised global economy.

Foucault uses a set of ideas which at first glance have a lot in common with the 'reflective' movement in teacher education. He discusses similar techniques of writing journals and so on as technologies of the self. But where the 'reflexive' writers assume that writing and thinking will self-evidently produce some kind of emancipatory or self-improving results, Foucault's technologies of the self are more firmly grounded in his theories of knowledge and power. The personal object of subjectivity is still 'subject' in three ways; classified into subject areas, subjugated by disciplinary blocs, and constituted as subjectivity, or self. These power-knowledge relations are to be analysed therefore, not on the basis of a subject of knowledge who is or is not free in relation to the power system. On the contrary, power-knowledge constructs and informs the subject, who can nevertheless become a subject who knows, and can discern the objects to be known and the modalities of knowledge. The knowing subject is affected by these fundamental implications of power-knowledge and their historical transformations. In short, it is not the activity of the subject of knowledge that produces a corpus of knowledge, useful or resistant to power, but power-knowledge, the processes and struggles that traverse it and of which it is made up, that determines the forms and possible domains of what is knowable.

Technologies of the self could be seen as the escape clause from the comprehensiveness of governmentality. Foucault's later interest in techniques of the self placed more emphasis on the 'spaces' or 'gaps' available for creating or exceeding known subject positions, without denying that the historico-discursive moment constitutes the self. It is the third aspect of the triumvirate: discourse-power-subjectivity. The difficulties of thinking in this fashion, outside or beyond our own historical and philosophical traditions are not to be underestimated. As Judith Butler says:

> ... the question of agency is not to be answered through recourse to an 'I' that pre-exists signification. In other words, the enabling conditions for an assertion of 'I' are provided by the structure of signification, the rules that regulate the legitimate and illegitimate invocation of that pronoun, the practices that establish the terms of an intelligibility by which that pronoun can circulate. (Butler, 2001, p. 111)

**The End of the Individual**

Although the end of the subject has been rather prematurely hailed—and dismissed, see for instance Derrida (1991), the dissolution of the conceptual apparatus of the 'individual', the rational, autonomous self of the enlightenment and liberalism ends the era of the essential soul. The 'individual' has constituted the basic building block for modernity, and as this edifice rumbles, the impact on the representations, the discourses, the institutions, the structures of human society will be immense. Our political struggles, our artwork, our use of resources, our capitalist systems and discursive foundations, utility, happiness—without the individual, all are liable to radical reassessment.

James Marshall has been as intrigued by agency as he was disillusioned with the neoliberal faith in a cast-iron individual. The complex integration of encounters between subjects and surrounding objects, the excess of causal elements that all contribute to the flow of events, the dynamics of power—or will—that are beyond any particular control; these all constitute the dynamic emerging and becoming of things into and out of existence. This scenario is not completely deterministic though. While never the sole cause, agency remains an integral part of the dynamics of change. Agency is not individuated freedom of will. It is the hesitant bringing forth of reflective thinking and practices on the contexts, the parameters, and the effects of modes of behaviour (individual and communal). As such, thinking can gradually initiate raised consciousness of particular events, issues, structures, paradigms. By entwining raised consciousness into already existing language, discourse can exceed the prevailing ways of imagining ourselves and our world. As educationalists, practicing reflection is one of our most active means of emerging from the globalisation of capital, the alienation of social systems from the environment, and the enframing of technology.

In schools it is still usual to act on the assumption that students are individuals despite the concerted effort to undermine that individuality in nearly every regard—by making students conform in their clothing, their conduct, and their learning. Failure to conform often elicits a stern speech based on the discourse of 'choice', and evoking the notion of autonomy. The child is admonished for not exerting their own will, that is to say, for not conforming to the expectations of adults rather than of their peers. It is extremely useful to be able to appeal to the individuality and autonomy of the student—it places blame on a relatively powerless person, and not on the teacher or parent, and therefore manages to avoid calling into question the practices of the school or classroom or home. By calling the attention of education students and others to the work of Michel Foucault, and the complexities, excesses and the construction of the self, James Marshall has done an enormous amount to destabilize a certain confident injustice in the way we treat young people, and to raise questions about the way in which we constitute ourselves and others in the game of education.

## References

Althusser, L. (1984) *Essays on Ideology* (London, Verso).

Buchanan, J. M. & Tullock, G. (1962) *The Calculus of Consent: Logical foundations of constitutional democracy* (Michigan, Ann Arbor Paperback).

Burke, E. (1790) Reflections on the Revolution in France, in: www.constitution.org/eb/rev_fran.htm (downloaded 10/1/2004).

Butler, J. (2001) Gender Trouble: From parody to politics, in: S. Malpas (ed.) *Postmodern Debates* (Hampshire, Palgrave).

Deleuze, G. & Guattari, F. (1988) *A Thousand Plateaus: Capitalism and schizophrenia* (London, Athlone Press).

Derrida, J. (1991) Eating Well, Or the Calculation of the Subject: An interview with Jacques Derrida, in: E. Cadava, P. Conner & J-L. Nancy (eds) *Who Comes After the Subject?* (New York, Routledge).

Foucault, M. (1977) *Discipline and Punish: The birth of the prison* (Harmondsworth, Penguin).

Foucault, M. (1978) Governmentality, in: G. Burchell, C. Gordon, & P. Miller (eds), *The Foucault Effect* (Chicago, University of Chicago Press, 1991).

Foucault, M. (1980) *Power/Knowledge: Selected interviews and other writings 1972–1977*, (ed.) C. Gordon (Toronto, Harvester Press).

Foucault, M. (1980b) Truth and Power, in: *Power/Knowledge: Selected Interviews and other writings 1972–1977* (New York, Pantheon Books).

Foucault, M. (1983) The Subject and Power, in: H. Dreyfus and P. Rabinow (eds), *Michel Foucault: Beyond structuralism and hermeneutics* (Chicago, Chicago Press).

Foucault, M. (1990) *The Care of the Self; History of sexuality*, Vol. 3 (Harmondsworth, Penguin).

Foucault, M. (1990a) *The History of Sexuality*, Vol. 1 (Harmondsworth, Penguin).

Foucault, M. (1991b) *The Foucault Reader*, (ed.) P. Rabinow (Harmondsworth, Penguin).

Foucault, M. (1992) *The Use of Pleasure; History of sexuality*, Vol. 2 (Middlesex, Penguin).

Glasser, W. (1992) *The Quality School: Managing students without coercion* (New York, Harper).

Goldstein, J. (ed.) (1994) *Foucault and the Writing of History* (Malden, MA, Blackwell Publishers).

Gruber, D. (1989) Thought of Michel Foucault; Foucault's critique of the liberal individual, *The Journal of Philosophy*, LXXXVI:II, pp. 615–621.

Hayek, F. A. (1988) *The Fatal Conceit, The collected works of Friedrich August Hayek* vol. 1 (ed.) W. W. Bartley III (London, Routledge).

Heidegger, M. (1973) *An Introduction to Metaphysics*, Ralph Manheim, (Trans: 1959, original publ.:1953) (Massachusetts, Yale University Press).

Heidegger, M. (1977) The Question Concerning Technology, in: *The Question Concerning Technology and other Essays* (New York, Harper Row).

Irigaray, L. (1975) The Power of Discourse and the Subordination of the Feminine, *Dialectiques*, 8, pp. 68–85.

Irwin, R. (2000) Nietzsche: Deleuze, Foucault, and genealogy as a method for education, in: M. Peters, J. Marshall & P. Smeyers (eds) *Past and Present Values: Nietzsche's Legacy for Education* (Westport, Bergin and Garvey).

Kant, I. (1933) *Critique of Pure Reason* (ed.) Norman Kemp (original publ.: 1781, revised edition 1787) (New York, Macmillan).

Kant, I. (1951) *Critique of Judgement*, J. H. Bernard (trans.) (Hafner Publishing, New York).

Kant, I. (1956) *Critique of Practical Reason*, (original publ.: 1788) (New York, MacDonald Publishing).

Lankshear, C. (1982) Personal Autonomy: a contemporary educational ideal, in: *Freedom and Education* (Auckland, Milton Brookes).

Marshall, J. (1997) The New Vocationalism, in: M. Olssen & K. Morris Matthews (eds), *Education Policy in New Zealand: the 1990s and beyond* (Palmerston North, Dunmore Press) pp. 304–326.

Marshall, J. (1998) Information on Information: Recent Curriculum Reform, *Studies in Philosophy and Education*, 17:4, pp. 313–321.

Marshall, J. (2000) Electronic Writing and the Wrapping of Language, *Journal of Philosophy of Education*, 34:1, pp. 135–149.

Marshall, J. (2000) Nietzsche's New Philosopher: The arts and the self, in: M. Peters, J. Marshall & P. Smeyers (eds), *Past and Present Values: Nietzsche's Legacy for Education* (Westport, CT, Bergin and Garvey).

Marshall, J. (1996) The Autonomous Chooser and 'Reforms' in Education, *Studies in Philosophy and Education*, 15, pp. 89–96.

Marshall, J. (1996b) *Michel Foucault: Personal autonomy and education* (Dordrecht, Kluwer Academic Publishers).

Nietzsche, F. (1979) *Ecce Homo: How one becomes what one is*, R. J. Hollingdale (trans. & intro.) (Harmondsworth, Penguin).

Nietzsche, F. [1883](1982a) Thus Spoke Zarathustra, in: W. Kaufmann, (ed. & trans., 1954) *Portable Nietzsche* (New York, Penguin).

Nietzsche, F. (1989) *On the Genealogy of Morals and Ecce Homo*, W. Kaufmann (ed. & commentary), with R. J. Hollingdale, (trans.), (originally published: 1887 and 1899) (New York, Vintage Books).

O'Loughlin, M. (1995) Intelligent Bodies and Ecological Subjectivities: Merleau-Ponty's corrective to postmodernism's 'subjects' of education, *Philosophy of Education* at http://www.ed.uiuc.edu/EPS/PES-yearbook/95_docs/o'loughlin.html

Peters, M. (1996) Poststructuralism and the Philosophy of the Subject: The Games of the Will to Power against the Labor of the Dialectic, in: *Poststructuralism, Politics and Education* (Connecticut:, Bergin & Garvey) pp. 21–45.

Peters, M. (1997) Neoliberalism, Welfare Dependency and the Moral Construction of Poverty in Aotearoa/ NZ, *NZ Sociology*, 12:1, pp. 1–34.

Peters, R. S., Rabinow, P. & Dreyfus, H. (eds). (1983) Afterword, The Subject and Power, in: *Michel Foucault: Beyond structuralism and hermeneutics* (Chicago, Chicago Press) pp. 208–226.

Rousseau, J-J. (1983) *The Social Contract* (Harmondsworth, Penguin).

# 3

# The Paradox of the Excluded Child

BRUCE HAYNES
*Edith Cowan University*

James Marshall's efforts to develop a post-analytic philosophy of education have, in part, centred on matters related to the punishment of children. James and Dominique Marshall (1997) presented the first extensive coverage of discipline and punishment in New Zealand schooling based on James' work on punishment in the 1970s and early 1980s, his work on Foucault in the 1980s and 1990s and Dominique's archival work.During this time, most attention of educators and the public in New Zealand and some other ex-colonies of Britain was directed to the issue of corporal punishment of children. In 1967 the Plowden Report recommended that corporal punishment be abolished in Britain, it was abolished in Victoria in 1983, it was suspended in New Zealand in 1987 and abolished in 1990, and in Western Australia abolition was officially recommended in 1972 but enacted in 1987. Insofar as consideration of this policy issue was informed by philosophical analysis, it largely considered the juridico-legal model of punishment as exemplified by Richard Peters (1966). Marshall (1997, p. 29) claimed that:

> There are problems with each of the conditions identified in the legal model which make talk of the punishment of children—in that legal sense -quite problematic. To be fair to Hart, he saw that point and talked of the punishment of children as involving a metaphorical use of the term.

Marshall did not accept this conclusion nor the means by which it was reached. He sought to develop an account of punishment of children based on his understanding of the work of Wittgenstein and Foucault. Marshall's (1997, p. 12) approach was to:

> start from practices rather than philosophical analysis. … If anything, the disciplinary 'home' of this work is philosophical, in so far as it works towards the meaning of a concept—disciplinary punishment—but on the way, it draws heavily upon historical data.

This paper is an extension of that work in a slightly different setting.

One of the puzzles facing a non-foundationalist philosopher of education is to determine what, if any, contribution such work should have to policy issues such as the punishment of children. For an analytic philosopher to identify, based on analysis of ordinary language, necessary and sufficient conditions for the use of the concept of 'punishment' is to provide rigorous constraints on the debate about policy issues. If an analytic philosopher's deliberations on the definition and justification of 'punishment' can help achieve clarity of language and relevance of evidence, then these are two solid foundations for the process of policy formation. Denying a second-order status for philosophy to establish foundations for practice is not sufficient to provide a role for philosophy of education. A philosopher, versed in a literature and tradition of examining the assumptions (and their alternatives) of traditions, may assist autonomous practitioners when faced with a problem arising from the fact that each act within a tradition contains the possibility of rule-following, rule-breaking or rule-changing as well as the possibility of ineptitude. One role for philosophy of education may be to point out when a problem is of such significance that it should be faced by the practitioners in the tradition. Another role is to elaborate the sense in which a practitioner is autonomous within the constraints of a tradition. A problem may arise, for example, when two practices contradict each other or when circumstances change such that the existing practice no longer fulfils its purpose. The paradox of the excluded child in a system of compulsory schooling has been noted for some time.

> The school laws compel attendance between certain ages, and the deliberate expulsion of a child by the school authority is incongruous with the idea of compulsory school attendance. (P. Monroe, 1911, II, p. 559)

Bureaucratic systems of compulsory schooling have coped with the paradox of the excluded child and some have been quite explicit in justifying the practice. The *Code of Public Instruction of the State of New-York* contains a detailed justification of a rule providing for exclusion from schooling. The rule states:

> Children may be excluded, not for punishment merely, but for the protection of others from such injurious example and influence as would entirely defeat the purposes for which schools are instituted. (Superintendent of Public Instruction, 1856, p. 311)

Exclusion is more related to broader social purposes and not focussed on the well-being of the individual. Exclusion, so justified, is not an extension of the practices of discipline and punishment as investigated by James Marshall. Marshall refers to Slee's (1988) account of punishment as tending to exclude rather than inclusion which Marshall (1997, p. 141) relates to Foucault's notion of governmentality. 'Slee is absolutely correct in seeing the importance of the inclusion/exclusion distinction'. (Marshall, 1997, p. 144) In this context, it is desirable that 'inclusion' and 'exclusion' are used with clear and constant referents. 'Inclusion' may be used in a classroom setting to refer to participation in the educational processes intended by the teacher as part of the curriculum. Some punishments may serve to exclude a student from such processes for a time and, upon completion of the punishment, the student resumes classroom activities in good standing. But these punishments may also be part of wider processes that serve to include the student, in the sense that they are subject to 'governmentality'. Such punishments may help develop the student's self discipline. Exclusion from schooling is a practice that has evolved as systems of compulsory schooling have developed and some exclusions may be intended to serve to include the student and others may exclude the student from formal education and other social activities.

Compulsion provisions were introduced in the first Education Act (1871) passed in colonial Western Australia only one year after it was granted a Legislative Council.

> 28. Every district board may from time to time, with the approval of the Central Board, make by-laws for all or any of the following purposes:
> (a) Requiring the parents of children of such age, not less than six years nor more than fourteen years, as may be fixed by the by-laws, to cause such children (unless there is some reasonable excuse) to attend school, which children do not reside beyond three miles from a Government School:

Reasonable excuses included the child being sick, having severe intellectual or physical disability, being needed for domestic or other work or being aboriginal. Exclusion from compulsory schooling takes two forms: deliberate exclusion of enrolled pupils and non-enforcement of the compulsion clauses for parents of children between the prescribed ages of attendance. The evolution of the practice of exclusion has seen changes in both these aspects.

## Evolution of the Practice of Exclusion

The evolution of the practice of exclusion from compulsory schooling in Western Australia has moved through several stages and a change of terminology. Up to the 1928 Act, a child was **expelled** from school without official provision for further education. After 1928, an expelled child may have been placed in an institution for incorrigible children. Since the 1960s, a child **excluded** from a government school may be: required to attend the school in a specified manner; relocated to another school; required to undertake an educational program in another kind of institution; or placed in the care of the parents to provide an appropriate form of home schooling.

From 1871 until 1928 in Western Australia, expulsion of an enrolled pupil terminated their engagement with educational institutions in much the same way as capital punishment or banishment terminated a criminal's engagement with the offended society. This consequence of expulsion was both recognised and taken seriously by those engaged in compulsory schooling, as is indicated by the official reasoning in support of the State of New York's rule regarding expulsion.

> It is to be remembered that among the objects of instruction is not only to deter from vice, but to reclaim those who are capable of reformation, and to correct bad habits which may result from parental neglect, or, what is more deplorable, from parental example. To deal gently with the erring, and especially with erring childhood, is the dictate of humanity, policy and duty. To abandon them to their evil courses is a step involving the most serious responsibility, never to be taken until remonstrance and persuasion have been exhausted. (Superintendent of Public Instruction, 1856, p. 311)

The Western Australian 1928 Education Act changed expulsion in that State in a particular way.

18. (1) If a child is constantly and habitually absent from school, the parent of such child may be summoned ... before a children's court under the Child Welfare Act 1907–1927, to show cause why such a child should not be sent to an institution under the said Act.

*Incorrigible children*

(5) This section shall, *mutatis mutandis*, apply to any child whose attendance at school would, owing to immorality or gross misconduct, be harmful to other children.

With the creation of the equivalent of prisons for incorrigible children, for habitual truants and for children whose parents deliberately withheld them from school for economic reasons, the practice of expulsion was changed. Children expelled from school could either be sent to another type of institution or could be released into the wider society and their parents freed of the requirements of the compulsion clauses. Regulations established under the 1928 Act set out procedures for expulsion of an enrolled child from a school. By 1960 the terminology had changed to exclusion and suspension.

21. The headmaster of a school may for such period as he deems necessary exclude from the school any child who is suffering from any contagious, offensive or infectious disease, or who is habitually of unclean habits.

35. No child shall be expelled from school, but if a headmaster considers that circumstances so warrant, he may suspend a child from attending school and report the suspension to the Director-General, who shall decide the action to be taken in respect to the child. (Education Department of Western Australia, *Regulations*, 1960)

The 'habitually of unclean habits' clause had been used frequently to exclude aboriginal children from school.

> State School, Quairading
> 23$^{rd}$. March 1914

The Director of Education

Sir,

I beg to report that owing to an outbreak of ringworm and sore eyes, the attendance of this school has decreased from 34 to 4 during the last three weeks. ...

One boy fainted twice in the school and is now on a farm recuperating for a month. The cause of his illness is said to be the abominable smell from the black children during hot weather. Two other children are ill from the same cause. Here, I beg to thank the Department for the Disinfectant sent to mitigate the smell. I regret to say that it was of no practical use. The proportion of black to white is too great ... As the black children are blamed for introducing these illnesses, the parents of the white children, are very dissatisfied with their presence in the school ... Awaiting your instructions. (Haynes et al., 1974, p. 50)

The Director of Education notified the teacher that 'the aborigines are to be excluded when the school re-opens next week'. In Foucault's terms, the symptom was transformed into a sign and the authorities sought to treat the smell and ignore aboriginal ill-health and other forms of difference.

From 1914 until 1940 aboriginal children were excluded from local government schools but could be enrolled at Native Schools that were often hundreds of kilometers away from their home. Special institutions to cater for children with severe intellectual or physical disability were established and these children were also excluded from local schools.

The School Education Act 1999 is the current legal basis for justifying exclusion of a child from a Western Australian school. Section 9 of the Act provides:

> (a) A child is to be enrolled in an educational programme for each year of the compulsory education period for that child.
> (b) A parent of a child must ensure that subsection (1) is complied with. Penalty $2,500

Section 91 of the Act provides:

> For the purposes of this Division a student may be excluded from attendance at a government school if—
> (a) he or she has committed a breach of school discipline in circumstances that—
> (1) have adversely affected or threaten the safety of any person who is on the school premises or participating in an educational programme of the school; or
> (2) have caused or are likely to result in damage to property;
> or
> (b) his or her behaviour has disrupted the educational instruction of other students.

Section 94 of the Act provides:

> (a) The orders that may be made by the chief executive officer are—
> (b) an order excluding the student from normal attendance at the school but directing him or her to attend the school for the purposes specified in the order;
> (c) an order completely excluding the student from attending the school;
> (d) an order directing the student to attend a specified government school or to participate in a specified educational programme;
> (e) an order determining the educational instruction the student is to be given, or a combination of 2 or more of those orders.

In effect, this Act compels parents to enrol and ensure the attendance of their children aged between 6 years and 15 years old in a school or be registered under Section 48 of the Act as the child's home educator. It further permits the Chief Executive Officer of the Department of Education to exclude a student from a government school on specified grounds. The Chief Executive Officer must consider making an order for an educational program for the excluded student. The current Minister is considering raising the age for compulsory attendance to 17 years.

## More Exclusions

A trend to more exclusion of compulsory school age children from government schools has been identified in both England and Western Australia. Harris and Eden (2000, p. 2) record that the number of permanent exclusions from English schools rose from 2,900 in 1990/1 to 11,084 in 1994/5 and 12,298 in 1997/8. They also noted the trend in England to legal protection of the rights and interests of children under the Human Rights Act (1998) and the trend to legislative prescription and legal review of decisions made by school personnel (e.g. School Standards and Framework Act 1998). Somewhat similar trends are evident in Western Australia. A number of explanations may be given for this trend.One explanation is that children's behaviour is now worse than in the past due to home background and less parental acceptance of responsibility for child behaviour. Evidence for this explanation may be cited in terms of weapons brought to school and assaults on teachers. Backing for this explanation may be that as children are accorded formal rights so parental responsibility is diminished thus resulting in worse behaviour by children.

An explanation may be given in terms of the process and procedures of schooling. The change in school attitude to truancy and unofficial exclusion is related to this kind of explanation. As school systems become less tolerant of truancy so it becomes more likely that the school will have to confront and exclude 'incorrigible children'. School systems have reduced the range of children unofficially excluded e.g. children in paid employment or domestic work, isolated rural children, children with significant disabilities and aboriginal children. Schools have also increased the age at which children may leave school. Thus it is more likely schools will confront children for whom schooling is a problem and so become a problem for school.

These types of explanation best account for long-term trends but the figures quoted above show a short term, rapid increase in exclusions. Explanations for such a trend require an identifiable change in procedure and/or a shift in basic assumption/s about schooling. In general, the changes in procedure seem to be responses to the trend to exclusion rather than an explanation of it. One change in procedure that may contribute to the increase in exclusions is the abolition of corporal punishment. Slee (1995, p. 59) cites Foucault as the authority for his claim that 'Suspension was to do what corporal punishment could not: maintain a docile student body in schools'. Short-term suspension from specific classroom activities, such as being sent out of the room, being interrogated by a school psychologist, or being sent home from school, are all forms of suspension that schools can use to replace corporal punishment. These practices are consistent with Foucault's account of the pathologisation of the student in which the expert improves the institutional situation by requiring the student to be 'cured', that is, become more docile. But as Dettman (1972, pp. 92 and 158) noted:

One very important consideration ... is whether suspension is a punishment or a period in which the allegations made against a pupil may be investigated and confirmed or modified. ...

If the suspension is being used as a punishment for the purpose of deterring extremely deviant behaviour, then it should be realised that it is relatively ineffective. The students most likely to incur this punishment are the students who dislike it least. ... The student's peer group may elevate him into a hero who easily manages to accommodate the worst the school can do.

This seems to be a case of Br'er Rabbit and the Briar Patch. If short-term suspensions are used as ineffective punishments then it is likely that both school and student will see exclusion as the desirable outcome. Slee (1995, p. 50) claims 'The abolition of corporal punishment simply translated into greater reliance on suspension and exclusion'. Even if this is so, are there other explanations for the increase in exclusions during the 1990s?

In particular, what kind of shift in assumption/s about schooling could produce a short term, rapid trend to exclusion? One shift is in the assumption about the function of schooling. Compulsory schooling was intended to counter the bad influence of some parents on their child (see Superintendent of Public Instruction, 1856, above) and to impose a view of schooling on those with a different view but who were voiceless. Such a school imposed its requirements on children. Those who lacked self-control, lacked required abilities or had a different view of the world, were failed. In a pluralist society, in which the government school is assumed to respect (to some extent) the views of the parents, both the school and the children/parents have difficulty in accepting the imposition of particular views. Such a school is expected to adapt its operation to meet the various needs of a diverse range of children and failure is that of the school. This leads to greater confrontation and, in more cases than in the past, exclusion. Such a shift in assumptions about schooling in Australia has occurred in the past thirty years.

A second type of explanation which is relevant to the trend to more exclusion is the shift from a set of assumptions about schooling as a bureaucratic organisation to a set of assumptions about schooling as a corporate or market organisation. A bureaucratic school was more likely to tolerate unofficial exclusion rather than to submit itself to the effort and stress of going through the official procedures leading to exclusion. Whatever the outcome of the exclusion process, those involved were always worse off. Just as it did not pay a school principal to try to dismiss an incompetent teacher (transfer to another school was an easier and better option), so it did not pay to exclude a student if some unofficial option was available. In a corporate system, but more so in a market system, the focus is on the efficient use of resources to achieve specified measurable outcomes. In each case, exclusion of some children from a school may be explained either in terms of the introduction of a quality control procedure for raw materials or a performance management system for members of the corporate team that happens to exclude non performers who have a deleterious effect on the school's outcomes. Where the excluded child is required to engage in an educational program provided at home then this form of exclusion is an extension of the privatisation of government schooling seen in Australia over the past thirty years.

## Conclusion

The circumstances of schooling have changed significantly in Western Australia since compulsory schooling was introduced in the late nineteenth century. The conception of schooling as a bureaucratically run, state imposed obligation on parents and children, has undergone significant change in the past thirty years. In a corporate or market school environment, the state has moved both to privatise the responsibility for schooling for some children and, at the same time, taken on additional responsibility for schooling. So, while governments have encouraged the provision of private schooling at subsidised prices and given increased recognition to home schooling as forms of privatisation, they have also increased the range of provision for children excluded from local schools. The increase in the numbers of compulsory school age children excluded from their local school is symptomatic of wider changes in schooling. The extent to which these changes reflect the purposes of schooling is important in any consideration of exclusion from compulsory schooling. For, as has been noted earlier:

> Children may be excluded, not for punishment merely, but for the protection of others from such injurious example and influence as would entirely defeat the purposes for which schools are instituted. (Superintendent of Public Instruction, 1856, p. 311)

James Marshall (1995, p. 343) asked 'How, as educationalists, are we to talk meaningfully about the punishment of children'. Marshall (1997, p. 128) was concerned to question traditional and humanistic explanations of changes in practices of punishment and to consider alternative explanations based on Foucault's notion of disciplinary power as applied in schools to 'constitute individuals in certain ways'. His concern was to treat it philosophically rather than merely historically or psychologically, so that the historical detail is there as an archaeology of perception rather than a description of events. One concern of this paper is to highlight the point that exclusion from compulsory schooling differs from punishment. A punishment imposes a penalty on a participant according to the rules of a tradition. Exclusion from compulsory schooling is not a penalty, it is a termination of participation and the rules of the tradition no longer apply to the excluded person. Explanation of the practice of exclusion from compulsory schooling relates more to the capacity of schools to fulfil the 'purposes for which (they) are instituted' than to the welfare of individual students. Justification in terms of broader social purposes of schooling is a way of dealing with the apparent paradox of the excluded child.

## Acknowledgement

I appreciate the improvements made to this paper as a result of Felicity Haynes' comments.

# References

Dettman, H. W. (Chair) (1972) *Discipline in Secondary Schools in Western Australia* (Perth, Education Department of Western Australia).

Education Department of Western Australia, *Regulations*, Reprinted from *The Government Gazette 26 July 1960 et seq.* (Perth, Government Printer).

Harris, N. & Eden, K. with Blair, A. (2000) *Challenges to School Exclusion* (London, Routledge, Falmer).

Haynes, B., Barrett, G., Brennan, A. & L. (1974) *W.A. Aborigines 1622–1972*, (Third Edition) (Nedlands, History Association of Western Australia).

Marshall, J. D. (1995) Wittgenstein and Foucalt: Resolving philosophical puzzles, *Studies in Philosophy and Education*, 14, pp. 329–344.

Marshall, J. D. & D. (1997) *Discipline and Punishment in New Zealand Education* (Palmerston North, Dunmore Press).

Monroe, P. (ed.) (1911) *A Cyclopedia of Education*, Vol. 2 (New York, MacMillan).

Slee, R. (1995) *Changing Theories and Practices of Discipline* (London, Falmer Press).

Superintendent of Public Instruction (1856) *Code of Public Instruction of the State of New-York* (Albany, N.Y., Weed, Parsons and Co.).

*Western Australia: Elementary Education Act 1871* (Perth, Government Printer).

*Western Australia: An Act to consolidate and amend the law relating to Public Education*, (1928) (Perth, Government Printer).

*Western Australia: School Education Act 1999* (Perth, Government Printer).

# 4
# Emergencies and Emergent Selves

FELICITY HAYNES
*The University of Western Australia*

I see my hands holding this book. I have hands. How do I know they're MY hands? Silly question. They're fastened to my arms, my body. How do I know this is my body? I control it. Do I own it? In a sense I do. It's mine to do with as I like, so long as I don't harm others ... If I have this body, then I guess I'm something other than this body ... In any case, I and my body seem intimately connected and yet distinct. I am the controller; it is the controlled. Most of the time.

D. Dennett, *The Mind's I*, p. 5

Each waking day is a stage dominated for good or ill, in comedy, farce or tragedy by a *dramatis personae*, the 'self', and so it will be until the curtain drops.

C. S. Sherrington, *The Integrative Action of the Nervous System*

Imagine that a fire breaks out in an unsupervised classroom. Most of the students panic, but one child seizes the water cooler, smashes it against the wall and douses the flames. In such an emergency, there is no time to consider action, make rational choices. So what makes this particular child react or act thus? This paper will not construct a theory to explain functional action in an emergency, but rather examine Jim Marshall's brief account of 'self' and its implications for the way we think of the 'self as agent'.

## Is There an 'I'? No.

When Wittgenstein says (NB, 80e) 'The thinking subject is surely mere illusion ... The I, the I is what is deeply mysterious. The I is not an object. I objectively confront every object. But not the I', he denies the usefulness of the ghost in the machine, the homunculus in control. Despite Daniel Dennett's epigraph above, Dennett argues that the idea of a separate self in control is an illusion and the often chaotic army of sub-editors rushing around without a commanding general is motivated by sets of physiological brainstates. Marshall (1999, pp. 113–121) agrees that 'I' does not refer to a substantive self and that Descartes and Hume were wrong in asking to what does 'self' or 'I' refer, but he does not seek the recourse of reducing 'I' to neuronal sequences or memes of habituated brainstates.

Marshall says that he is trying to uncover 'what Wittgenstein could have been referring to when he spoke of himself as a "person", "self", "identity", "subject", and "subjectivity"' (1999, p. 9) but the 'what' in that phrase should not give the impression that these intertwining threads constitute the person named Ludwig who refers to himself as 'I'. 'I' can no longer be examined as if it were being used simply to express the collection of experiences that is LW, because that is still to try to name the referent of 'I'. The notion of an individuated self is a bump which Marshall wishes to smooth out, a fly which he wishes to release from the flybottle.

## What is 'I' Used For?

Marshall's contribution is to show how 'I' functions, not as a referent, but as an explanation for a name—' "I" *explains* a name, and "*I am LW*" has a different function in language from contingent identity statements' (Marshall, 1999, p. 115). His methodology is the Foucauldian one of looking at practices. In this case, he tries to 'explain a name' by looking at the conditions under which 'I' is learned and how 'I' is taught to children. In so doing, he looks at the **use** or function of the word rather than its **meaning** in a conceptual scheme. To do that he examines how concepts such as 'I' and 'conscious' and 'aware' are *used* to mutually support each other but this is a contingent matter rather than the naturalistic correspondence of statements to states-of-affairs that underpins most representational views of language. This marks a crucial shift in the philosophical activity. Marshall, following both Wittgenstein and Foucault, has shifted the issue of 'I' from a semantic one to an epistemological one, or even, given the centrality of power/knowledge in any educational institution, to a political one, and one which makes philosophy crucially relevant to educators.

## The Grammar of Self

Marshall, as Wittgenstein did, examines the grammar of first person psychological statements, and concludes (p. 117) that Wittgenstein 'considers them as *expressions* of natural feelings rather than *descriptions* of inner mental states' (*emphases in original*) and these expressions of natural feelings, including pain, are learned (p. 118). A child learns the use of 'I' and names such as 'Ludwig' almost simultaneously. But the child who learns how to use these terms must already be a language user and understand even if tacitly that intention is a necessary component of language. 'I' then 'functions' to remind people of certain things. 'I am LW' expresses an intention to associate, and have others associate, the name LW with criteria of identity such as 'the Austrian philosopher', the 'relentless truth seeker.' A 'centre of consciousness' that cannot be mistaken about 'I am LW' is associated with those criteria and 'I' has a certain world view as an eye at the boundary of the world of representation. Marshall concludes that the fact that a mouth is speaking saying that 'I am LW' identifies a centre of language and intentional use for Wittgenstein. Wittgenstein's use of 'self' or 'I' requires a set of mutually supportive and as far as possible coherent beliefs concerning intentionality, mind, autonomy, self-consciousness, and this web of mutually supporting beliefs is built up from shared practices in a social world.

## The Agency of Adaptation

Yet for Marshall, Wittgenstein has a curiously deterministic notion of the construction of this grammar is. Because there is no *dramatis personae* or homunculus, there can be no actor or agent. He concludes that Wittgenstein was deeply pessimistic about the ability of the self to do anything but adapt to a 'decadent' world, so that it becomes a passive acceptor of the shared conventions and practices that contributed to its very formation. 'In Wittgenstein, the world as I found it is essentially the world as I will leave it' (Marshall, 1999, p. 120). By some irony, this traps him in the same sort of reductionism practiced by Dennett, that we construct the idea of being the controller, or the self empowered to act, but that the separation of the 'I' from its expression of the body is fanciful. I argue that the emergence of a constructed 'self' will protect him from this determinism.

## 'I' as Emergent Institutional Fact

The constructed or emergent self is not inconsistent with Marshall's focus on the conditions under which 'I' is learned and how 'I' is taught to children. We may have to look more closely at the evolutionary epistemologies offered by Piaget, Vygotsky, Toulmin, Popper, or, more recently, Searle. Realist that Searle (1998) is, he can retain the notion of a mind, consciousness and intentionality as biological, and explain an epistemologically objective social reality such as self as being partly constituted by an ontologically subjective set of attitudes, because he believes that collective intentionality is a primitive, demonstrated whenever people cooperate. 'Collective intentionality is the foundation of all social activities and occurs whenever you have people sharing their thoughts, feelings and so on' (Searle, 1998, p. 120). To construct institutional reality Searle does something that Wittgenstein does not do directly, that is he assigns functionality to human action. The student who uses the water cooler to extinguish the fire is an agent assigning a function to, or imposing a function on some object even where it is not done consciously. An agent exploits some natural feature of the object to achieve a purpose. To relate the notion of a brute reality to an institutional reality, Searle appeals to constitutive rules which seem to have much in common with Wittgenstein's shared conventions or 'knowing how to go on'. habituated through use and functional.

This crucial difference of intentional functionality makes a difference to how we learn the conventions of self and identity. Searle proposes that our institutional structures evolved out of actions. He tells the story of primitives individually assigning functions to individual objects, such as using a stump as a seat and then perhaps together building a wall around their shelters to keep intruders out. The wall has an assigned function in virtue of its physical features and it has collective intentionality because a function has been assigned to it. Even if the wall were to gradually decay, we can imagine that the inhabitants would continue to treat the line of stones as if it still served the function for which it was built, that they treated the line of stones as if it was not to be crossed. The wall now serves its function not in virtue of its physical structure but in virtue of the collective acceptance or recognition by the individuals acting collectively. Similarly the mechanism of collective intentionality whereby X counts as Y in C can be iterated over time so that in complex societies, the C term (context) is typically a Y term from an earlier stage. Searle's favourite example is paper money which serves a status function, but he shows how institutions such as marriage (implying heteronormativity) can be built up out of iterative contextualization of specific speech acts and collective intentionality for procreation. Such institutional facts are emergent events, similar to the emergence of human language (Popper) and of the human brain.

The consequence is that we do not have separate and mutually exclusive classes of brute and institutional facts. The whole point of having institutional facts such as money, marriage, theories (or selves) is to gain social control of the brute facts. While we are embedded in practices of inclusion and exclusion, such practices direct us in our self-awareness of ourselves, sometimes presenting agonizing stress for homosexuals like Wittgenstein and Foucault.

## Education of the 'I'

Is Foucault as deterministic as Wittgenstein appeared to be? Marshall contrasts Wittgenstein's pessimism with 'the philosophy of hope' carried in Foucault's 'care of the self' but does not elaborate. Foucault's ongoing concern with the three modes of objectification which transform human beings into subjects indicates that as individuals we have very little power to change either the world or ourselves. Yet Foucault's notion of power/knowledge allows resistance to institutional hegemonies, even where unconsciously expressed by fidgeting in class. Resistance is not inconsistent with the institutional fact of self as agent being presented with other possibilities, perhaps through education in the arts, or presentation of different cultural practices, or even global culture on mass media*. It may be that in learning institutional facts through shared conventions practices, individuals do adopt a trial-and-error testing of hypotheses, and consider more than one hypothesis at a time. Our ability to jointly construct institutional facts gives us equal ability to change or resist them through imagination or philosophical hypothesis, once we have built a self sophisticated enough for knowledge systems. The process need not be as rational as Popper suggested in his three worlds or as solipsistic as Piaget believed. If we interpret Foucault's injunction to 'take care of the self' in a way which uses 'taking care' in its widest sense of paying heed to unanticipated possibilities, we can choose to join, adapt or resist prevailing hegemonies through reflection. Foucault's concern with institutional power and subjectivities still leaves the way open for teachers to consider in what way they help constitute the identity of students qua students, or citizens, or commodities or autonomous beings. If it does not, then there is no point in philosophising.

## Acknowledgment

* My thanks to Bruce Haynes for this point.

## References

Dennett, D. C. (1978) *Brainstorms* (Vermont: Bradford Books).
Hofstadter, D. R. & Dennett, D. C. (1981) *The Mind's I* (Sussex: Harvester Press).
Marshall, J. (1999) Wittgenstein on the Self, *Educational Philosophy and Theory*, 31:2, pp. 113–121.
Popper, K. R. & Eccles, J. C. (1981) *The Self and its Brain* (Berlin, Springer International).
Searle, J. (1998) *Mind, Language and Society* (New York, Basic Books).
Sherrington, C. S. (1947) *The Integrative Action of the Nervous System*, 2nd edn (Cambridge, Cambridge University Press).

# 5

# Education as Liberation: The politics and techniques of lifelong learning

Bert Lambeir

## The Learning Society

'The "information" in the last decade of the twentieth century is that we are entering the age of information and that our social and cultural life will become restructured as we "evolve" into the information society' (Marshall, 1996, p. 268). This may be a widespread rumour, a self-fulfilling prophecy, a blessing, a deeply rooted fear, or just the simple 'truth', but it *is* something that mobilizes us. Politicians, economists, and educationalists are inventing and providing us with ways in which we can face this new challenge, in order to become adjusted inhabitants of the modern society.

It is taken for granted that the complexity of the information society has to do with such factors as the unstoppable growth of knowledge, the omnipresence of information and communications technology (in all its facets), globalisation and the shrinking of the world into what McLuhan called our 'global village'. Consequently, a reorientation of our being in this world seems to be required. We need to learn to retrieve, select and use the most suitable information; we have to master new techniques and different languages in order to communicate on a larger scale; we must become part of a flexibly available work force, adapted to the changing work climate and economic indicators.

Not surprisingly, the call to become lifelong learners gets louder and more intense every day. For how can we be citizens of a rapidly changing world, if we are not capable of changing along with it? Do we not need to update our knowledge and skills again and again in order to keep up with the pace of the ongoing transformations? Should we not explore, develop and exploit our (hidden) talents to apply for or keep our standing in respectable places in our social environment? Inevitably, the bond between the information society and the learning society appears to be a very tight one.

Not surprisingly either, in the meantime the call for permanent education has become an institutionalised one. Lifelong learning is a magic spell in the discourse of the educational and economic policymakers, as well as in that of the practitioners of both domains. The Flemish minister of education for example declares lifelong learning to be one of the government's priorities. She argues for equal learning opportunities for every individual, to encounter the threatening duality between those who did learn and still do, and those who do not use the educational facilities. In order to meet this goal, individualized learning advice and support will be necessary. In this respect, we might consider the following: first, learning activities must be presented as enjoyable, and related to the adult's curiosity and to the creation of new opportunities. Second, there is the need to set up a 'digital learning mall', a database which provides an overview of the learning activities offered in the country. Finally, the opportunity to use information and communications technology to offer more flexible and need-oriented learning facilities, must be explored. (Vanderpoorten, 2002).

The government's aspiration is elaborated in detail by educational scientists and economists. The economists emphasize a more market oriented supply of courses, and speak in terms of providers and buyers in the learning marketplace (see for instance *De Financieel Economische Tijd* (*The Financial Economic Times*), 2003). The educationalists stress the need to perceive learning as everyone's opportunity, and emphasize the importance of key qualifications, basic skills and primary knowledge. To actualise this, we need to promote 'self-managed learning', and the acquisition of cognitive and meta-cognitive skills, to develop an integral remedial program for schools in which most children face learning difficulties, and to prevent youngsters from leaving school too early. Another central idea outlined in the research report *Contouren beleid levenslang leren Vlaanderen* (Baert, et al.), is the necessary shift from an offer-oriented towards a question-oriented approach to lifelong learning. Stated otherwise, more attention should be paid to the expression and the analysis of the learner's learning needs. This implies in its turn, to transform the implicit question into an explicit one, the creation of better conditions for people to enable them to learn continuously, allowing the learner to see or experience the 'profit' of her efforts, and last but not least to stimulate on a large scale the question or need for learning by a variety of methods. (Baert, et al.)

One may wonder whether lifelong learning is indeed desirable at all ages, or whether this is the kind of life we *want* to live for a lifetime. It seems problematic to be content with what one has realised (or not) at a particular moment in one's life. One may also wonder whether almost everything we undertake, experience, or encounter during our lifetime, needs to be labelled as learning in accordance with the contemporary hype, or whether some of these things just have to do with *living* a life. It is, on the other hand, hardly contestable that creating equal opportunities for personal development, encouraging the autonomous individual in developing her own capacities, and motivating a large number of people to learn are worthy goals. Alphabetisation courses or introductory lessons in the use of computers, for example, are undeniably valuable.

Yet there are two comments I want to make here when lifelong learning—as expressed nowadays—is at stake. The first remark concerns the concept of learning, and the related idea of the learner as a human being herself. This will lead us to the heart of the problem itself, namely the illusion that it is the subject's individual choice to learn.

## Learning to Manage, Managing to Learn

As Marshall rightly observes: '... knowledge has been replaced by skills and *learning*. Everything which might have been seen as obtaining knowledge—an *object* of an activity—seems to have moved into an activity mode, where what is important is *process*' (Marshall, 1996, p. 269). Learning, and with it education, are redefined in terms of a process, since what once was perceived as knowledge, has now become *information*. 'And because it is (merely) information it has to be continuously "relearned", readjusted and restructured to meet the demands of the consumer in the service information industry' (ibid.). This means, as already became clear in the description of lifelong learning itself, that the concept of learning itself is altering. In curriculum documents the emphasis is on skills related to information retrieval, dissemination and evaluation. Additionally, cognitive and critical skills are perceived as necessary. Learning is an ongoing acquiring, and thus the permanent addition of competences. At the same time, what does not seem to be obviously useful at first sight, namely knowledge and understanding, evaporates and is discounted by the new educational forms. Put differently, we face a frightening constriction of our concept of education into a permanent training in information management. Learning now is the constant striving for extra competences, and the efficient management of the acquired ones. Education has become merely a tool in to the fetishisation of certificates.

Taking into consideration this altered concept of learning, what kind of human being is this lifelong learner? This learner is related to herself as an entrepreneur: what she becomes depends on what she undertakes, which means in its turn that what she becomes depends on her choices. (Masschelein & Simons, 2003) As an entrepreneur, the subject is expected to be capable of showing her personal records (scores, skill profiles and self descriptions) at any time. In sum, we become countable and manageable by others and by ourselves. No doubt this is an accurate analysis of the lifelong learning discourse: we have to emancipate and create ourselves; we need to become independent individuals who develop, update and refine their potentials constantly in order to earn a respectable place in society (i.e. among all the other learning undertakers). We are the investors in and traders of ourselves. Another, and perhaps even more frightening constriction now appears. Together with the shift from knowing *that* to knowing *how*, the subject becomes a public collection of competences and appears to be, along with all the courses on offer, a commodity on the labour market. (Compare this with Heidegger's analysis of the world and its inhabitants as *standing reserve*.)

But why criticise all the efforts to educate the individual subjects and to ensure they get the chance to develop their capacities? It seems a truism to respect and even stress the freedom of the subject to learn, to stimulate the autonomy to take ones life in one's own hands and to do something 'worthwhile' with it. Education (and thus lifelong learning as well) is—by providing all the opportunities one can think of—the liberation of Man ...

## Lifelong Learning as the Human Condition

There is however something going on with this *autonomy* of the individual learner. The debate of lifelong learning indeed emphasises the importance to orient the courses on offer toward the particular questions of the learners/consumers and the 'needs felt' by them. And thus apparently, the learner is choosing independently what to learn and according to this, which capacities to develop and train and which to ignore. For Foucault this lifelong learning hype would be a perfect example of coercive power structures which are imposed upon us. The way in which our society is organised, with its schools, hospitals and companies for example, installs certain control mechanisms. These techniques lay '... down for each individual his place, his body, his disease and his death, his well-being, by means of an omnipresent and omniscient power that subdivides itself in a regular, uninterrupted way even to the ultimate determination of the individual, of what characterizes him, of what belongs to him, of what happens to him' (Foucault, 2003, p. 590). What we are faced with are mechanisms that aim to discipline society by disciplining each of its inhabitants. This results in the society as a collection of individuals, a multiplicity of subjects that can be ordered, numbered and supervised (see also Marshall, 2000; Masschelein & Simons, 2003).

Remarkably, this has nothing to do with a kind of tyranny. On the contrary, since everything is visible and accessible (think of the personal records named above), the control is a very 'democratic' one. For '... it arranges things in such a way that the exercise of power is not added on from the outside, ... but is so subtly present in them as to increase their efficiency by itself increasing its own points of contact. ... The discipline mechanism [is] that must improve the exercise of power by making it lighter, more rapid, more effective, a design of subtle coercion for a society to come' (ibid. pp. 594, 596). People themselves become the bearers of the power structures and disciplining politics, while at the same time these mechanisms are automatized and disindividualized.

It appears that the whole idea of lifelong learning fits nicely into this framework, albeit not with Foucault's notion of biopower—the exercise of power on the body. It is Marshall's alternative notion of *busno-power* that sheds light on the educational policies and practices under concern. Busno-power 'is directed at the subjectivity of the person, not through the body but through the mind, through forms of educational practices and pedagogy which, through choices in education, shape the subjectivities of autonomous choosers. ... In producing and reproducing the form of human nature—autonomous choosers—this busno-power also impinges upon the population as a whole, as individual consumer activity "improves" both society and the economy' (Marshall, 1995, p. 322).

According to Marshall, the exercise of busno-power coincides with a total change in culture. This has to do with the merger of the economic, the social and the governmental activities on the one hand, and the attempts '... to break the distinctions between education and training, research and learning by discovery, knowledge and skills, knowledge and information, and in definitions of quality in education' on the other hand (ibid., p. 323). This rearticulation of the relations between society and its individuals, and the accompanying new forms of governmentality penetrate, still according to Marshall, the basis of human nature itself. It is the emergence of the *busnocratic rationality*.

Finally, for Marshall the central notion to busno-power is that of the *autonomous chooser*. Normally one would expect that this concept refers to, for example, a student who makes her *own* choice, that she does so independently, and that her needs and interests have not been manipulated or imposed upon her in some way. However two things are at stake here: first, since the economic, social, political and educational have merged, '[w]hat is perceived as being worthwhile in education, and what is perceived as quality education, are being imposed ... from outside the traditional educational institutions' (ibid., p. 325). This is to say, in part, that we are deluded in our notions of 'good' (rational) and 'wrong' choices, and that the way we choose is subtly directed in some way. Second, precisely as the result of busno-power and within the framework of the busnocratic rationality, the 'individual' is not merely acting *as* an autonomous chooser, but does so *because* of its nature. In other words, '[t]here is almost a postulation of a human *faculty* of choice, which is both part of human nature and which humans need to exercise to be "proper" human beings' (ibid., p. 326). We are not only or simply confronted with our freedom to choose; this freedom is imposed upon us, and we are expected to see our lives as 'the making of choices' (Masschelein & Simons, 2003).

It becomes clear then in what sense Foucault's analysis of subtle power techniques and Marshall's related notion of busno-power, help us to understand what this lifelong learning policy implies. We are encouraged to see our life as an enterprise, one of the autonomous chooser. This is to say the notion of the self is thoroughly influenced by this rationality. To be a human being is to choose to learn this and to learn that for the rest of one's natural life. We can not choose *what* we choose, neither *that* we choose (to choose). We are expected to be willing to learn for years to come, because resisting to do so is putting oneself outside our complex and rapidly changing lifestyle—apparently not wanting to survive. According to Foucault, it is not '... that the beautiful totality of the individual is amputated, repressed, altered by our social order, it is rather that the individual is carefully fabricated in it, according to a whole technique of forces and bodies' (Foucault, 2003, p. 596). The popular and concrete idea of lifelong learning incorporates mechanisms that discipline and therefore normalise people instead of emancipating them. The orientation towards the market ensures that specific economic needs will be fulfilled; the melting together of the social and the economic guard the lifelong learners against eventual irrational choices. The resulting normalisation provides society, not so much with well-educated, liberated *persons*, but rather with inter- and exchangeable units. We are faced with a kind of individualism that our society needs to survive. And it becomes easy to manipulate the needs, interests and choices, for the autonomous chooser is, as Marshall puts is, highly manipulable and easy to pick off. And again, the irony is that the individual—as an entrepreneur—will keep on developing and updating her competences, in order to be wanted.

*This being wanted* as a unit in contemporary society differs strongly from being respected as the person you are. The latter is why I feel honoured to have the opportunity to write this essay for Jim Marshall. I met him in the first month of my research fellowship, when he visited our university for three months. During his visit, we shared an office. Though at that time I was a layman in the domain of philosophy of education and had great difficulties with the English language, Jim treated me with great respect and sympathy. (Indeed, no need here for further improvement of the 'social skills'!) Together with his work, in which he always takes a critical and personal stance, his personality and style made a great impression on me, for which I am grateful.

And then it becomes clear why Marshall's theoretical and political analyses of the contemporary educational landscape, and perhaps this essay here, are relevant to those who are occupied with education. For they force us to question the kind of education we really want, and the path we have followed towards this ideal until now. Is this client-centred education thing, this lifelong learning hype, the only way we can think of education? Is this what counts for us? Is it our (only) frame of reference when we talk of education and learning? No need to say I feel uneasy with this one-sided concept that guides all our actions.

Suppose lifelong education is more than the provision of skill modules, freedom to choose and to switch. Could it be? It is hardly revolutionary to perceive education as raising the child and giving her the opportunity to make something of her life. It might be fruitful to see this as an opportunity for the educator to engage in a personal relationship wherein she can show the child what it means to live a life. Educating thus implies showing the necessity to make choices and trying to choose authentically what one finds worthwhile. This includes the recognition of all the pleasures and the constraints one faces, and their inclusion in the educative process. In other words, education is not—or at least not in the first place—about acquiring skills as much as possible, but about life itself. That is what we must teach children.

As a consequence, there can be no chance for the educator to hide behind exercises for cognitive and metacognitive skills, or to mask herself with an impressive offer of fast-food for the brain. She has to educate, not so much as the facilitator and instructor, but as the person she is. But who do we want to be? And then the question what kind of person she wants the child to be, pops up unavoidably. Who do we want the other to be? What disturbs me most in the contemporary *busno-rationality* is the base whereon people are found (and labelled) interesting and worthwhile, or not. Respect is equated with obtained certificates, recognition is levelled to acquired grades. This installs an enduring 'hunger' to 'learn' more, and the subtle coercion upon those who are endangered to fall by the wayside, to jump on the carrousel. As such, it has become a part of the human condition to be frustrated for the things one cannot realize, and to try to distinguish oneself fruitlessly from the uniformed, grey mass of 'autonomous learning entrepreneurs'. Is this constant striving, and the expansion of one's certification collection, what *counts* most? Is this what makes us think of those whom we respected most? Obviously not the skills of the other but the person she is, is what impresses us, what sticks in our memory. If so, this might have to do with finding and sharing meaning, with developing a personal stance, with creativity, with *wisdom*, with being captivated and interested, with joy and with being content, with taking time for oneself and the other, and with caring for oneself and the other.

Education then, as challenging learners, does not only mean providing them with more packages to collect, or with more complex exercises to improve and maintain their capabilities. It means to be a live example, or to encourage learners to find one. It means addressing them in a way that stimulates exploring their own ideas and wants. This too is learning for life—a continuous process that in the end may be very worthwhile. For the educator it takes the courage to face and recognize the human (all too human) concerns, to take them into account and to disrupt the attending learner. Taking this kind of risk transforms the relationship into a personal encounter and engagement, which is an opportunity to free education partly from its mechanistic, cognitivistic and dull character. And there is a good chance that a lot of educators will not mind at all. At least Jim would not …

## References

Baert, H., Kusters, W., Scheeren, J., & Van Damme, D. (n.d.). *Contouren beleid levenslang leren Vlaanderen.* Retrieved April, 2003, from http://www.kleurrijk vlaanderen.be/

FET (2003) Iedereen wil de Vlaamse Opleidingsmarkt Reoganiseren. (28/03/03) available: http://www.kleurrijkvlaanderen.be/

Foucault, M. (2003) Panopticism, in: R. C. Scharff & V. Dusek (eds), *Philosophy of Technology: The technological condition* (Oxford, Blackwell) pp. 589–602.

Marshall, J. D. (1995) Foucault and Neo-liberalism: Biopower and busno-power, in: A. Neiman (ed.), *Philosophy of Education 1995*, Proceedings of The Philosophy of Education Society, Illinois: Philosophy of Education Society, pp. 320–329.

Marshall, J. D. (1996) Education in the Mode of Information: Some philosophical considerations, in: *Philosophy of Education 1996*, Proceedings of The Philosophy of Education Society, Illinois: Philosophy of Education Society, pp. 286–276.

Marshall, J. D. (2000) Electronic writing and the wrapping of language. *Journal of Philosophy of Education*, 34, pp. 135–149.

Masschelein, J., & Simons, M. (2003) *Globale immuniteit: een kleine cartografie van de Europese ruimte voor onderwijs* (Leuven: Acco).

Vanderpoorten, M. (2002) *Een leven lang leren.* Available at: http://www.kleurrijkvlaanderen.be/showpage.asp?iPageID=538

# 6

# Testing Resistance: Busno-cratic power, standardized tests, and care of the self

CRIS MAYO
*University of Illinois*

James D. Marshall has given us multiple accounts of the problems of power and resistance in education and helped us to deeply trouble the current talismans of educational reform. He has argued that autonomy is 'unfreedom' and that educational choice is 'demeaning'. And for all of that, he has left us with much to do and suggested quite strongly that we get busy resisting rather than relying on stale concepts that prevent freedom. His work insists upon the challenging difficulties of 'care of the self', which he explains is 'a very active form of resistance'.[2] Following Foucault, Marshall understands the care of the self to be neither a passive undertaking, nor one without immense political and community responsibilities. Indeed, one cares for oneself in the process of taking account of one's power effects on others, as well as deeply problematizing the central discourses and relations through which one had understood oneself to have meaning. Marshall has also pointed to the difficult contexts in which the self as a problem must negotiate its self-overcoming and responsibility to community. Arguing that there is a new player in addition to Foucault's bio-power, Marshall contends, 'This new form of power, which I call *busno-power*, is directed at the subjectivity of the person, not through the body but through the mind, through forms of educational practice and pedagogy which, through choices in education, shape the subjectivities of autonomous choosers. Education, embedded in the frameworks of busno-power and busnocratic rationality, is the first step in the individualizing and totalizing functions of busno-power'.[3]

Arguing that the consumer has been installed where the previous, and also problematic, autonomous subject stood, Marshall argues that busno-cratic rationality uses the mechanism of consumer choice to create a new subject, one whose choice-making abilities and drive are well beyond that of the traditional liberal chooser. He argues, 'There is almost a postulation of a fundamental human *faculty* of choice, which is both part of human nature and which humans need to exercise to be 'proper' human beings. He argues that the old form of autonomy in traditional liberal theory could or could-not be exercised. 'Now, it seems, choice cannot be resisted. It is not just that human beings are autonomous, or that their autonomy can be developed, or that it is a duty to exercise autonomy, but instead there seems to be a constituent *faculty* of choice which is necessarily exercised continuously on commodities, and which sweeps aside or over-rides the traditional categories and frameworks of the human sciences on human nature'.[4] As Marshall reminds us, what is at stake in the new form of autonomy is the development of a subjectivity that 'has no theoretical need for the other, for the needs of self and the other, and social justice'. I will argue in what follows, following the insights of Foucault and Marshall, that resistance is already well underway, potentially problematic, and potentially transgressive (in Marshall's words 'a reflective reconstitution').[5] The self is not only a chooser in busno-cratic land, it is also re-commodifying itself and in so doing, beginning to struggle at the limits of its commodified situation. I will argue that commodified selves, as much as they are constrained, are also potent sites for resistance. Part of that resistance is being waged in the terrain of the high stakes test, where the self that could 'choose' runs headlong into a product that definitively limits its range of choice. In order to trace out resistance, I examine the cracks in the monolithic power of testing, cracks that point to the uncertainty of numbers and the ambivalent anxieties of test takers.

The constrained version of autonomy offered through busno-cratic 'choice' is the twin of the form of administered intelligence spawned by tests. Where one might have previously found a lever of critique in the subjective nature of grades deeming one 'lower performing' or 'average', the clean lines and mass practice of standardized tests are yet another form of wide ranging population control and management.

Like other sure-fire commodities, 'tests' have a mythic quality and their attendant statistics take on lives of their own. As Sherman Dorn argues, statistics have become the expected standard in reporting about education and in the public's understanding of how well educational systems are doing. He contends that test scores, percentiles, and other statistical measures that were once highly contextual, specific pieces of information are now doing broader work and standing for more than they actually, factually stand for.[6] The Committee on Appropriate Test Use argues that testing itself is now doing more work symbolically and practically (or impractically) than it was originally intended. Tests that were meant to provide aggregate data are being used to assess individual students and identify low-performing schools, for instance.[7] Like statistics, 'tests' are subject to rich and varied strategies of interpretation and are going far beyond authorial intention. When Time magazine reports on the SAT scores of prominent citizens, including Jennifer Lopez and George W. Bush, we can probably guess that tests are turning into a popular form of entertainment and a form of readily identifiable status, somewhat like a Rolex. (There is hope, though, that not everyone is under the spell of standardized tests. Lopez, when asked by the New York Post what she got on the SAT, replied, 'nail polish'.)

Of course the problem with high stakes testing is that it commodifies education even more than it is already commodified. As Marshall's analysis of busno-cratic 'choice' so nicely helps us to see, once Stanley Kaplan arrived on the SAT scene, intelligence comes more closely to mean the intelligent consumer, capable of purchasing the techniques of test-taking. The ability to intelligently purchase is as close as one gets to intelligence proper in this market-driven, test-driven economy. According to the Committee on Appropriate Test Use numerous studies indicate diverse support for high stakes testing, with many believing that higher standards will encourage achievement, and that few students will do poorly.[8] Clearly though, without a purchased intelligence, many students do poorly and consumer confidence is beginning to wane in the face of high numbers of 'low performing' schools. Educational consumer dissatisfaction is driving the anti-testing movement and fueling widespread test anxiety.

In what may strike us with the same ambivalent joy as the potential release of 'Chicken Soup for the Foucauldian Soul', the anti testing movement has made gains in a number of states. In what Foucault would likely take to be a better version of 'test ethics' than the usual 'do not copy your neighbor's work', parents, students, teachers, and other community members are encouraging students to stay home on test day, publicly protesting, and demanding legislative reconsideration of the tests. Some of these critiques are made within existing discourses of excellence and merit, others are critical of the funding patterns, and still others critique the technocratic rationality implicit in standardized tests. Some test-resisting parents argue, for instance, tests do not adequately measure gifted children because tests have yet to extend their evaluation to all schools subjects. But most other counter-testing movements criticize educators for penalizing under-funded school students. Further, test resisters argue that the entire school community is threatened when invidious and high stakes distinctions are made among students. No one likes to see their entire district labeled 'low performing', even if they had previously lived comfortably within a system that labeled some students in the same way. In other words, the scale of labeling, as it extends to whole populations and not just some students, is raising the ire of concerned community members who may not have even considered their membership before. A centrally administered label, then, has begun a reconsideration of the bonds of community in some areas. Further, like the resistances that have accompanied school choice, vouchers, and charter schools, testing has restarted important conversations in communities about the aims and practices of education, the range of knowledges students ought to know, and the forms of accountability that might better take the diversity of students and knowledges into account. As Marshall cautions, these are difficult processes that call into question many ideals about education long held dear, but the resistances against the machinery of testing hold promise for care of the self and its attendant care of the community.

Another form of care of the self, and thus resistance to busno-cratic power and the power of standards, is evinced in 'test anxiety'. Whether one sees test anxiety as an indication that the subject matter being tested is not central to one's intelligence, that is, does not measure (or could not measure) what one takes to be one's best interests; or one sees test anxiety as an unwillingness to conform one's intellectual efforts into a particular activity, test anxiety is an indication of the limits of 'objective testing'. Further, while forms of test anxiety may be experienced as highly individual matters, 'test anxiety' itself is a widely recognized and socially understood phenomenon. The seemingly individualized inability to conform intelligence to test taking practice may even make test anxiety a form of social identity. To paraphrase Foucault, 'the test failure was a temporary aberration, test anxiety is a species'. This is borne out by the Stanford study that found that black students taking tests in the presence of white students did considerably worse than they previously had because the social dynamics of race differential outcomes was raised in their minds by the presence of whites who are 'well known' to do better. On the one hand, the study indicates the very real effect social pressure has on test takers. But on the other hand, the study also indicates a form of 'test nullification' that some students of color explain as the reason they did so spectacularly poorly on standardized tests. They 'opt out' of competition in what they understand to be a socially and politically dangerous apparatus, and willfully opt out rather than take a test that will only confirm the social knowledge that 'black students do poorly on this test'. While the costs to the students for this practice is high, it is nonetheless a reminder that students do read the context of their activities and understand their refusal to conform as a critique of the context. That students are also able to articulate—or are encouraged by teachers to articulate—different areas of intelligence means that their ethical stance against testing may open them to 'becoming intelligent' in other areas, to making their capacities an object for scrutiny and enhancement. This 'becoming intelligent' is analogous to Foucault's contention that the gay movement should not get stuck in a concretized, unexamined form of gayness, but should instead work on 'becoming gay'. Keeping 'intelligence' open in ways that encourage the difficult process of care for the self is one way test resisters turn commodification back on itself. They are, in fact, dissatisfied consumers whose disappointment in the product offered challenges the value of the product and uses a hyper-form of choice to resist.

So standardized testing and accountability potentially can 'negatively' provide a moment for critical reflection and redefinition of what it means to 'become intelligent' as opposed to what it means to 'do well on a test'. Before I go into this I want to underscore that 'test anxiety' or poor test taking skills also bring with them norms of what good test taking ought to look like and that those norms in turn define particular forms of learning disability. So while moments of on-the-ground refusal of test 'validity' may create in students a fuller understanding of alternative knowledges and counter disciplines, they also provide a site for the further production of 'diagnoses' like disgraphia and the like.

More than a few states (though interestingly, not all) recognize that the public also has 'test anxiety', their web sites attempt to allay that anxiety by explaining the technology of the test, what it measures and what unethical school response to accountability anxiety would look like. These web sites, then, help parents and teachers to also become ethically critical of the very machinery being described. The first anxiety the sites often address is that of 'public misunderstanding' or 'myths about end of course test', indicating that accountability experts are well aware that 'objective testing' has taken on a vast variety of meanings for everyone involved. Colorado's web site[9], for instance, is aware that teachers and administrators have a stake in improving test outcomes by providing more formal and informal instruction on test material than they really should. This is more than a double bind of course because it both points out that the test is not all of knowledge but it also reminds us that the test is high stakes otherwise why would good hearted teachers and administrators be willing to sacrifice 'knowledge' for 'the test'?

> An unethical assessment practice is anything that would knowingly and deliberately harm a child or will not support or enhance student learning, such as teaching the specific content from an assessment instrument. For example, teaching a specific test or developing curriculum based on a particular test narrows the curriculum and does not enhance student learning.[10]

Among other unethical practices are, 'Developing curriculum based on the content of CSAP' as opposed to 'Preparing students for the assessment by aligning curriculum and instruction to district content standards' which is ethical. It is unethical to engage in 'Preparing instructional objectives based on specific CSAP items and teaching accordingly, rather than developing instructional objectives based on the content standards,' but ethical to 'Using CSAP released items for professional development purposes and as examples in the classroom'. Also unethical is 'Copying the vocabulary words from CSAP test items, reading passages, or writing prompts (as opposed to words from the test 'Directions'), and using them as the basis for or incorporating them into language arts instruction' and 'Leaving visible "word walls," vocabulary posters, spelling words, multiplication tables, or any other aids that could artificially inflate student scores or that are expressly forbidden in the CSAP Administration Manual'.[11]

Test policy makers are also keenly aware of how inequalities among student affect school outcomes and further, how teachers and administrators attempt to deal with these inequalities by sending them off on field trips on the day of the test. This is, of course, not ethical, but arguably neither is testing all the students, 'Encouraging lower-performing, special education, or limited English proficient students to stay home during the testing period to artificially boost apparent school performance' and 'Sending on field trips or dismissing lower-performing, special education, or limited English proficient students during the testing period to artificially inflate apparent school performance'.[12]

While I have been optimistic about resistance, standardized tests have also disciplined teachers quite effectively. While not all teachers at all times have learned to stop worrying and love the test, when classes get into discussions about testing and accountability one gets a clear sense that the teachers are learning a very strong lesson from their own working conditions and are not shy about translating what they have learned into the graduate curricula they encounter. They want more opportunity for assessment on how they are achieving the objectives of their graduate curricula. Not that they really in their heart of hearts want quizzes but they do want more of a sense, especially in the shifting discussions of philosophy, of exactly where they are and where they should be going. In other words, being practitioners has increasingly become test-oriented and thus their own educational aspirations and desires are marked by the forms of discipline they purvey in daily practice. At the same time as they can regale one another for hours with the minutiae of testing, they very clearly feel that testing is destroying the creativity of teaching and they themselves articulate the degree to which this destruction also shifts their own interrogation of educational materials into consumption of educational materials.

Still, testing also encourages resistance among teachers and administrators. They can easily see that it is not fair, for instance, that a test was originally designed to measure their teaching ability and is now being used to measure student outcomes and affect school funding. They are further frustrated by demands that improvement occur every year, even if their schools were near perfect to begin with or continue to be severely under-funded. For teachers, then, the tests are symbols of their own limitations in economically constrained circumstances and reminders of the tragedy of teaching. As they watch the shifting values of pieces of information and practices of pedagogy, they can often only wonder at the instability of 'knowledge'. Because testing is also so closely connected with the evaluation of individual students, test taking abilities have come to outline a kind of individual. Like Marshall's critique of the problematic individual formed by consumer choice and the all too unfree autonomous individual touted by educational plans, this test-defined individual is criss crossed by power and counter strategies. But as Marshall tells us, while busno-cratic power may occasionally seem monolithic, there are cracks. Likewise, as standardized tests continue to flourish, the ripples of resistance also continue.

## Notes

1. Marshall, J. D. *Michel Foucault: Personal Autonomy and Education* (Dordrecht, Kluwer, 1996), pp. 107–108.
2. Marshall, J. D. (1996) *Michel Foucault: Personal autonomy and education*, (Dordrecht, Kluwer), pp. 107–108.
3. Marshall, J. D. (1996) Foucault and Neo-Liberalism: Biopower and busno-power, in: A. Neiman (ed.), *Philosophy of Education 1995*, Urbana, IL: Philosophy of Education Society, retrieved from http://www.ed.uiuc.edu/EPS/PES-Yearbook/95_docs/marshall.html, accessed 1 May 2003.
4. Marshall, J. D. Foucault and Neo-Liberalism, retrieved from http://www.ed.uiuc.edu/EPS/PES-Yearbook/95_docs/marshall.html
5. Marshall, J. D. *Michel Foucault*, p. 219.
6. Dorn, S. (1998) The Political Legacy of School Accountability Systems, *Educational Policy Analysis Archives*, 6:1, 2nd Jan., p. 2 (web journal, accessed 14 Mar. 2001).
7. Heubert, J. P. & Hauser, R. M. (eds) (1999) Committee on Appropriate Test Use, *High Stakes: Testing for Tracking, Promotion, and Graduation*, (Washington, D. C.: National Academy Press,) p. 30.
8. Heubert & Hauser, *High Stakes*, pp. 43–44.
9. Colorado Department of Education, Ethical and Unethical Practices in the Administration of CSAP, http://www.cde.state.co.us/cdeassess/as_ethical.htm, accessed 14 Mar. 2002.
10. Ibid.
11. All of the above quotes are from Colorado Department of Education, 'Ethical and Unethical Practices in the Administration of CSAP,' http://www.cde.state.co.us/cdeassess/as_ethical.htm, accessed 14 Mar. 2002.
12. Ibid.

## References

Colorado Department of Education. Ethical and Unethical Practices in the Administration of CSAP http://www.cde.state.co.us/cdeassess/as_ethical.htm, accessed 14 Mar. 2002.

Dorn, S. (1998) The Political Legacy of School Accountability Systems, *Educational Policy Analysis Archives*, 6:1 (web journal, accessed 14 Mar. 2001).

Heubert, J. P. and Hauser, R. M. (eds) (1999) *High Stakes: Testing for Tracking, Promotion, and Graduation*, (Washington, D. C., National Academy Press).

Marshall, J. D. (1996) *Michel Foucault: Personal Autonomy and Education* (Dordrecht, Kluwer).

Marshall, J. D. (1996) Foucault and Neo-Liberalism: Biopower and busno-power, in: A. Neiman (ed.), *Philosophy of Education 1995*, Urbana, IL: Philosophy of Education Society, retrieved from http://www.ed.uiuc.edu/EPS/PES-Yearbook/95_docs/marshall.html, accessed 1 May 2003.

# 7

# Foucault, Educational Research and the Issue of Autonomy

MARK OLSSEN
*University of Surrey*

Foucault has had a major impact on the social sciences and a smaller, yet growing, impact on educational studies. In 1989 James Marshall (1989, p. 98) could note that 'educationalists had little to say on the subject'. In reviewing the works influenced directly by Foucault, Marshall refers to studies by Jones & Williamson (1979), Hoskin (1979), as well as the critical psychology of Henriques, Hollway, Urwin, Venn, and Walkerdine (1984). In the few years after Marshall made this observation, the situation began to alter. Publications by Cherryholmes (1988), Ellesworth (1989), McLaren & Hammer (1989), Walkerdine (1989), Davies (1989), Marshall (1989, 1990), Ball (1990), Miller (1990), Pagano (1990), Anyon (1991), Aronowitz and Giroux (1991), Britzman (1991), Lather (1991), McLaren (1991), Giroux (1991), and Olssen (1993), to name just some, established a veritable explosion of works influenced by Foucault or by post-structuralism generally. Indeed, since 1993 the influence of Foucault and post-structuralism on education has continued to grow, affecting almost every area of study, although Marshall's (1989, p. 98) observation that 'it is far from clear that the theoretical radicalness of the work has been grasped' would still seem to be relevant. In addition, notwithstanding an increasing volume of literature, in many places Foucault's ideas are still marginalised within the mainstream discourses of educational scholarship.

Many of the works that appeared in the late 1980s and early 1990s relating Foucault to education simply sought to explain the relevance of Foucault's distinctive orientation to education, or of post-structuralism generally (e.g. Cherryholmes, 1988, or Marshall, 1989). Others sought some sort of integration of synthesis between post-structuralism and critical theory (Giroux, 1991; Aronowitz & Giroux, 1991; Lather, 1991; Ellesworth, 1989), proposing post-structuralism as a theory of emancipation towards a more equitable society. The appeal of Foucault, as of other post-structuralist writers, was that he problematised the meta-narratives of the enlightenment and advocated the possibility of treating all knowledge and forms of pedagogy as *contingent, specific, local* and *historical* (Aronowitz & Giroux, 1991, p. 81). It permitted too the realisation of historically constituted forms of knowledge and pedagogy as 'regimes of truth' (Gore, 1993, Ch. 6) without resorting to 'top-heavy' critical meta-narratives such as Marxism. More recent works in the last decade have sought to expand the horizon, applying Foucault's approach to both substantive and methodological issues (Biesta, 1998; Popkewitz, et al., 1998; Olssen, 1999; Gale 2001; Peters, 2001; Popkewitz et al., 2001; Varela, 2001; Edwards, 2003; Marshall, 2003; Baker and Hayning, 2004; Edwards, 2004; Edwards and Nicoll, 2004; and Olssen, Codd and O'Neill, 2004).

In this paper I intend to limit my review and application of Foucault to the issue of personal autonomy, extending the work of James Marshall with that of my own 'Foucauldian-inspired' approach to the subject. In a number of papers and books spanning several years James Marshall (1989, 1990, 1995, 1996a, 1996b) has presented a Foucauldian analysis of liberal education principles focusing upon (1) personal autonomy, (2) notions of identity, (3) the adequacy of the liberal concept of authority, and (4) the notion of the improvement or progress of human beings through education or in society.

Maintaining the Foucauldian thesis that the autos or self has been constructed politically by power-knowledge, Marshall critiques the view that education is involved in the pursuit of personal autonomy, or that rational autonomy is the aim of education. For Foucault, says Marshall, the pursuit of personal autonomy in such Enlightenment terms is a social construction and is destined to fail because it masks the fact that any such persons have been constituted by political acts. As he puts it (1996a, p. 113), 'the notion of a self able to deliberate upon and accept laws so as to act autonomously as opposed to following laws heteronomously is a fiction, furnished upon the western world post-Kant as the basis for moral action but, for Foucault in the cause of governmentality'. Rather, for Foucault, says Marshall, our conception of ourselves as 'free agents' is an illusion, and he argues that liberal educators like Kenneth Strike, R. F. Dearden, Paul Hirst and R. S. Peters who advocated personal autonomy as a fundamental aim of education do not understand how modern power, through the technologies of domination and the technologies of the self, has produced individuals who are governable. As he states (1996b, p. 70):

> For [R.S.] Peters education becomes essentially the development of mind through the search for truth, essentially in the traditional academic disciplines ... In thinking rationally a person thinks on their own, autonomously. This person, the autos, is the source of law, the nomos.

For Marshall, the very concepts which we use to construct our identities are such as to make independence and autonomy illusory. Hence education via governmentality effects the production of a new form of subject—one who believes they are free. Such an education simply introduces a new form of social control and socialisation and new and more insidious forms of indoctrination where a belief in our own authorship binds us to the conditions of our own production and constitutes an identity that makes us governable. In that 'selves' do emerge it is as 'pathologised' into certain types of human beings which are discursively constructed.

The human sciences have been pivotal here as technologies of the self in the construction of human subjects as autonomous. The human sciences have produced knowledge about man during the period of the Enlightenment. This, says Marshall (1996a, p. 120), entails a 'messy involvement':

> Man enters the scene as both speaking subject and as an object that is spoken about. As speaking subject, Man represents the very conditions of

possibility of content knowledge about the object man. Foucault argues that Man as subject in the human sciences has a continuous messy involvement in knowledge about the object Man. Or, to put it another way, whereas the very conditions for the possibilities of knowledge should be separate from the contents of knowledge, or that there should be a dividing line between the transcendental and the empirical, Foucault believes that in the human sciences they are not and *cannot* be so divided.

In a related sense, utilising Foucault's concept of governmentality, Marshall (1995, 1996a, 1996b) and Peters & Marshall (1996) examine the neo-liberal notion of the autonomous chooser as embodying a particular conception of human nature, as a model of the security of the state, and as a particular model of surveillance and control. Focusing upon the massive changes in political policies regarding education, as well as other social services, which have taken place in countries such as America, Britain, Australia and New Zealand since the late 1970s, he develops a Foucauldian analysis of the reforms in terms of notions such as 'choice', 'quality', 'freedom', and 'autonomy'. In a way similar to his analysis of autonomy as a liberal educational goal, what is presupposed in the notion of the 'autonomous chooser', says Marshall, is that the notion of autonomy needed to make choices, and the notion of needs and interests entailed as a result, have not been manipulated or imposed in some way upon the chooser, but are the subject's own. A Foucauldian critique rejects such a possibility.

## Problematising Autonomy

What I want to do in the rest of this paper is extend Marshall's Foucauldian critique of autonomy to contemporary work in the political philosophy of education. Two contemporary American liberals utilising the concept of autonomy are Rob Reich (2002) and Meira Levinson (1999). Both define autonomy as the end or goal of a liberal education. For Reich the prime task for the liberal state is the creation of political virtues, such as trust and reasonableness, and these in turn presuppose that each citizen is autonomous. Reich defines autonomy as:

> A person's ability to reflect independently and critically upon basic commitments, desires and beliefs, be they chosen or unchosen, and to enjoy a range of meaningful life options from which to choose, upon which to act, and around which to orientate and pursue one's life projects. (p. 46)

Unlike Kant or Mill, or many within the liberal tradition, Reich is at pains to point out that autonomy is not a natural quality of humans but is something that is learnt. In this he has clearly taken on board many of the communitarian criticisms of liberalism, regarding the importance of an 'embedded' conception of the self, and the need not to presume a natural 'already formed' view of the human being. In order to get citizens to be autonomous, the liberal state must educate them in the political virtues. So, says Reich (p. 43), the political virtues 'imply at least that citizens are autonomous'. Reich's conclusion at this point is that autonomy must be planned for, educated for, and is not culturally neutral.

The weight Reich gives to autonomy, or as he will eventually qualify it, 'minimalist autonomy', causes serious problems for much of multicultural political theory. Here he criticizes a long list of writers in what is an impressive survey of the field, including William Galston (1995), the more staunch multiculturalists Avishai Margalit and Moshe Halbertal (1994), and Chandron Kukathas (1995, 1997). While Reich is prepared to tolerate diversity, it is only on the basis that autonomy is not compromised. Arguments, and cultural groups, that fail to respect autonomy are thus not acceptable. William Galston, who celebrates diversity over autonomy, is criticized on the grounds that the value of autonomy remains central even to Galston's project, for 'Galston packs into his account a concern for autonomy which evinces itself specifically in his discussions about civic education' (p. 52). Yet, Galston sees autonomy as only one possible mode of existence. While it needs respecting and safeguarding, what is really important is the protection of social diversity. As he puts it (1995, p. 523) 'liberalism is about the protection of diversity, not the valorization of choice'. Because some cultures may not value choice, Galston, adopts the familiar tactic among multiculturalists of allowing for a 'right to exit'. Reich indicates he is unhappy with arguments of this sort for any 'right to exit' *presupposes autonomy*, for autonomy underlies such abilities as critical independent judgement which are necessary in order to make decisions about whether one wants to exit ones cultural group or not. In this way, Reich keeps coming back to his argument that because autonomy is central to the creation of the political virtues, it cannot be compromised, and must assume a fundamental role—for all cultural groups.

Theories of the liberal multiculturalists, and theories of group rights, are also criticized (Reich, Ch. 3). His objection to group rights is not on the usual grounds that group rights threaten common citizenship values, but rather that with regard to group rights, groups trump individuals, and hence individuals—frequently children— become sacrificed to the interests of the group. Although the 'right to exit' is usually held up as the bulwark of a minimal liberalism, in Reich's view, it can not perform the task required of it. Such arguments apply even against 'sophisticated' liberal multiculturalists like Kymlicka (1989, 1995) who also takes the concept of autonomy seriously. But group rights don't effectively give children a meaningful right of exit, even in Kymlicka's theory. In this sense, Kymlicka's conception of autonomy is unsatisfactory and his defense of rights to separate schooling for some cultural minorities is weak in that it constitutes a punitive restriction for children by confining them *within* a particular cultural group. Meaningful autonomy, as Reich will argue, presupposes *inter-cultural awareness*, which Reich maintains (in an unfair characterization of Kymlicka's views) Kymlicka's theory fails to acknowledge or resolve.

Clearly Reich's view of liberalism as a doctrine grounded in autonomy, based on the respect for individuals and the choices they make, has radical implications for multicultural theory of education. Recognising historical problems with autonomy as developed by writers like Kant and Mill, where it assumed the role as an overarching metaphysical postulate, Reich limits his conception to what he terms 'minimalist autonomy'. Minimalist autonomy, he claims, avoids the troublesome effects of the 'strong' conception, avoids being 'rarefied' or 'elitist', and doesn't assume an important role in the architecture of the political theory. As he tells us:

> Minimalist autonomy will not insist that an autonomous life be one that makes the person both author and subject of universal moral laws, nor will it insist that people create for themselves a life like any other. What is important for a minimalist conception of autonomy is that autonomous persons are self-determining, in charge of their own lives, able to make significant choices from a range of meaningful options about how their lives will unfold. (p. 100)

Reich then makes three important distinctions. The first concerns the fact that autonomy does not apply to reason, but to the 'a person's life or character'. As he states:

> When we ask whether or not people are autonomous actors or agents, we normally mean to ask about the extent to which they are able to lead the life they desire for themselves, to act upon the commitments, values, wishes and beliefs they deem worthy: we are asking whether they exhibit an autonomous character, a character that is exhibited in the way that a person adheres to his conception of the good life. Autonomous persons are discernable not on the basis of any particular act but on the basis of an overall shape they give to their lives, the freedom this has in making decisions for themselves that relate to fundamental aspects of their lives. (p. 92)

Reich's second point is that autonomy is a matter of degree, not an all or nothing state. People he observes are not born autonomous:

> Furthermore, the exercise of autonomy will vary by degree not only within each person and over a lifetime, but also by degree across persons. Individuals are variously capable of leading autonomous lives, some more so than others. (p. 93)

Reich's third distinction concerns the difference between autonomy and liberty. Central to autonomy is 'reflection' rather than 'the fidelity of tradition'. But being autonomous is not reducible to acting freely:

> Autonomy carries with it an implication of directing ones' life through choices made independently and reflectively. To be free or to have liberty involves on the other hand, an absence of constraints (negative liberty) or organisation of character (positive liberty) that enables choice making, but says little about the actual course and character of a person's life. (p. 95)

Meira Levinson (1999) also develops the notion of autonomy as central to her weak perfectionist brand of liberalism and claims this is essential to liberal education.

According to Levinson, the problem with political liberals like Rawls is that they cannot argue convincingly from (1) the fact of pluralism over values and ideologies; to (2) fair and neutral criteria that justify liberal procedures, to (3) the substantive realisation of institutions that support constitutional democracy. Rawls, she says, radically underestimates the extent and depth of pluralism and reasonable disagreement, and seeks artificially to constrain it through his arguments concerning the 'burdens of judgement'.[1] The fact is, however, that there is no way to argue from pluralism to liberal proceduralism, and from there to constitutional democracy, unless one establishes liberal autonomy as a value the state must be committed to. Such a concept must indeed be 'thick' enough to justify state support for constitutional democracy, and 'thin' enough that the vast majority of people agree.

Levinson defines autonomy as 'the capacity to form a conception of the good, to evaluate ones values and ends with the genuine possibility of reviving them should they be found wanting' (p. 15). A few pages later (p. 19) she defines it as 'the capacity to evaluate one's values and ends self-critically with the possibility of revising and then realising them'. She claims that any liberal justification of substantive liberal institutions and freedoms rests on such a value. And, in parenthesis she notes (p. 33) '*incidentally*, that the achievement of autonomy requires that individuals basic needs be fulfilled, including the provision of food, shelter, clothing, affection, and self-esteem, to give a partial but representative list' (emphasis added). Clearly, neither Reich, nor Levinson, would see their support for autonomy as excluding support for a welfare state.

Levinson's justification for using the concept certainly indicates the seriousness of the cause, for as she explains it, there is need for a perfectionist principle if liberal institutions and values are to be justified. It is certainly correct, given the way she proceeds, that there is need for some principle or other, if the liberal state is to be justified, and the concept of autonomy builds in the idea that each individual will have an equal space and be in charge of their life. That individuals' rights to make decisions over their lives be recognised and respected and for such rights to be enshrined in law is the basis of the principle. This is important for liberals, and it is a worthy ideal, but we should note that the idea of justifying liberal institutions is not unimportant for Foucault, and for that matter, all non-totalitarians. What Foucault would suggest is that concepts other than autonomy can do this just as well, and with far fewer negative effects than use of the concept of autonomy brings with it. While the concept of autonomy may convey ideals that are important, it *misrepresents* at the same time. A Spinozist, for example, might suggest that 'self preservation and well-being' (*conatus*) could provide such a principle, where a concern for freedom and security are seen as integral to such a principle, and thus become important in justifying the types of institutions we live with. Spinoza, like Foucault, did not develop a specifically liberal philosophy, or not one commonly recognised as within the liberal tradition of political philosophy, but nevertheless was concerned ultimately with the values of democratic justice and freedom. 'The true aim of the republic is freedom', said Spinoza (1985, Chp. XX, p. 241). I mention this because Spinoza influenced Deleuze, and Foucault, and (with some adaptation) can be used to supplement Foucault to provide scope for a normative political theory, and overcome the problems of epistemological and moral relativism.[2] It is as well to point out that liberals have no monopoly on a concern with such values. Indeed, the perfectionism of self preservation and well-being would surely be better, and one could argue, as I have endeavoured to do elsewhere (Olssen, *et al.*, 2004) that these dictate a conception of democracy which has multiple values including *freedom*, *security*, *equality* and *inclusion*. In such a conception, the concept of *autonomy* is not necessary. Not because autonomy does not, as a conception, contain values of importance, but rather for two reasons. Firstly, because the term contains too many ideas of importance, and yet fails to differentiate between them, i.e., because the term is too diffuse, too abstract, and in short too indeterminate; secondly, because it grounds political obligation to the individual's private arena, underemphasising the social relations, ethical duties and responsibilities, and the complexities of the individual-collective interaction. In this sense, utilisation of the concept in political philosophy has distorting effects of an ideological nature.

To start with the idea that the concept is too diffuse, let me point to a few possible meanings that it is not sensible to run together. First, as people are interdependent and inter-connected in the structures of social support, and to other people, the concept is—when applied to people, rather than city-states—technically inappropriate, as I will comment further below. Second, while autonomy is the basis of freedom, it is also the basis of the competitive market order. That is, it is the privileged and protected space in which competitive entrepreneurial conduct takes root, and one might say, is in this sense both the normative underpinning of *homo economicus*, and more generally of white Anglo Saxon protestant middle class values. In this sense, autonomy has served to link the freedom of individuals in the history of liberalism to natural law theories of property rights, to government strategies of laissez-faire, to arguments for a minimal state, and for support for policies of low taxation. While it is unfair to accuse Reich or Levinson of advocating these types of policies, it is difficult to dissociate these various ideals within the expansive semiotic possibilities of the concept, especially when considered in relation to the history of its usage. Third, it is also the model of *personal health* (for Levinson extremely needy people cannot be autonomous) and thus a political ideal is confounded with a psychological and medical one; Fourth, it is also the model, or principle of a *healthy polis*. By this, it refers to a political formula of legitimate as opposed to illegitimate state action, concerning the issue of individual freedom or liberty. Fifth, relatedly, the concept is also used to support a notion of individual rights as fundamental. The conception of rights supported by Reich and Levinson is implicitly a traditional one with connotations of self-ownership and exclusive sovereignty, which sees the self as existing in a natural arena with exclusive rights of ownership and control over private decisions, set against the artificiality of society, and the danger of the collective. Sixth, notwithstanding an explicit concern to distance autonomy from Kant, autonomy is invoked to refer to 'critical judgement', both in a cognitive and moral sense. As Reich (p. 95) says, '[a]utonomy carries with it an implication of directing one's life through choices made independently and reflectively'. This ability to make decisions which are assumed to be the individual's own, unrelated to the social and historical milieu is evident in both writers works. To some extent, this independence of judgement coalesces with the first point, concerning separateness or independence of a life, but it would seem to me that the first point contains an economic and political dimension while the second refers more directly to mind or consciousness. But, whether this is so or not, it would appear that the concept of autonomy is something of a Trojan horse that carries a number of different riders. When cultural groups such as the Amish with to withdraw from public system of education, their rejection of the concept of autonomy may well be related to *the other work done in its name*, rather than any opposition to the development of independent thinking skills in its children. They might also claim that one's liberal freedoms, if taken literally within certain versions of the harm principle, sanction types of behaviour which liberals themselves do not permit their children to engage in.[3] They may claim that it carries unfortunate associations with traditional models of property rights and self-ownership, or that it allows for and promotes forms of behaviour which are arrogantly disrespectful of community traditions and norms. Or it may claim, as I will, that it implicates liberal underpinnings which are in contradiction to recent extensions of democratic theory in a global direction.

From a Foucauldian perspective, it should be noted at the outset, that the objections are not to the value of freedom, or of constitutional democracy, or to the value of rights. Rather, the objections are to the theoretical and methodological function of the concept of autonomy within liberal philosophers' theories. It is claimed that such a concept in seeking to ground liberal polity also misrepresents and distorts the character of social existence. Although it alludes to and identifies important qualities (freedom, control, rights, etc), it does so in a way that distorts the overall frame of reference in a particular political direction. One of its drawbacks is the very expansiveness of the possible meanings such a concept conveys. Hence, while it identifies some values which many people hold to be important, it is also ideological. Further, I will argue that the methodological work such a concept does to justify democracy can better be done by other means—means which preserve what is valuable in 'autonomy', but are more specifically focused and include other important dimensions and values as well.

What can be noted from the outset is how the word is in many instances inaccurate when applied to individuals. Such a concept, originally applied to city-states, made sense in that the city-state *was* independent.[4] Kant used the term to apply to the fact that reason operated in the noumenal realm and was *unconditioned* by sensuous experience, hence, quite literally, *it was autonomous*.[5] Reich, as we have seen, criticizes the transcendental sense in which Kant uses the term. Both he and Levinson use the term in a different sense to refer to the overall quality or character of a life, and in the ability of individuals to engage in reflective critical thinking determining the overall form of a life. But lives do not develop in separateness, and independence from the world. People may be capable in dealing with the world, but this is a far cry from saying they are autonomous or separate from it. Indeed, it is not inaccurate to say that autonomy is precisely what people—who are interdependent as the empirically ascertainable condition of their being—*do not have*. As the word is commonly used, it is what many people—the disabled; the mentally impaired; the sick; the elderly, the young—cannot even aspire to. But I do not want to refer specifically to special groups, as I will maintain that nobody is autonomous in this sense. To define the perfection of the state in terms of such a value therefore will obviously short-change many groups. To make it the foundation value of the state also potentially exonerates the state from responsibility to assist its citizens when in need. It is not so much of a slippage, after all, from arguing that 'the state should assist people to become autonomous' to arguing that 'they expect all to *be* autonomous'.

Levinson, like Reich, can of course acknowledge that as a capacity autonomy is a matter of degree. It is not seen as a natural condition but as something to be achieved. Both have bought into, and acknowledged, most of the communitarian criticisms of the early Rawls, and see the self as 'embedded', and therefore concede that people are only partially autonomous. Reich sees the problem here in the following way: if autonomy is never fully realised and is only a potential to be achieved, it can hardly function as the locus of state respect for individuals. Hence, Reich states (2002, pp. 93–94) that as well as being a *capacity*, it must also be a *condition*. As a capacity it is partial. But as a condition it is total, and is always 'on'.

One is still left wondering 'why autonomy?', rather than, say, 'respect' or 'dignity' or 'well-being', 'freedom', 'integrity' or even just plain simply 'rights'? While it makes sense to suggest that individuals should have rights to challenge or contest authority, and even that they have the freedom to do so, it is far from clear that they are ever 'autonomous' in the sense that is clearly conveyed in this term, of being 'self-sufficient', or 'independent'. While many people may aspire to become self-sufficient, not all groups have this aim, and those that profess to—including one suspects liberal philosophers—frequently mistake the ideology of the society for the reality, as the ideal. Even when we profess autonomy as ideal, we delude ourselves; people are far less independent that they feel, or claim. It is really that we suffer the myth of the 'self made' person, believing that we are far more independent than we are. As Hobhouse (1911) made clear there is a social factor in achievement which is frequently unacknowledged, and sometimes unrecognised. We start from a situation of non-autonomy, and end in one as well. Some of us attain what appears as reasonable partial autonomy, but is in fact more dependent on the structures of social support than possibly believed. Even for those who do so aspire, what is really meant in such an ideal is a degree of reasonable self-sufficiency, of mature judgement, and reasonable detachment of perspective, as they balance the interests of themselves and their families with those of the community, and the polis. In that it is autonomy, it is of a highly relative and qualified nature.

This last comment raises yet another concern about use of the concept, and this concerns the sense in which it functions *ideologically*. Are the skills that Reich and Levinson and others associate with it as residing under its banner really indicative of 'autonomy'? Or, to put it differently, are western liberal societies so independent and self-critical, self reflective about their lives and goals. Is it really true that certain minorities all follow tradition and we all think for ourselves? Do we really educate children for critical reflective selfhood? Certainly, individuals exercise free choices within specific constraints, and with varying degrees of success, they manage and control much of their own lives. Such freedom is exercised as choice over fairly ordinary options in day to day living, which are the same types of choices exercised in all cultures by all peoples. It's called living. Such freedom is also seen as the legitimate basis of the way societies in the west should be organised. But, as I will argue, one does not need the concept like autonomy to serve this function. It can be argued that the very use of the concept assumes a degree of 'self-reliance' which is illusory, however, for the very concept embodies the self-reliant and individualistic conception of the person that has been the hallmark of western liberalism, and which is avidly promoted through its popular forms of entertainment and media. It not only understates the degree of interconnectedness and interdependence that characterizes relations in societies; but it exaggerates the extent to which people are independent and self-legislating. Every individual depends far more than they probably imagine—and far more than liberal political philosophers have traditionally acknowledged—on the structures of social and institutional support. Even those few who finally end up being highly competent at achieving life's goals cannot really be said to be 'autonomous' in anything but a highly qualified sense. It is rather that their privileged capabilities depend on a whole network of complex structures and supports.

Related to this, citizens—both adults and children—are far more the products of normalization and socialization than they believe, or claim. But in individualistic cultures, the normalized representations are to models of 'choice', where the choices which are much of the time between the 'colours and the brands', are to a large extent illusory, or at least not significantly different from the choices made by people in all sorts of different cultures of the world. And in that people are socialized, they are 'responsibilized' through strategies of 'power-knowledge' to believe they are freer than they really are. The liberal middle classes manifest far more respect for the 'fidelities of tradition' than they believe, or at least claim. With relation to children, it can be claimed that education is structured not so much as to critically inform their minds, or to get them to engage in reflective practice, but rather to 'protect' their minds and adopt 'appropriate' middle class values. What is evident is that the very use of such a concept resonates the arrogance and self-deceiving nature of western phallocentricism, ethnocentrism and class-centrism. It helps create and perpetuate the illusion that we are more self-reliant than we are, that we are (solely/largely) responsible for our own achievements, and that we are the 'self-originating sources' of our values and goals. For contemporary liberals like Reich and Levinson, if this is no longer realistic as an originating idea, it is still operative as an end goal for education to pursue. Here I would claim they frequently seem to confuse autonomy with privilege.

In addition, and as a consequence of this, as both Reich and Levinson develop their case for autonomy-based liberalism, notwithstanding their denial, it assumes a metaphysical status within the theories they develop. Not only does it potentially harbour unacknowledged bedfellows such as market man, thus inadvertently contextualising autonomous critical development in an enterprise society, but it assumes an unhistorical and formal character which empties it of much significance. When Reich argues (p. 94) that as well as being a 'capacity', it must be respected as a (total, always 'on') 'condition', he is inserting it as a foundational ontic premis for which he has not a single scrap of evidence or support. It serves then a purely normative function within his theory, a matter I will address below.

Both may claim that in arguing for 'minimalist' autonomy, they themselves recognise the sociological objections I have raised above. If it is to do the important work in relation to both education and normative political theory it must be strong enough to justify a constitutional democracy, and yet 'thin' enough to apply to and appeal to almost all people. To support this they recognise the rights of groups to be 'non-autonomous' if they wish.[6] Another argument both maintain in order to support their arguments for 'minimal' autonomy is to draw a distinction between *self-determination* and *self-creation* or *self-authorship*. Individuals, they claim, are self-determining, but not self-creating. The inference is that self-determination is somehow 'less than' self-creation. Yet, I would argue that no real distinction can be made here, and they fail to justify grounds to differentiate the two. As most poststructuralist philosophers who have utilised the Nietzschean conception of self-creation maintain that every action has a *novel* aspect, self-determining actions *are* self-creating. The idea of self-determination, like that of self-creation, needs careful qualification, as it still implies *total control* of the individual over their environment. While the individual as a bearer of rights of citizenship is a vital stakeholder, any actual determinations reflect a complex balance of forces and strategies. As Foucault (1977a) explains, 'the man described for us, whom we are invited to free, is already in himself the effect of a subjection much more profound than himself'. Although he utilises practices of the self in the tasks of invention, 'these practices … are not something that the individual invents by himself. They are patterns that he finds in the culture and which are proposed, suggested, and imposed on him by his culture, his society and his social group' (1991, p. 11). Underpinning the determinations of individuals is a mix of shaping and conditioning forces and necessities. While this doesn't mean that freedom is not possible, and is possibly cumulatively successful over time, the agency of the self is intermittent and only one of a variety of factors affecting the course of a life.

A further related problem concerns the act of endeavouring to clarify what sort of personality-type 'autonomy' really describes. This is a problem that entangles Levinson, who disagrees with Dworkin (1988) over who is and who is not worthy of being called autonomous. Complaining that Dworkin's conception is purely formal, and not substantive, Levinson objects to Dworkin wanting to consider Harry autonomous when he is 'deeply psychologically dependant on his mother's approval' (p. 27), and similarly for people who 'abdicate control over the direction of [their lives]' (p. 28). A further point of contention emerges over 'Sister Susan' (p. 33) who devotes her life to the obedience to God. Whereas Dworkin would see Sister Susan as autonomous, Levinson doesn't see how she could be. She concludes that 'Dworkin's notion of autonomy is untenable as it currently stands, and further that it cannot provide a fruitful foundation for liberal freedoms'(p. 29). To his credit, Dworkin recognises the problems created when one considers the concept of autonomy in the light of basic human connectedness. As he puts it (1988, p. 21), 'the conception of autonomy that insists upon substantive independence is not one that has claims to our respect as an ideal … [it is] inconsistent with loyalty, objectivity, commitment, benevolence, and love'. Levinson (1999, p. 30) admits that 'such a notion of autonomy, if truly inconsistent with these virtues, is highly unappealing'. Yet, in contrast to Dworkin, her own more substantive conception ends by classifying only those who are psychologically independent, or as tending to independence, as being fit candidates for classification as autonomous. Although her tone is cautious when she notes that 'certain conditions, such as extreme neediness or dependence, can never be compatible with autonomous action' (p. 32) she creates the unfortunate 'sense', as a consequence of such a line of analysis (which coalesces with the general image of the Hollywood action-hero), of representing both social and psychological independence as the new figure of health in the brave new world of 'autonomy-based' liberalism.[7]

In relation to the issue of philosophical justification for the liberal state, and system of education, one real and important question that liberals wish to answer, and invoke autonomy to try to answer, is the issue of individual versus state discretion over jurisdiction. As Keynes (1931, pp. 312–313) put it in a different context, but one that highlights the real question being addressed here, the central issue concerns: 'what the state ought to take upon itself to direct by the public wisdom, and what it ought to leave with as little interference as possible to individual exertion?'. For John Stuart Mill (1859, p. 13), this was embodied in his formulation of the harm principle, which determined, in brief, that individuals are free to do anything they like, so long as their behaviour does not harm the interests of any other person, or group. Fundamentally, this concerns the issue of rights. In theory, to decide that individuals are, or ought to be, autonomous, means that the state has a duty to respect that autonomy.

That liberals utilise 'autonomy' to endeavour to solve this question is worthy. Both Reich and Levinson do a credible job in terms of the liberal philosophy they proffer. One suspects that this is the real reason that they seek to justify autonomy, not particularly because it has anything particularly to do with children, or psychological or cognitive independence, but because it defends *a way of life*. It's a particular form of 'rights-talk'. My argument is, however, that one does not need to 'invent' autonomy in order to safeguard individual rights and freedoms. Individual rights and freedoms are important to everyone's security and well being, even without autonomy. The concept of freedom, which is different to autonomy, is all that is required as far as John Stuart Mill's 'harm principle' is concerned. For Foucault, while rights are important, there are no rights antecedent to society. Moreover, Mill's presumption that some actions of individuals are 'self-regarding' and therefore of no concern to other people or society, as if individuals operated in some sort of 'nature-reserve', or exclusively private domain, would be untenable for Foucault. Given the self is social—by nature as it were—the issue of what a person can regard as their own, and claim 'rule' over is not directly what does not 'harm' others, but what may potentially harm others, what is even of concern to others in terms of its long-term, short-term, or even possible effects. In this sense, while Mill's principle may be a useful 'rule of thumb' given avowed goals of freedom and well being as the aims of the republic, as a principle it will always *underdetermine* any possible application in practice. What fills the gap is deliberation, contestation, and *public* arbitration made possible through a more expansive conception of democratic control.

In that Reich and Levinson invoke autonomy to defend a conception of rights however, it builds in a particularly liberal conception of individual rights as foundational. Hence Reich objects to Kymlicka privileging group rights over individual rights, on the grounds that 'individuals—frequently children—become sacrificed to the interests of the group'. Yet I find it problematic in Reich's account that individual and group rights are treated as mutually exclusive. There is an important sense again that we all live within groups, and our interests are to varying extents if not sacrificed, certainly effected by the groups within which we live. This is necessarily so, and that Reich objects to the influence of the group on individuals, simply reflects his liberal philosophical heritage. From Kymlicka's perspective, while he supports a conception of group rights, it had not occurred to me before reading Reich that he therefore excluded individual rights. In New Zealand certain group rights were given to Māori with reference to seats in Parliament, places in schools and higher education institutions, but these did not cancel the ordinary rights of citizens under the law. Reich says that acknowledging a 'right to exit' (which Kymlicka does) is not adequate, for prior to exercising an option of 'exit' a child would need to make a 'critical judgement', and this presupposes 'autonomy' as basic. Such an argument is fallacious on several grounds. First, children's ability to recognize abuse, or violence, or to think for themselves when confronted with unpleasant necessities, does not indicate 'autonomy', and the very application of this term—now in relation to children's mental faculties—shows clearly the paucity of the concept. Second, in that Kymlicka (as Reich concedes) acknowledges an 'exit' option, he clearly *is* recognizing the mutual co-existence of individual with group rights. The realistic issue is not concerning 'exit' of course, as children of all groups rarely have such an option in actual life. But the right is important, in that a right to 'exit' is also a right to complain, to appeal, to telephone a 'help line', to originate legal redress, and so on. In recognizing a right to 'exit' therefore, Kymlicka is not expressing a 'minimal liberalism' but acknowledging the importance of individual rights under the law as a general condition. Similarly, Reich criticizes Kymlicka for promoting group rights to the exclusion of inter-cultural awareness. But again, these two are not mutually exclusive. It is a case of both/and, not either/or. The more that one probes, the more such a conception of rights appears as a reinvention of traditional natural rights of the solitary (autonomous) individual of classical liberalism.[8] For Foucault, rights are important, not because any such foundation exists, but because they have proved historically important in protecting individuals and groups relative to the imperatives of well-being and survival. They save lives.

The real point here, however, is that while autonomy may well invoke some important values, to the extent it does so, it brings with it a number of other problems. Related to the points considered above, it may, indeed, seek ideologically to 'stack the deck' in advance, to expand the entitlements and responsibilities of the individual as against the collective, and one can suspect that liberal and neo-liberal arguments coalesce here. Such arguments historically have done a great deal to maximize individual and private entitlements to wealth, and understated the

values of equality and collective determination. If the 'autonomy' of each is emphasised, one also, by definition as it were, underplays the responsibilities and duties
which we owe to each other, individually and collectively. In fact, one could say
that an emphasis upon 'autonomy' denies such responsibilities. If we are autonomous we are not interdependent; if we are not interdependent we do not owe
each other anything. Such viewpoints have also been linked to campaigns to erode
welfare state ('individual's should be responsible for themselves'); to argue for a
reduction of state size and functions (laissez-faire) and to mobilise for free trade
(which is what richer nations demand when their own economies are in order).

None of this, however, argues against rights, individual and group. That a constitutional democracy legislates a protected space, a system of rights and entitlements, is also important; that individuals require certain capabilities to function
effectively in such a society can be acknowledged and accepted. But these are
characteristics of the *political system* which defends and protects freedom and security. They concern the *socio-institutional* sense in terms of which freedom is exercised, and pre-suppose certain *institutional* and *political* arrangements. Autonomy in
this sense is akin to the stability generated by a system of equal legal rights. In
Kymlicka's usage, this seems understood, but with both Reich and Levinson there
is a confusion of the personal with the political.

In this sense, rather than autonomy being privileged, inhering in the protection
of individual against the demands of other individuals, or of society as a whole, it
would be more appropriate to emphasis *democracy*, which by origin, attests to 'rule
by the people', but which is better construed as a discourse which specifies rights,
entitlements and obligations, and the protection of individuals and groups, both
against each other and against their leaders, or those in power. In addition, as I
have claimed, we must also balance the demands of freedom against those of
equality, security, inclusion, participation, and social justice. While we can agree
that societies exist for the individuals who make them up, it is unwise to reify any
one term as a central ontological postulate. This is especially so in relation to
education, for while children develop, and hopefully realise their potentials, what
is needed to be understood is what freedom means, and how it can be expressed
in the context of social, national and global *connectedness*. Rather than consider
them as autonomous, or as potentially autonomous, it is preferable to consider
what is owed them, and what they owe. In the educational context, my own
preference is to speak of 'capabilities', such as critical reason, cognitive and cultural
capital and resources, emotional and social capital, and so on. Capabilities also
linked with needs, where resources and the structures of support are emphasised.
Martha Nussbaum (1992) refers to such capabilities as constituting a 'thick vague'
conception of the good. Such a conception comprises 'the most important functions of human beings in terms of which human life is defined' (p. 214) Such a
conception is not metaphysical in the sense that it does not claim to derive from a
source exterior to human beings in history, or to privilege a single term or concept
as grounding educational development. Rather, such a conception is 'as universal
as possible' and aims at 'mapping out the general shape of the human form of life,
those features which constitute life as human wherever it is' (p. 216). This sort of

approach also has the virtue of balancing freedom with equality and the concerns of justice. Now, if we are to educate for the political virtues required for democracy, in my view education must pursue a capabilities approach.

## Towards a Foucauldian Conception

Ultimately, from a Foucauldian point of view, autonomy 'over-individualises' and confuses the effects of a certain form of power by which individuation takes place. By focusing on 'autonomy' as a personal trait, what the liberal philosophers do is to reduce the political domain as a trait of individuals (autonomous selves), thus perfecting the philosophical *interiorisation* that Foucaucalt (1997) traced to Descartes, and that Charles Taylor (1989) also traces in *Sources of the Self*, from the external to the internal; from Plato to modernity, involving both a *pyschologicization* and a *social abnesia*, not recognized in some cultures, possibly, inversely with the extent to which individualistic values have become sedimented into the deep structures of normalisation within the culture. What is being complained of here is a tendency to attribute what should be described at the level of the system or culture, to being a characteristic of individuals. What should really be meant by autonomy, is not a personal attribute of individuals with relation to their conduct, but *one* aspect of a democratic state. When, in other words, liberal philosophers talk of 'autonomy'; they are essentially speaking of democracy, with its implication of equal rights for all.

This is another way of saying that the concern with autonomy is a specifically modern exercise. During the seventeenth and eighteenth centuries morality and conduct was conceived in terms of obedience, which came to be increasingly contested and replaced with emerging conceptions of morality and life as an exercise in self-governance (Schneewind, 1998). This newly emerging individualism principally derived from four sources: (1) from the protestant reformation of the fifteenth and sixteenth centuries (2) from the scientific revolution of the sixteenth and seventeenth centuries, (3) from political and economic liberalism's emerging in the seventeenth century; and (4) from the industrial revolution of the eighteenth and nineteenth centuries. In each of these areas, specific proposals (religious worship, political obligation, scientific method) confounded various senses or forms of individualism—descriptive, moral, religious, political—asserting what in essence was a *metaphysic of individualism* against the more social and communitarian metaphysic of the *ancien regime*. The implication of this was to fashion a conception of the individual as 'owner and creator of his own capacities' (Macpherson, 1962). The ontological priority of the individual was reinforced by a broad spectrum of social and political theory and is closely tied to social, religious, economic and political changes from the sixteenth century onwards. The Reformation and the attendant protestant religion gave rise to a new spirit of individualism whereby each individual could communicate directly with God and was solely responsible for his (or even her) salvation.[9] With the expansion of empire, the growth of science and the enlightenment belief in progress, the idea that the individual was master of their fate was further encouraged. Partly this was inspired by the successful methods of the physical sciences which employed mathematical laws, measurement quantification, and based itself on a metaphysic of atomism, reducing complex physical phenomena to its smallest component particle. Believing that the social world could be studied in the same way was to generally endorse the search for the truth of life in the individual.

Classical liberal individualism encompassed all aspects of life. In *The Wealth of Nations*, published in 1776, Adam Smith sought to explain laissez-faire capitalism as a consequence of the natural competition of the individual in very much the same way, with respect to basic postulates, that Darwin later sought to explain the processes of natural selection at work in the origins and evolution of species. In political philosophy John Stuart Mill was to frame a political conception of liberty to safeguard political freedom within a laissez-faire approach to capitalism. Others such as Jeremy Bentham and Herbert Spencer were to legitimise 'non-intervention', 'individual liberty' and 'unregulated competition' as being part of the *natural order of things*, reinforcing what was an ascendant view of society as a consequence of solely individual initiatives.

C. B. Macpherson has described the strain of thought in his book *The Political Theory of Possessive Individualism* (1962) and describes how, through a variety of thinkers from Thomas Hobbes to John Stuart Mill, English political and social thought from the seventeenth century to the nineteenth century is characterised by the idea of possessive individualism. This idea, says Macpherson, became axiomatic to liberal democratic thought and to scientific movements. In the nineteenth century it became an underlying and unifying assumption. Its 'possessive' quality is found in the condition of the individual as essentially the proprietor of his (or presumably her) own person or capacities, owing nothing to society for them. Thus for theorists such as Hobbes, Locke, Adam Smith, Herbert Spencer, Bentham, Mill, Galton, the individual 'pre-figures' society and society will be happy and secure to the extent that individuals are happy and secure. Not only does the individual own his/her own capacities but also, more crucially, each is morally and legally responsible for him or herself. Freedom from dependence upon others means freedom from relations with others except those relations entered into voluntarily out of self-interest. Human society is simply a series of market relations between self-interested subjects. For Adam Smith it is guided by an 'invisible hand'. For John Locke society is a 'joint stock company' of which individuals are shareholders.

From a Foucauldian view this process of political individualism led to individualistic explanations at the level of the social and psychological sciences. Thus in his earliest published book, *Mental Illness and Psychology*, first published in 1954, Foucault (1987) traced how dysfunctions in the structure of societies, or environments, were represented as the pathologies of individuals—as 'conformity-disorders', 'behaviour problems' and the like.

With the liberal political philosophers there was a shift in the locus of political obligation from the community (obedience) to the individual (self-governance), although this transition was never as 'cut and dried' as it is often represented. From the time of Socrates individual rights have been argued about and violated, just as they have been from the seventeenth to the twenty-first centuries. What Foucault recognised was that the individual was never as autonomous or independent as modernity had represented them. The ideology of individualism may well have been useful in many arenas—science, religion, capitalist expansion—but it misrepresented the origins of identity, and the social and historical nature of selfhood. It obscured, also, the ontological independence of the social, as Wittgenstein (1953) had pointed out with his writing on 'forms of life' and our mistaken attributions regarding the private origins of language.

While the community defines identity through its objectified social practices, this doesn't deny the individual rights, however. But the rights of individuals do not emerge from nature, but through the common aim to survive. Thus, Foucault speaks of 'human rights' to 'confront governments' which is beyond the limits of nationality. As he puts it:

> There exists an international citizenship that has its rights and its duties, and that obliges one to speak out against every abuse of power, whoever its author, whoever its victims. After all, we are all members of the community of the governed, and thereby obliged to show mutual solidarity. (Foucault, 2001, p. 474)

International organisations have, says Foucault, 'created this new right—that of private individuals to effectively intervene in the sphere of international policy and strategy' (p. 475). The basis for such a cosmopolitan network, he perceived, was emerging, if only embryonically at the time he wrote, with the rise of NGOs and global conferences on trade, war, population and environment, which suggested the emergence of a new global public sphere. The emergence of public institutional forums, both national and global,[10] enabled deliberation and contestation, and ensured rights. Rather than educate children to be autonomous, one must give them the political capabilities to act in public and global arenas. It is by strengthening public institutions that democracy will work and that equal legal rights can be enforced.

In such a global system, new dimensions of democracy serve to transform traditional notions of rights, and freedom. *Transparency* is one such practice. As Anderson (2005, p. 9) observes:

> It was the principle of transparency, abolishing *arcana imperii* that had always characterized the foreign policies of democracies and tyrannies alike, under the pretext that affairs of state were too complex and delicate to broadcast to the public, and too dangerous to reveal to the enemy. Such secrecy could not but erode democracy itself, as innumerable actions— at home and abroad—as the national security services of contemporary states testified. Here a vicious circle was at work. States could only become fully democratic once the international system become transparent, but the system could only become fully transparent once every state was democratic.

Such transparency, extended as an operating principle of democracy at all levels— individual, national, global—interferes with, erodes and transforms, the very forms of sovereignty that traditionally defined 'privacy' and 'autonomy'. Both become undermined as a new relation of individual to collective is enacted. This recognises what has always been profoundly true: that nobody is autonomous; but that every one can have rights.

Democracy for Foucault does not rely on or need autonomy. Rights are given, and capabilities provided, in its absence. In fact, in Foucauldian terms autonomy is a strategy for decreasing the role of the state and increasing individual responsibility for welfare. As Jim Marshall (1996, p. 83) puts it, 'to believe that personal autonomy in modern times is liberating is mistaken—according to Foucault ... its pursuit leads to unfreedom'. According to Marshall, 'from Foucault's perspective the political has become *masked* and the true nature of this alleged autonomy and its role in governmentality hidden' (p. 85). In this sense, to advocate greater autonomy is to advocate greater individualisation in society and greater 'responsibilisation' of individuals and families.

In addition to expanding the public sphere, Foucault would encourage educational policies that represent it as a relation of power that develops agency and resistance. For Foucault, it is not autonomy, but *mature judgement* on the basis of existing terrain of forces. What are required are the arts of criticism. In a pluralistic universe, contradictory possibilities need to be analysed. They are analysed in relation to survival, from a particular point and place. They are mature, and not arbitrary. Discursive historical possibilities can be referenced to other mature discursive systems, that have generated confidence over time, as well as to practical issues and possibilities. Although through appeal to other mature discursive systems and rules of practice, one obtains a type of 'distance', of 'perspective', a perspective is nevertheless always historical, always expressed in relation to its relevance a particular time and place.

That education should intellectually and charactorlogically empower all individuals is a worthy ideal, and one that is important for the development of democratic values, but again, if power is the essence, in what sense is it accurate or meaningful to identify 'autonomy' as the foundation of the architecture to the neglect of other important goods and values, or social processes like social class.

If the concept of autonomy were to mean anything, it represents an equally balanced network of spaces, or points of reference, where the arts of criticism are safeguarded, and where freedoms can be exercised, and power relations enacted. As a particular strategy, it may have 'responsibilisation' as a developmental ideal to a certain extent, but its real value is that it ensures equalisation of power between people: that is an equalisation of entitlement to rights to live and develop. This theme of equalisation which ensured a distribution of power is what rights protect. It is what was argued for by Montesquieu (1900) in *The Spirit of the Laws*, and it is the essence of Foucault's relational approach.[11] It ensures conditions for the development of capabilities; for rights and entitlements to develop freely, without interference, and so on. But none of these qualities is it really helpful, or accurate to call 'autonomy'. The equalisation is not of 'autonomy' but of 'power', which renders agency effective. As Foucault states:

> One must observe also that there cannot be relations of power unless the subjects are free. If one or the other were completely at the disposition of the other and became his thing, an object on which he can exercise an indefinite and unlimited violence, there would not be relations of power.

> In order to exercise a relation of power, there must be on both sides at least a certain form of liberty. ... That means that in the relations of power, there is necessarily the possibility of resistance, for if there were no possibility of resistance—of violent resistance, of escape, of ruse, of strategies that reverse the situation—there would be no relations of power. (Foucault, 1991, p. 12)

Yet another thing autonomy neglects is the strategic sense in which agency is exercised. For Foucault the game is a useful metaphor to express his sense of freedom. The game illustrates the political nature of freedom as pertaining to possibilities under specific conditions. In a game one is both free and constrained. Players find themselves at points where they must respond. In addition, movements in a game are infinitely variable and fluid. While players are confined by rules, indefinite numbers of possibilities and options exist within them. In addition, through effective strategies players can utilise the rules to their own advantage; they can invent and improvise; within a system of constraints, moves are numerous. Freedom and constraint co-exist. Such a view expressed Foucault's conception of freedom, as something political, expressed, or mobilised, through the exercise of power. Mind develops and works politically, i.e., *through power*.[12] In this view, there are constant necessities, but they are obstacles to 'got round', 'pushed against', 'maneuvered', 'fought', and 'tamed'. Freedom to be effective requires moral problematization. In a Foucauldian sense, what autonomy really constitutes is a form of power, or 'cultural capital' in Bourdieu's sense.

Ultimately, too, it requires individual and collective agency. To manifest effective agency is often a complex matter: it involves devising elaborate plans; implementing them through successive stages; and in many instances acting collectively (e.g., to achieve goals on climate change, or in relation to the community). On such a view necessity (rules, constraints) and freedom (agency, initiative, choices) co-exist. Thus, at critical junctures, in certain circumstances, given certain conditions, 'free' agency is rendered, in some instances more possible, and in others more effective in relation to goals. Ultimately, this is the view I think Foucault accepts. Freedom develops, and is difficult. It involves not just recognition of necessity, but a taming, of necessity.

What is clear is that neither freedom nor autonomy exists as a birthright prior to engagement in the historical process. The human subject is socially and historically constituted and develops a capacity for freedom and decision-making slowly, progressively, and with differential success. Freedom is a political skill to be exercised. But as a skill it holds out great promises. Like Spinoza, Foucault was ultimately an optimist. As he says (Martin, *et al.*, 1988, p. 10):

> My role is to show people that they are much freer than they feel, that people accept as truth, as evidence, some themes which have built up at a certain moment during history, and that this so-called evidence can be criticised and destroyed.

The role of education is important here for the exercise of power involves resources, capacities, skills, acumen, technē, eristic, and an understanding of rules. These are the tasks of education.

## Notes

1. Rawls argument concerning the 'burdens of judgement' is presented in several places in his writing, see *Political Liberalism* (1993, p. 60). Also see Levinson (1999, pp. 18–22).
2. I cannot go into this relationship here except to say that the emphasis on power, on constitutive praxis, and on self-creation are all present within Spinosa. See Negri (1991); or my forthcoming book Olssen (2005).
3. John Stuart Mill thought that taking drugs was within the private domain protected by the harm principle, in that such activity did no harm to others. Similarly, depending on how it is defined, gun-collecting or knife collecting could be so defined. The notion of autonomy seems to protect this idea of an exclusively private domain, which is frequently used by libertarians to defend an expansive understanding of private rights.
4. The idea of autonomy goes back to ancient Greece. The root meaning derives from the Greek word auto, which means self, and nomos, which means rule. Thus, autonomy was understood as 'self-rule or 'self-governance' and originally applied not to individuals but to Greek city-states (see Marshall, 1995; Reich, 2002, p. 90).
5. See Kant (1929, A5535/B562) where he says: 'There is in man a power of self-determination, independently of any coercion through sensuous impulses'. It was in the sense that it was independent of experience that determined it as autonomous, and it is in this sense that autonomy, for Kant, was tied to a 'pre-social', historical and metaphysical conception of the person. For in Kant's view an Individual can reason Independently of social and historical locatedness. Notice that for both Reich and Levinson, it is not reason but the overall character and course of a life that is 'autonomous'.
6. The policy while noble is clearly likely to depend upon repressive tolerance. For if the tolerated 'non-autonomous' groups become a majority, or hegemonic, then the viability for the support for autonomy would be 'questioned'.
7. This conclusion is strengthened by Levinson's language. She frequently qualifies her argument in a way that she may claim gives her an escape clause. For example, (p. 33) she claims that it is 'virtually impossible for Sister Susan to be thoroughly autonomous'. This tends to reinforce that there is a hierarchy of autonomy, and that 'thorough' autonomy represents the highest and most independent state of being.
8. To suggest, as Reich does, that children from different cultural groups should be as familiar with other groups as their own is of course impositional. It would be better to suggest open power relations and lines of communication as the solution to this problem.
9. Part of Luther's assertion in the *Ninety-Five Theses* was that the Bible, not the Church, was the final authority for belief and conduct in life. If this was the case then any individual who could read the bible became the locus of interpretation and an independent authority in religion. Hence Luther's promotion of individualism was a factor supporting the general individualist surge in economics (the capitalist spirit) and in other areas of life.
10. Foucault statement initially published in *Libération* in June 1984 was to mark the announcement in Geneva of the creation of an international Committee against Piracy. In the article, Foucault refers to Amnesty International, Terre des Hommes, and Médecins du monde. See Foucault (2001).
11. Charles Eisenmann (1933) maintained that the 'separation of powers' thesis was a myth, and that Montesquieu really advanced an 'equalisation of powers' theory, where he was concerned with issues of 'balance', of 'combination', rather than separation.
12. The analogy of the state works well in relation to mind: mind has its exchequer; its defensive arm; its home secretary; its consultative apparatus; and so on. The self *is* political.

## References

Anderson, P. (2005) Arms and Rights: Rawls, Habermas and Bobbio in an age of war, *New Left Review*, 31, Jan.–Feb., pp. 5–42.

Anyon, J. (1991) The Retreat of Marxism and Socialist Feminism: Postmodern and poststructural theories in education, *Curriculum Inquiry*, 24:2, pp. 115–133.

Aronowitz, S. & Giroux, H. (1991) *Postmodern Education: Politics, Culture, and Social Criticism.* Minneapolis: University of Minnesota Press.

Baker, B. M. & Heyning, K. E. (eds), (2004) *Dangerous Coagulations: the use of Foucault in the study of education.* New York: Peter Lang.

Ball, S. J. (ed.) (1990) *Foucault and Education: Discipline and Knowledge.* London: Routledge.

Biesta, G. (1998) Pedagogy Without Humanism: Foucault and the Subject of Education, *Interchange*, 29:1, pp. 1–16.

Britzman, D. (1991) *Practice Makes Practice: A critical study of learning to teach* (Albany, SUNY Press).

Cherryholmes, C. (1988) *Power and Criticism: Post-structural investigations in education* (New York, Teachers College Press).

Davies, B. (1989) *Frogs and Snails and Feminist Tales: Preschool children and gender* (Sydney, Allen & Unwin).

Dworkin, G. (1988) *The Theory and Practice of Autonomy.* (Cambridge, Cambridge University Press).

Edwards, R. (2002) Mobilizing lifelong learning: governmentality in education practices, *Journal of Educational Policy*, 17:3, pp. 353–365.

Edwards, R. (2003) Ordering Subjects: Actor networks and intellectual technologies in lifelong learning. *Studies in the Education of Adults*, 35:1, pp. 55–67.

Edwards, R. & Nicoll, K. (2004) Mobilizing Workplaces: actors, discipline and governmentality. *Studies in Continuing Education*, 26:2, pp. 159–173.

Eisenmann, C. (1933) *L'Esprit des Lois et la Séparation des Pouvoirs* (Mélanges Carré de Malberg, Paris), pp. 163–92.

Ellesworth, E. (1989) Why Doesn't This Feel Empowering: Working through the repressive myths of critical pedagogy, *Harvard Educational Review*, 59:3, pp. 297–324.

Foucault, M. (1977) *Discipline and Punish* (trans. A. Sheridan). New York: Pantheon.

Foucault, M. (1987) *Mental Illness and Psychology* (trans. A. Sheridan). Berkeley: University of California Press.

Foucault, M. (1988) *Technologies of the Self* (L. Martin, H. Gutman, & P. Hutton eds) (London, Tavistock).

Foucault, M. (1991) The Ethic of Care for the Self as a Practice of Freedom: An interview (trans. J. D. Gauthier), in: J. Bernauer & D. Rasmussen, *The Final Foucault* (Cambridge, Mass., MIT Press).

Foucault, M. (1997) On the Genealogy of Ethics: An overview of work in progress, in: M. Foucault, *Ethics, Subjectivity and Truth: The essential works* (P. Rabinow ed., R. Hurley trans.) (Allen Lane, The Penguin Press), pp. 253–280.

Foucault, M. (2001) Confronting Governments: Human rights, in: James D. Faubion (ed.), *Michel Foucault: Power, the essential works 3* (Allen Lane, The Penguin Press), pp. 474–475.

Gale, T. (2001) Critical Policy Sociology: Historiography, archaeology and genealogy as methods of policy analysis, *Journal of Education Policy*, 16:5, pp. 379–393.

Galston, W. (1995) Two Concepts of Liberalism, *Ethics*, 61:3, pp. 516–534.

Giroux, H. (1991) Modernism, Postmodernism and Feminism: Rethinking the boundaries of educational discourse, in: H. Giroux (ed.), *Postmodernism, Feminism and Cultural Politics: Redrawing educational boundaries* (Albany, SUNY Press).

Gore, J. (1993) *The Struggle for Pedagogies* (New York, Routledge).

Henriques, J., Hollway, W., Urwin, C., Venn, C. & Walkerdine, V. (1984) *Changing the Subject: Psychology, social regulation, and subjectivity* (London, Methuen).

Hobhouse, L. T. (1911) *Liberalism* (London, Williams and Norgate).

Hoskin, K. (1979) The Examination, Disciplinary Power and Rational Schooling, *History of Education*, 8:2, pp. 135–46.

Jones, K. & Williamson, K. (1979) The Birth of the Schoolroom, *Ideology and Consciousness*, 5:1, pp. 5–6.

Kant, I. (1929) *Critique of Pure Reason* (trans. N. K. Smith) (London, Macmillan/St. Martin's Press).

Keynes, J. M. (1931a) [orig.1926]. The End of Laissez-Faire, in: John Maynard Keynes, *Essays in Persuasion* (London, Macmillan).

Kukathas, C. (1995) Are There Any Cultural Rights?, in: Will Kymlicka (ed.), *The Rights of Minority Cultures* (Oxford, Oxford University Press).

Kukathas, C. (1997) Cultural Toleration, in: Ian Shapiro and Will Kymlicka (eds), *NOMOS 39*, (New York, New York University Press).

Kymlicka, W. (1989) *Liberalism, Community, Culture* (Oxford, Clarendon).

Kymlicka, W. (1995) *Multicultural Citizenshiip* (Oxford, Oxford University Press).

Lather, P. (1991) *Getting Smart: Feminist research and pedagogy within the postmodern* (New York, Routledge).

Levinson, M. (1999) *The Demands of Liberal Education* (Oxford, Oxford University Press).

McLaren, P. & Hammer, R. (1989) Critical Pedagogy and the Postmodern Challenge: Toward a critical postmodernist pedagogy of liberation, *Educational Foundations*, 3:3, pp. 29–62.

McLaren, P. (1991) Schooling and the Postmodern Body: Critical pedagogy and the politics of enfleshment, in: Henry Giroux (ed.), *Postmodernism, Feminism and Cultural Politics: Redrawing educational boundaries* (Albany: SUNY Press).

Macpherson, C. B. (1962) *The Political Theory of Possessive Individualism* (Oxford, Clarendon Press).

Margalit, A. & Halbertal, M. (1994) The Right to Culture, *Social Research*, 61:3, pp. 491–510.

Marshall, J. (1989) Foucault and Education, *Australian Journal of Education*, 2, pp. 97–111.

Marshall, J. (1990) Foucault and Educational Research, in: S. J. Ball (ed.), *Foucault and Education: Discipline and knowledge* (London, Routledge).

Marshall, J. (1995) Skills, Information and Quality for the Autonomous Chooser, in: M. Olssen & K. Morris Matthews (eds), *Education, Democracy and Reform* (Auckland: New Zealand Association for Research in Education/Research Unit for Maori Education).

Marshall, J. (1996a) Personal Autonomy and Liberal Education: A Foucauldian critique, in: M. Peters, W. Hope, J. Marshall & S. Webster, *Critical Theory, Post-structuralism and the Social Context* (Palmerston North, The Dunmore Press).

Marshall, J. (1996b) *Michel Foucault: Personal autonomy and education* (Dordrecht, Kluwer Academic Publishers).

Marshall, J. (ed.) (2003) *Postructuralism, Philosophy, Pedagogy* (Dordrecht, Kluwer Academic Publishers).

Mill, J. S. [1859] (1956) *On Liberty* (Currin V. Shield, ed.) (Indianapolis, Bobbs Merrill Library of Liberty Arts).

Miller, J. (1990) *Creating Spaces and Finding Voices: Collaborating for empowerment* (Albany, SUNY Press).

de Montesquieu, C. (1900) *The Spirit of Laws* (Thomas Nugent, trans.) (New York, The Colonial Press).

Nussbaum, M. (1992) Human Functioning and Social Justice: A defence of Aristotelian essentialism, *Political Theory*, 20:2, pp. 202–46.

Olssen, M. (1993) Science and Individualism in Educational Psychology: Problems for practice and points of departure. *Educational Psychology*, 13:2, pp. 155–172.

Olssen, M. (1999) *Michel Foucault: Materialism and education* (Westport, Bergin and Garvey).

Olssen, M., Codd, J., & O'Neill, A.M. (2004) *Education Policy: Globalisation, citizenship, & democracy* (London, Sage).

Olssen, M. (2005) (forthcoming) *Michel Foucault: Materialism and education.* (Second enlarged ed.) (Boulder, Paradigm Publishers).

Pagano, J. (1990) *Exiles and Communities: Teaching in the patriarchal wilderness* (Albany, SUNY Press).

Peters, M. (2001) *Postructuralism, Marxism and Neo-Liberalism* (Lanham, Rowman and Littlefield).

Peters, M. & Marshall, J. (1996) *Individualism and Community: Education and social policy in the postmodern condition* (London, The Falmer Press).

Popkewitz, T. & Brennan, M. (eds) (1998) Foucault's Challenge: discourse, knowledge and power in education. New York: Teachers College Press.

Popkewitz, T. S., Franklin, B. M. & Pereyra, M. A. (eds) (2001) *Cultural History and Education: Critical essays on knowledge and schooling* (New York, Routledge/Falmer).

Rawls, J. (1993) *Political Liberalism* (New York, Columbia University Press).

Reich, R. (2002) *Bridging Liberalism and Multiculturalism in American Education* (Chicago, Chicago University Press).

Schneewind, J. B. (1998) *The Invention of Autonomy: A history of modern moral philosophy* (Cambridge, Cambridge University Press).

Spinoza, B. (1985) *Collected Works* (Edwin Curley, trans.) (Princeton, Princeton University Press).

Taylor, C. (1989) *Sources of the Self. The making of modern identity* (Cambridge, Mass., Harvard University Press).

Varela, J. (2001) Genealogies of Education: Some models of analysis, in: T. S. Popkewitz, B. M. Franklin & M. A. Pereyra (eds) *Cultural History and Education: Critical essays on knowledge and schooling* (New York: Routledge/Falmer).

Walkerdine, V. (1989) *Counting Girls Out* (London, Virago).

Wittgenstein, L. (1953) *Philosophical Investigations.* (G. E. M. Anscombe, trans.) (Oxford, Blackwell).

# 8

# Marshalling the Self: James D. Marshall as Educational Philosopher

MICHAEL A. PETERS
*University of Glasgow*

> Gradually it has become clear to me what every great philosophy so far
> has been: namely, the personal confession of its author and a kind of
> involuntary and unconscious memoir; also that the moral (or immoral)
> intentions in every philosophy constituted the real germ of life from
> which the whole plant had grown.
>
> —Friedrich Nietzsche, *Beyond Good and Evil*

> Working in philosophy—like work in architecture in many respects—is
> really more like working on oneself. On one's own interpretation. On
> one's way of seeing things. (and what one expects of them).
>
> —Wittgenstein, *Culture and Value*

> How one becomes what one is.
>
> —Nietzsche, *Ecco Homo*

## Biosophy

It is difficult having as a friend someone who one has intellectually grown up with.
I was recruited from the philosophy department at the University of Auckland,
New Zealand, where I had completed an MA by Jim Marshall, after returning to
full time study following seven years as a secondary school teacher. I had worked
with Jim on a philosophy of education paper as part of the MA and as a result we
had produced a couple of academic papers on the debate between Richard Pring
and Michael Young for the *Journal of Philosophy of Education*, arguing for Young's
position, or least trying to provide some philosophical arguments for his position
(I seem to remember). I was fresh from completing an MA where I contrived to
do most of my papers on the philosophy of Wittgenstein. I was particularly interested in the latter Wittgenstein, *The Philosophical Investigations* and works published
posthumously like *On Certainty*. I had already decided to go on to do a PhD but
found little sympathy for my project on Wittgenstein in the philosophy department,
even though I had scored a first. In fact, much to my surprise I found an ideological bias against the latter Wittgenstein, especially by one lecturer, who found his
philosophy odious. I had expressed a desire in one paper to examine the doctrine of

cultural relativism in latter Wittgenstein; we ended up not so obliquely by studying the *Theatetus* and celebrating the triumph of Socrates/Plato's self-refutation argument against Protagoras' measure hypothesis as an object lesson. In a fit of bloody-mindedness I had taken Protagoras' side and argued that Plato's arguments didn't go through. Much to my chagrin when I found out my mark for the assignment and even though I had especially dedicated myself in particular to this assignment. Thus when it came to the prospect of completing a PhD in the philosophy department I baulked.

Jim Marshall, by contrast, was obliging and while trained in the analytic school— he had completed his PhD at Bristol on identity theory with Stephan Körner—he was tolerant of other perspectives and in those days—the late 1970s when analytical philosophy of education was at its high point—entertained and even relished the prospect of an argument against foundational epistemology. Jim was different from any other academic I had met. He was widely read, curious, and someone who knew his way around an argument—not so unusual perhaps—but he was also genuinely collegial with students and prepared to work collaboratively with them. The first couple of papers we wrote together we did so by sitting in front of his computer and formulating it sentence by sentence. This was a terrific education: one-on-one, face-to-face, intensive hours together writing—what better training could one receive? He was so impressive that I decided to complete a PhD thesis under his supervision, working on the latter Wittgenstein. I have to say that as a young graduate I was more interested in those days in Wittgenstein than in philosophy of education, and even looked on the field with some distain.

I toiled away for a couple of years visiting Jim periodically to shape up the text and thesis. He always read what I had written and we had seemingly endless sessions discussing the ideas, him forcing me to elaborate and to defend what I had written. It really was superb training. Denis Phillips, a close friend of Jim's, who spent a year at Auckland, also read everything and commented on it. Jim knew many of the international 'stars'.

Even while completing the PhD Jim and I wrote together. We developed a writing partnership that survived from 1978 through until his retirement in early 2003— twenty-five years! In that time we co-authored or co-edited several books, including edited collections on Nietzsche (Peters, Marshall & Smeyers, 1999), critical theory and poststructuralism (Peters *et al.*, 1996), educational policy (Marshall & Peters, 1999) as well as co-authored books on Wittgenstein (Peters & Marshall, 1999) and political philosophy of education (Peters & Marshall, 1996). As well as these collaborative works we have written many book chapters, papers, research reports and special journal issues together. On a rough count I calculated that we had written some 50 papers or chapters together. (And that is a lot of time to spend in one another's company!). Of course this is in addition, to the considerable corpus of work that Jim produced on his own (see Jim's bibliography appended to this issue) including work on Dewey, Wittgenstein, Nietzsche, Foucault, science, punishment, educational policy, curriculum issues, management, technology and so on. He was a profilic academic author. By commenting on our collaborative work I am establishing my credentials as someone who knows Jim and his work well. I am also testifying to his wide-ranging philosophical interests and his status as a teacher. He inspired me and would always welcome an intellectual conversation. I loved the way we would pursued a conversation in first decade of our relationship. He is a great conversationalist and an expert at argument.

Intellectual biographies are notorious for their conflation of the man and his works, even this division, at least from a poststructuralist view, is open to question. In what academic and pedagogical language-games does the professor or lecturer learn to tell the truth about him- or herself? How central are these language-games to the language or narrative creation and reconstruction of the self? What cultural forms of autobiographical truth-telling are represented in language-games that are both pedagogical and academic?

Jim so closely identified with his work, his *oeuvre*—as he said work on the self is not easy and I think he was attracted to Wittgenstein and Foucault because they are great stylists as philosophers. They sought not to emulate anyone but to become themselves through reading and writing. This notion of reading and writing the self—perhaps we could add teaching the self—has such an easy resonance with Jim. Not only did it increasingly define the man, the author, the style, self-stylisation, but that over the years Jim became more interested in this question—self-writing, self-stylisation, self-assertion through writing, reading and teaching—a particular trope following Foucault's 'aesthetics of existence' and his Nietzschean notion of turning oneself into or becoming a work of art. (Does it mean anything more mundane than this?).

From the outset Jim was in revolt. While a team member, even at school, on the rugby field or as captain of a vessel he could demonstrate a will to rebel against convention and established ways of doing things. In part, this also was his fate as a New Zealander who can be naturally disobedient. Jim certainly could lead as well as be a member of a team but he is a very private man and complex. How well do any of us know ourselves? Doesn't philosophy in the Western tradition begin with the question of self-knowledge and self-deceit? Why is it a question of self *knowledge* rather than *understanding, communication* or *dialogue, existence, expression* or any of a dozen other possibilities? Is truth a predicate of the self? And what of the lie?

I can not answer for Jim's private self but his public self as teacher, professor and academic author certainly played with the Wittgensteinian and Foucaultian problematic of the self in relation to philosophy so much so that I think his Francophilia was a kind of existential quest for ontological security—not foundations but for some self-image, some coherent persona. In the reminder of this paper, part intellectual biography, part stocktaking, part elucidation of intellectual themes that preoccupied Jim, I shall comment on only two specific projects that represent Jim Marshall's approach and interests: Wittgenstein and Foucault.

Jim was well aware of the connections between the two thinkers. He wrote a paper that later became a chapter in our Wittgenstein book entitled 'The Self: Wittgenstein, Nietzsche, Foucault'. There he clearly indicates that Wittgenstein leaves us with a mystical and pessimistic notion of the self which can be rectified by advancing an expressivist approach to identity statements. Such statements for Wittgenstein, Jim maintained, were based upon the notion that first person states like 'I am in pain' *express* pain and do not describe a mental state. Jim also held that Foucault, whilst believing in Wittgenstgeinian fashion that the self refers to nothing substantial, nevertheless shows us how we can care for or nurture the self. Jim also noted stylistic, thematic and historical parallels in their thought. Not to put too fine a point on it, Foucault knew of and even used Wittgenstein's work though without explicit acknowledgement.

## Wittgenstein as a Pedagogical Philosopher

I attribute a view to Jim that he may never have explicitly held although I know that he had contemplated it even if he had not formally expounded it: Wittgenstein was a pedagogical philosopher. It is a view that I also subscribe to and one that in essence underlies the substance of our book. By 'pedagogical philosopher' I think he meant that Wittgenstein was not concerned with advancing truth or even propositions, rather he was more concerned with inventing a new way of *doing* philosophy and this way of doing philosophy—philosophy as a kind of style— involved different kinds of writing, the act of *composition*, and an experimentation with writing and teaching that bought into view the new possibilities of philosophical genres. Not just the treatise or the thesis—in fact one does not deconstruct the picture that holds us captive through argumentation—but also the confession, the autobiography, the album, the poem. Wittgenstein's work was full of jokes, parables, thought experiments, examples and counter-examples, puzzles, mathematical equations, aphorisms, little dialogues with the self. His work represented an attempt to wrestle himself free of prevailing philosophical forms—forms of writing that contained or constituted the self. This was the exercise of freedom on the self as Foucault might say, as Marshall might say. It was in Wittgenstein's case deeply personal, perhaps incommunicable to another human being—not said but shown, made manifest in the work.

Marshall begins by noting that for the early Wittgenstein influenced by Schopenhauer the self is a mysterious entity and he quotes from the *Notebooks*: 'The thinking subject is surely mere illusion. But the willing subject exists ... The I, the I is what is deeply mysterious. The I is not an object. I objectively confront every object. But not the I' (80e).

Later Wittgenstein was to develop a form of language philosophy as a kind of therapy of the self. And Jim would quote Wittgenstein from the *Investigations*:

> Philosophical problems ... are not empirical problems: they are solved, rather, by looking into the workings of our language, and that in such a way as to make us recognise those workings: in despite of an urge to misunderstand them. The problems are solved, not by giving new information, but by arranging what we have always known. Philosophy is a battle against the bewitchment of our intelligence by means of language. (PI, §109)

But if, as Wittgenstein argued, philosophy puts everything before us because everything lies open and what is hidden is of no use to us why are selves so difficult to understand and why has it become the central problem in the western tradition? Apart from mentioning that the work of philosophy therefore 'consists in assembling reminders' (PI, §127) about our language and therefore, the language-game of the self, I'm not sure that Wittgenstein or Marshall got any closer to resolving the issue. In the chapter I mentioned Jim also talks about personal identity and about identity theory (thus circumnavigating himself). But I am not about to go into this matter here.

Jim's work on the self—his academic work, for he wrote chapters on Schopenhauer and Wittgenstein, Wittgenstein and Freud, Wittgenstein, Nietzsche and Foucault—served in that book as a 'Prolegomenon to a Pedagogy of the Self', the final chapter. It is, I think a profitable idea and one that can work, although we did it too quickly.

## Foucault as Naturalised Kantian

James Marshall was one of the first scholars and certainly among the most systematic in his approach and appropriation of Foucault. In his influential book *Michel Foucault: Personal autonomy and education* (Marshall, 1996) Marshall tends to discuss Foucault in terms of the challenge that he represents to analytic philosophy (and analytic philosophy of education), especially in relation to traditional topics of autonomy and punishment. He says in the Preface that the book 'provides a Foucault based critique of a central plank of Western liberal education, the notion of the autonomous individual or personal autonomy'. He provides this snapshot of his own position: The writer started reading Foucault from a position in education which was in the liberal framework, somewhere between Dewey, Freire and Habermas, but with an interest in punishment, authority and power and he states that it is his intention 'to show that he [Foucault] provides the basis for a powerful critique of the post-Enlightenment ideal of personal autonomy'—'not just that this ideal is difficult to attain but that it is fundamentally incoherent; instead of liberating the individual and guaranteeing independence it promotes dependence, subjection and domination' (Marshall, 1996, p. 1). In part this reflects Marshall's own training as an analytic philosopher. He completed a PhD thesis in philosophy on identity theory with Stephan Körner at Bristol before taking an appointment in teacher education first in the UK and then at the University of Auckland in New Zealand.

Marshall explains the philosophical influences on Foucault (Chapter 1), elaborates notions of liberalism and liberal education (Chapter 2), and focuses on personal autonomy as an aim of education by reference to Kant and interpretations of Kant by liberal philosophers of education (Barrow, Dearden) which argue for two antithetical views. (I have reorganised Marshall's representation of the streams, see page 89).

(1) autonomy is part of human nature; autonomy is socially constructed
(2) autonomy and morality are/are not necessarily linked
(3) the development of autonomy presupposes or is compatible with freedom which involves the acceptance of universal laws/to act in accordance with universal laws is to be inauthentic and not be free

On Marshall's reading the development of autonomy in the sense attributed to liberal thought does not for Foucault presuppose or entail freedom rather such 'development' (education) is both a negation and denial of freedom, at least in his early or middle work of, for example, *Discipline and Punish*. (In his later work, freedom becomes a condition for 'development'). Marshall drawing on Foucault— his notion of power/knowledge and governmentality—argues that 'liberal education, in its pursuit of personal autonomy, masks the power relations operating, and hence the thrust for governmentality, by its talk of authority and the development of mind' (p. 215). Perhaps, more important for 'new directions' than Marshall's reading of Foucault and the critique of personal autonomy is his extended Foucauldian critique of neo-liberalism and what he calls the 'autonomous chooser' as a neo-liberal substitutive for personal autonomy. He writes:

> This is not the notion of an independent and free chooser but someone whose choices have been structured through the manipulation of the needs and interests by what I call busno-power. (Marshall, 1996, p. 213; see also Marshall 1995a, 1995b)

It is perhaps this major development of Foucault that Marshall's work has ongoing significance above the level of an introduction to Foucault's thought and critique of autonomy as an aim of liberal education. Though there is also a positive side to Marshall's reading that leads him to emphasise the Kantian ethos in Foucault's later work to interpret 'freedom as an exercise upon the self'.

Marshall consistently reads Foucault as a naturalised Kantian, as he writes in a recent essay:

> For Foucault the point of philosophy, insofar as he classified himself as a philosopher, was that philosophy was concerned with the self; it involved working on the self. (Marshall, 1998, p. 68)

Education and teaching on this view 'should allow the individual to change at will'. It involves work on the self and Marshall leaves room for forms of non-manipulative education that do not simply collapse into neo-liberalism's autonomous chooser or substitute traditional liberal notions of personal autonomy for that former. Jim, there is still some work to do. It has been a great privilege working with you.

## References

Marshall, J. D. (1989) Foucault and Education, *Australian Journal of Education*, 2: 97–111.
Marshall, J. D. (1996) *Michel Foucault: Personal autonomy and education.* London: Kluwer Academic.
Marshall, J. D. & Peters, M. A. (eds) (1999) *Education Policy*, International Library of Comparative Public Policy, General Editor, B. Guy Peters, Cheltenham, UK, Edward Elgar, 828pp.
Marshall, J. D. (1995a) Foucault and Neo-Liberalism: Biopower and Busno-Power, *Philosophy of Education Yearbook*: http://www.ed.uiuc.edu/EPS/PES-Yearbook/95_docs/marshall.html
Marshall, J. D. (1995b) Skills, Information and Quality for the Autonomous Chooser, in: M. Olssen & K. Morris Matthews (eds), *Education, Democracy and Reforms.* Auckland: NZARE.

Marshall, J. D. (1996) Education in the Mode of Information: Some Philosophical Considerations *Philosophy of Education Yearbook*: http://www.ed.uiuc.edu/EPS/PES-Yearbook/96_docs/marshall.html

Marshall, J. D. (1998) Michel Foucault: Philosophy, Education, and freedom as an Exercise upon the Self, in: M. A. Peters (ed.), *Naming the Multiple: Poststructuralism and Education.* Westport, CT. & London: Bergin & Garvey.

Peters, M. A. & Marshall, J. D. (1996) *Individualism and Community: Education and Social Policy in the Postmodern Condition*, London, Falmer Press.

Peters, M. A. & Marshall, J. D. (1999) *Wittgenstein: Philosophy, Postmodernism, Pedagogy*, Westport, CT. & London, Bergin & Garvey.

Peters, M. A., Marshall, J. D. & Fitzsimons, P. (eds) (1997) *Education and the Philosophy of the Subject*, Special issue of *Educational Philosophy and Theory*.

Peters, M. A., Marshall, J. D., Hope, W. & Webster (eds) (1996) *Critical Theory, Poststructuralism and the Social Context*, Palmerston North (NZ), Dunmore Press.

Peters, M. A., Marshall, J. D. & Smeyers, P. (eds) (2001) *Nietzsche's Legacy for Education: Past and Present Values*, Westport, CT. & London, Bergin & Garvey.

# 9

# Marshall—Making Wittgenstein Smile

ROBERT K. SHAW
*The Open Polytechnic of New Zealand*

Here I set out a personal account of my work with Jim Marshall and Michael Peters and I admit to some prejudices that I hold as a manager of government development projects. Comments are made about the New Zealand Government's contract research programme and Marshall's contribution to national education policy through research.

## The State Services Commission

I was seconded to the New Zealand State Services Commission (the organisation that employs all central government employees) to manage the public service's response to new official information legislation. The legislation was enacted in 1982 but I did not arrive until 1984 when concern about the legislation had passed. Hence, there was money tagged 'decision-making at the top of the public service' and I had to spend it. On Pukerua Bay beach I decided to teach ethics to chief executives and change their behaviour. I also decided I would persuade Jim Marshall to work on the project.

Why did I ask Marshall, at that time a senior lecturer at the University of Auckland, to work on the development of a model of decision making, trials of its teaching, and an evaluation of learning? First, the combination of disciplinary skills was vaguely as required: ethics, adult education, teaching/learning, and evaluation. Second, for years I had been trying to have philosophers of education more involved in policy research. This I had been doing in my role as the manager of the Department of Education's research programme (New Zealand Department of Education, 1982; 1990). Third, I had always found Jim easy to deal with from the time I was his student. Fourth, and most important by far, I believed he would have credibility with senior officials.

I sat in Jim's tiny office and he asked if I would mind having Michael Peters involved because Michael needed the money. If there were other reasons, I cannot remember them.

Marshall was a public servant before he was an academic. He rose through the ranks in a very conservative part of the civil service, the British navy. Perhaps that was why he was invariably understanding when the public service constricted me, information had to be provided immediately, we had to placate the Minister of

Education, or budgets had to be held. Nothing is more important when you contract academics.

The academic literature records the project, so I am excused the task of describing it (Shaw, 1983; Shaw, 1985; Marshall & Peters, 1986; Peters, Marshall & Shaw,
1986). What became clear to me as we worked though nine trial courses, each with
six participants presenting half-day case studies based on actual decision-making
in their organizations, was Jim Marshall's dedication to duty. He read every page
of every case study and wrote down all the dialogue with his fountain pen. I
successfully defended the Marshall-Peters report to my colleagues because the
theory was clear, the report's limitations were set out, and each conclusion was
substantiated by evidence in a massive appendix. In addition to the main report,
there were academic papers that began to work on concepts that were to become
important in later practical work. The course produced has been presented by
several people, all of whom were trained as a part of the original project. The Open
Polytechnic of New Zealand funded further research on the model of decision-
making in 1999 (Shaw & Burns, 1999). It proved to be robust although the
terminology needed updating to take account of the fashion of risk. I have yet to
find another course that teaches officials how to implement policy, although
courses on how to develop policy are common.

## The Department of Education

I did not know what to do. In Maori terms his behaviour was acceptable, even
proper, certainly welcomed, but this may jeopardise the project's immediate goals,
which meant the project itself would collapse, and it could kill his reputation with
the civil service. I did care about his reputation as a friend, but I was also conscious
of other effects regarding my reputation and the delicate interplay of the civil
service and academics that were contracted as advisors. The situation related to
one of those philosophers whom I wanted included in the government's contract
research programme, and who now was leading a major evaluation, at a time when
only research with numbers seemed acceptable in head office.

It was the late 1980s and the décor was 1960s. Heavy motel style furniture,
patterns that would not show stains, polished dark and sometimes light woodwork,
low ceiling, and heavy commercial drapes, all a bit oppressive. Large bright square
lights built into the ceiling, it was hot, and it was about 6 or 7 p.m. The room was
full of people, most of them with brown faces, and the Pakeha looked very noticeable.
Obvious because they were white, but obvious because they dressed formally and
represented power. Apart from Jim Marshall and Michael Peters that is, for they
were in a separate category.

Jim was making a plea for more money for Maori education, for the reform of
the education system, and for a better acceptance of Maori values. Unfortunately,
he was a little unsteady on his feet.

I moved over, trying to be inconspicuous, put my arm around Jim, and we
lurched between tables and left to go into a bedroom. We sat on the bed, in this
small room. Tears down his face, later tears down mine, as we considered the

situation and its causes. (I regret I did not take longer at that time, but felt it was important to get back to the *hui*. At least I now know that instinct was wrong for three different reasons.) We spoke of cultural traditions, love, wives, children, commitment, power and peoples and of the real purpose of being an academic. The questions of who am I, what do I stand for, and commitments that go beyond the contract and the role. 'Robert, I had always thought that ...' he said many times. This catharsis (to use a word Jim liked) had been building for at least a year. Looking back I can see its origins—the Maori struggle, the deeper under-standing of cultures that the Maori brought with them, thoughtful and articulate people, and the enormous ability of Maori to accept people regardless of their failings.

Jim Marshall, whom I thought of as a New Zealand Englishman, had emotionally connected to Maori culture. The moment it all broke through was a critical one for our project: we were being visited by officials, our purpose being to convince them of the worth of what we were doing and to ask them for money. Jim in his asking became passionate and then abusive. Alcohol was part of the mix but not a particularly significant part in my view then or now. The senior official was Lyall Perris who went on to become the chief executive of the Ministry of Education before he retired to become an Anglican Minister.

The events described were at the last of three Burma Lodge *Hui* (Burma Lodge was a conference centre in Johnsonville, Wellington). They were a part of the project that became known as *Te Reo O Te Tai Tokerau*, although that was but the concluding part of the whole project. Again, I am excused from describing the project because it is in the literature (Peters & Marshall, 1988; Marshall & Peters, 1989; Marshall & Peters, 1989; Peters & Marshall, 1989; Peters, Para & Marshall, 1989; Peters, Para & Marshall, 1989).

When a team works closely together it is hard to identify individual contributions and so it is difficult for me to identify what was contributed by Jim Marshall, Michael Peters, Robert Shaw, Dave Para, Monte Ohia, Vervise McCausland, John Matthews, and about 24 other secondary school teachers of Maori, Maori elders and students from throughout New Zealand.

When I designed the project, I thought about the problem of centre/periphery, central control/local control, head office/district office, government/community. The money and power of decision-making always reside overwhelmingly with the central authority. Yet, programmes that do not accord with the values at the periph-ery will be undermined, intentionally or unintentionally, and you have to have motivated people. How can central agencies release the power of decision and money, when they have accountability requirements and are locked into legal and institutional constraints? But, the most significant consideration is that the ability of the periphery to innovate is very limited unless a central control agency provides resources and opportunity. (I had first faced this question when I designed and contracted the evaluation for Prime Minister Robert Muldoon's Committee on Gangs projects.) My solution was to employ evaluators, who were really to be 'honest brokers' or arbitrators, voices of reason, standing separate from the com-munity and head office and thus forming a triangle. My notion was any two together could move the third. Remember, the problem cut both ways: the community needed to convince the government, but the government also needed to convince the community.

Where does the project manger stand in this? You have to be a Jesuit. You are in the world, but you pursue your own goals. You have to want to construct something yourself. When Marshall and Peters wrote on empowerment and the role of the evaluator as educator, those papers stayed in my desk drawer for years, although I thought they could have said more on the position of the official in the hierarchy (Marshall & Peters, 1985; Marshall & Peters, 1986). Subsequently, over the last decade, the official's moral responsibility has become a topic in the literature of public agency decision-making.

Rory O'Connor, Assistant Secretary (Tertiary Education) gave me the brief for this project. He said the Minister of Education was concerned about the number of complaints he received about the School Certificate examination subject Maori (School Certificate was a national norm-referenced examination where most students took 5 subjects; the subject Maori was a small subject with about 2,000 candidates a year). O'Connor and I agreed the problem was 'complex' (meaning unlikely to be meaningfully addressed) because it involved Maori culture and associated sensitivities, *te reo* Maori, examinations, and a norm-referenced system that was in effect an intelligence test that disadvantaged both lower socio-economic level students and culturally different students.

With Monte Ohia, I convened meetings with the teachers of Maori from throughout the country to identify the problems and produce a development proposal. The first task was to take an 80% written/20% oral examination and make the oral component 80%. The challenge of this was to get the oral assessment accurate. The second task was to take the subject Maori out of norm-referenced examination system and to report on levels of achievement with special certificates for the candidates. The third task was to have the oral assessment done on *marae* and thus to involve the whole Maori community in the assessment of candidates. Looking back it is easy to see the logic of it all, but at the time we had to find our way and convince others. Marshall and Peters were involved in the project through the three tasks. I can remember Jim saying to me 'I do not know anything about School Certificate' but I cannot remember my reply. Peters had been a secondary school teacher, so I suppose that helped.

The problem when you pursue your own goals from within the civil service is that you need to be sure you are right. New Zealand is a small country and a determined individual well placed can actually alter national policy.

Policy development carries a responsibility and that is one of the reasons I needed Marshall and Peters—to provide assurance on the goals. It is said that one of the problems with public administration is that no one is morally or legally responsible because so many individuals are involved in the construction of a new policy (sometimes called the 'many hands' problem). Sometimes in New Zealand in the 1980s, the opposite was true. The official was left alone to decide and act. A Director-General of Education once remarked 'Robert's projects cost little money, involve a cast of thousands, address major issues, and always worry me and the Minister of Education excessively'. Well, Mr. Director-General, they were not my projects—they were a team effort.

What I find interesting was the way that the goals were developed and the practical problems were solved. The language of argument between us was the language of the philosophy of science. It was analogy and metaphor—Wittgenstein, Popper and Toulmin contributed.

Something of the Maori perspective on the project appears in a paper prepared for the New Zealand Council of Educational Research (Shaw & Ohia, 1988). It seeks to bridge the gulf between the Maori world and the Pakeha bureaucracy and begins with a tentative 'guiding statement' by Paki Para:

> Consideration as an official guiding statement for the project:
> *Te Taitokerau—Te Hiku o te Ika nui a Maui*
> *Ko to reo he mana—he wehi—he ihi—he wairua*
> *whangaia a tatou tamariki mokopuna i te taonga tupuna nei*
> *Kia tupu ake ratou i roto i te korowai o te reo a o tatou matua tupuna.*
> *Ko te timatatanga of te kauri rangatira*
> *Ko te kakano nohinohi.*
>
> People of the North the tail of Maui's Great Fish
> Your language is pride-prestige-power-spirit
> Nourish our children with this sacred treasure of our ancestors.
> The beginning of the majestic kauri
> Is the humble (tiny) seed. (p. 1)

Then Ohia and Shaw continue:

> In 1986, when the project was first considered, there was recognition of the need for participants to understand their own role, to understand the role of others and to assist others to maintain those roles. Whilst our team might appear at New Zealand Council for Educational Research's conference as one group we are three separate interest groups, with distinct and often different responsibilities. We are united in our concern for both Maori children and *Te Reo*. Nevertheless, we operate from different bases—power and influence are derived from different sources, and accountability structure and issues are different. We are:
> * the community,
> * the evaluators,
> * the department.
>
> As members of these three groups we each have different roles to fulfill. At the same time we are also citizens, with some understanding of, and emotional involvement with, the needs of our country. Questions of role definition make demands upon our own integrity, and our willingness to accept the constraints under which others must operate. (pp. 2–3)

The paper also lists the conclusions drawn by Monte Ohia and myself regarding what we learnt from the project. It would be inappropriate to revise them now:

The history of *Te Reo O Te Taitokerau*, from the perspective of departmental development officers, suggests the following principles of project management:

a) Complex problems which involve the community are best resolved by an iterative model of evolutionary decision-making. The essence of this approach to policy development is that concepts are developed and they are subject to scrutiny in appropriate forums. This results in good decision-making with commitment to ideas, and in turn ensures practical outcomes.

b) Useful progress can result from a department's undertaking policy development as a series of smaller steps. Evolutionary approach is often more rapid than the more extensive, embracing review of policy.

c) Within the department, procedures need to be established to enable knowledge of the project to be brought into focus whenever it can contribute to policy-making.

d) Funding for implementation stages, should the project be successful, needs to be planned for in advance.

e) The department's leadership role in this approach to policy development largely relates to two matters: (i) fostering the development of new concepts to address problems, and (ii) the obtaining of commitment of participants to both the broad policy objectives and the specific actions necessary to operate the project.

f) Officials wishing to operate a programme which involves community responsibility can begin by reviewing the exact parameters of the department's responsibility as set down by statute.

g) When attempting to involve the community in a project, positive steps must be taken to balance the power structures.

h) Evaluators can be established to play a professional political role in project development. They are useful as advocates for arguments, which they consider to be sound, both in the community and in the department.

i) All effects, both within the department as well as in the community, should be taken into account before judging the worth of a project such as Te Reo O Te Taitokerau.

These principles are indicative of the values held by some officials.

They are also suggestive of a particular relationship between community—department—evaluators. We hope that they may further discussion of both the project Te Reo O Te Taitokerau and management theory. (pp. 6–7)

Education is littered with projects that work well, perhaps are recorded, and then are abandoned, or corrupted, or subsumed by other things. So it was with our work on School Certificate Maori.

When the Department of Education was restructured into a Ministry and a Qualifications Authority, I was appointed to the Ministry and told to work out if Government should fund *kura kaupapa* Maori (schools teaching only in the Maori language). The assessment of School Certificate Maori was found to be expensive, if I remember rightly $40 a candidate, compared with less than a dollar for subjects like English, and the officials that replaced us began their own projects.

However, Marshall and Peters had recorded much more of the project in reports to the Department, and in published academic papers, than is usual. Theoretical and practical experience met. Maori teachers pursued degrees; other projects in education were started by the teachers of Maori who had worked with us; school principals, Ministers of the Crown, and other government officials approached us to discuss their proposals; and enduring friendships were made between Maori and Pakeha. I remember two Maori teachers, both about 50 years of age, saying of Marshall and Peters that they were the first Pakeha to really listen to them and understand them. It is a considerable tribute.

## Policy, Development Projects, and Research

There were other projects that we worked on together for the Ministry of Education, Ministry of Research, Science and Technology, and the Wellington Regional Council. Let me provide a few reflections on the whole experience.

When agencies of state have money with the tag 'evaluation' they advertise for evaluators and expect 'impartiality'. In the two projects described above I did not advertise. I selected the evaluators, using one main criterion. I needed people who would be totally committed to making the projects a success. The quality of the goals required nothing less.

I am convinced that good academic skills, and an academic background, are essential in any practical educational development project. Academic work is a tool, not an end in itself. Marshall, to me, always saw it that way.

Marshall's writing on Maori can demonstrate the sympathy that comes only from real experience (Peters & Marshall, 1988; Marshall, 1991). He sometimes grasps opportunities to do things in a manner consistent with Maori culture and consistent with the values that were so stark at Burma Lodge. He begins one paper with an account of how he relates personally to the topic and seeks to find the sympathetic compromise or synthesis (Marshall, 1999).

When the emotional base drives Marshall the result is powerful. Consider his attempt to advance the practical problem of sovereignty for Maori:

> But in order to get two different language users to agree on how to use a term like 'sovereignty' in a different manner, there must be some concept of self and the other that permits an interchange which is not power laden, manipulative, and dependent upon some notion of language use which is either universal and liberal (Rorty), or that of the scientific community (Dewey), or that of a community of (competent) language users (Habermas). It must recognize difference explicitly, but also recognize a form of communality. Thus, language is not mine but shared and one is initiated into it without it being imposed, or at least imposed so that it is closed off … (1999)

This paragraph is a part of an academic paper. But, consider how a policy analyst could put this paragraph to work. It begs to be used. The author is as important as the words—he has credibility as a New Zealander, credibility with a significant number of Maori, and credibility through the appointment at Auckland University. In the fast, personal, intuitive world of policy, the person counts as much as the text.

Academics who see their positions as an opportunity to contribute to the country impress me. In the 1970's and 1980's empirical studies received most of the research funding and people asked, what could a philosopher do to assist education? The ability of philosophers to contribute to the country seemed quite limited. Marshall proved one thing for his discipline—philosophers should be included in governments' social science research programmes. He established the worth of the philosophy of education in both the work for the State Services Commission and the work on Maori education. And, incidentally, he may have made Wittgenstein smile.

## References

Marshall, J. & Peters, M. (1985) Evaluation and Education: The ideal learning community, *Policy Sciences*, 18:3, pp. 263–288.

Marshall, J. & Peters, M. (1986) Administrative Discretionary Justice: A report on the development of a model of decision-making, *Public Administration*, 64, pp. 453–459.

Marshall, J. & Peters, M. (1986) Evaluation and Education: Practical problems and theoretical perspectives. *New Zealand Journal of Educational Studies*, 21:1, pp. 29–41.

Marshall, J. & Peters, M. (1989) Te Reo O Te Tai Tokerau: A community approach to the assessment and promotion of oral Maori, *Pacific Education*, 1:3, pp. 70–89.

Marshall, J. & Peters, M. (1989) Te Reo O Te Tai Tokerau: The assessment of oral Maori. *Journal of Multilingual and Multicultural Development*, 10:6, pp. 499–514.

Marshall, J. D. (1991) *The Treaty of Waitangi, Educational Reforms and the Education of Maori* (Auckland, University of Auckland).

Marshall, J. D. (1999) The Language of Indigenous Others: The Case of Maori in New Zealand (a response to Egéa-Kuehne), *Philosophy of Education Yearbook 1999*. <http://www.ed.uiuc.edu/EPS/PES-yearbook/1999/marshall.asp> (12 September 2003).

New Zealand Department of Education (1982) *Annual Research Report* (Wellington, Research and Statistics Division).

New Zealand Department of Education (1990) *Annual Research Report* (Wellington, N.Z., Research and Statistics Division).

Peters, M. & Marshall, J. (1988) Te Reo O Te Tai Tokerau: Community evaluation, empowerment, and opportunities of oral Maori language reproduction, in: *Future Directions: Report of the Royal Commission on Social Policy, volume 3.* (Wellington, Royal Commission on Social Policy), pp. 703–44.

Peters, M. & Marshall, J. (1989) *Nga Awangawanga Me Nga Wawata A Te Iwi O Te Tai Tokerau: Final report of the project, Issues Concerning the Schooling and Retention of Maori Secondary Students in Tai Tokerau (Northland) 1989: report to the Directors, Research and Statistics Division, and Qualifications and Assessment Directorate, Department of Education* (Auckland, University of Auckland).

Peters, M., Marshall, J. & Shaw, R. (1986) The Development and Trials of a Decision Making Model, *Evaluation Review*, 10:1, pp. 15–27.

Peters, M., Para, D. & Marshall, J. (1989) Te Reo O Te Tai Tokerau: Language evaluation and empowerment, *New Zealand Journal of Educational Studies*, 24:1, pp. 141–158.

Peters, M., Para, D. & Marshall, J. (1989) Te Reo O Te Tai Tokerau: The need for consolidation and national implementation, *Access*, 8:1, pp. 10–25.

Shaw, R. (1983) Beginning the Administrative Decision-Making Project, *Step*, 1983.

Shaw, R. (1985) Administrative Discretionary Justice, *Public Sector*, 8, pp. 19–26.

Shaw, R. & Burns, C. (1999) *Let's Teach Managers How to Implement Policy: Executive Decision-making Skills Project* (Wellington, The Open Polytechnic of New Zealand).

Shaw, R. & Ohia, M. (1988) *Te Reo O Te Taitokerau: He tirohanga na nga kaimahi.* The First Research into Educational Policy Conference (Wellington, New Zealand Council for Educational Research).

# 10

# The Labouring Sleepwalker: Evocation and expression as modes of qualitative educational research

PAUL SMEYERS

I'll teach you differences.

—King Lear; from the correspondence between Wittgenstein and Drury,
in R. Rhees (ed.) *Recollections of Wittgenstein*

## Introduction

Jim Marshall and I met first in 1990 at the second Conference of the International Network of Philosophers of Education (INPE) in London. Since then I have benefited enormously from the numerous discussions we had at the occasion of the projects we were both involved in or the conferences we attended. We share an interest in Wittgenstein and Nietzsche, in postmodern authors, in philosophy and philosophy of education, and in each other's company, and above all in long discussions in which Jim would point me to one two simple things which often throw a whole new light on what we are talking about. His philosophical craftsmanship and strength really lies in the intellectual honesty to search again and again for what is presupposed in this or that argument, and where it will lead us thus combining the very best of the Nietzschean and Wittgensteinian legacy with courage of Foucault.

He and I were always captivated by Wittgenstein's 'theory of meaning' and the possibilities generated for philosophy in general, and for philosophy of education in particular. But, we were also aware of the fact that there is more than one interpretation of his works. Indeed, they can be placed on a scale with at one end an emphasis on the importance of an actual (linguistic) community and, at the other end, a contrasting position of the possibility of giving personal (and maybe new) meaning to situations and phenomena. Both are dangerous: if the touchstone of meaning in the end is the community to which one belongs, there is a threat of conservatism and conformism—as the possible meaning is limited to the hitherto existing meaning; on the other hand if the touchstone is the individual, one has to delineate the boundaries of meaning so that not 'anything goes'. Jim has always been more receptive to the threat posed by the existing order, than I have been, which at least partly explains his interest in Foucault and in analyses of the neo-liberal society and an educational system that embraced that. Hence his penetrating critique of 'output' and 'performativity' that rules in New Zealand and elsewhere. Not only meaning and understanding, but *significance and relevance*, and therefore how power is distributed and dealt with in society, are at stake.

In this paper I chose to focus on the other arm of the opposition and will deal with the highly personal way an individual makes sense of the world in a way that avoids the pitfalls of the so-called private language. For Wittgenstein following a rule can never mean just following another rule, though we do follow rules blindly. His idea of the 'form of life' elicits that 'what we do' refers to what we have learnt, to the way in which we have learnt it and to how we have grown to find it self-evident. But the reference to the 'bedrock', to what was originally learnt, is however the only kind of situation for which it makes sense to ask whether the meaning of a concept is correctly stated. Dialogue, conversation, and exchange of ideas are the right ways to characterize all the other situations. The challenge of Wittgensteinian philosophy is therefore that of a balance of the individual and the community, of language and the world. His insistence on the third person (or the intersubjective level) is countered by the importance he gives to each individual's personal stance: persons must speak for themselves and do what they *can* do. Given the growing interest for the kind of educational research where the 'personal' is focused on, I will try to take up the challenge to see how here as elsewhere 'language' works. By making clear what it does for us, it will gradually become clear how this kind of research may itself have to be reinterpreted.

## Disturbing the Unified Picture of Research

Within social sciences the qualitative approach enjoys a new *élan*. Witness to this are the many studies within sociology and psychology, as well as within the educational sciences. Particularly as regards research concerning schools and educational policy, it can be argued that for the major part of this kind of research within the U.S.A.—where, incidentally, one finds the largest concentration—the qualitative approach is the dominant paradigm. There are different methods used within this kind of research in educational contexts: participatory observation, narrative and biographical research and action research as well as clinical interviews, case studies and analysis of experiences. Setting aside the differences between these ways of investigating a particular reality, there are some presuppositions which are shared by all of them, in general: that it is not meaningful to speak of a world which is independent of or separated from the subject; that child rearing and education are primarily concerned with individuals and the way they make sense of the world; that knowledge of the particular rather than knowledge of the universal is to be aimed at. The legitimacy of these presuppositions can be made more explicit within an anthropological (Taylor) and an epistemological frame (Wittgenstein). But this point of departure also generates a number of problems: the degree of universality of the insights, the meaningfulness of this kind of enquiry, the differentiation between argumentation and evocation and what should be understood by the improvement of a particular practice. These problems emerge preeminently within narrative educational research where a narrative is central and is explicitly recognized as a 'story', problems which are furthermore similar to those one is confronted with in other kinds of qualitative research. Is the result something still to be called 'science' or is it no more than 'expression'? And is what one envisages with research a kind of evocation? Does one not presuppose without good reason that there is more coherence in someone's personal story than actually is the case?

This directs us to a first question, whether the enigmatic nature of narrative inquiries can be further elucidated by Wittgenstein and Taylor. By indicating the limits of our dwelling on reality (whether through empirical or philosophical research) and what occurs in novels and poems, the attention is focused on language, on expression and evocation themselves. What exactly is the role of each and every individual? How does she find a balance between what expression constructively contributes, and what is 'given', the passive element in all of this. Another question I want to ask concerns the manner in which contemporary literary theory reflects on the language of literature itself as a particular kind of expression and evocation of human existence. With this in mind, the debate within literary theory is scrutinized with a view to confronting the lines of force within the debate that concerns the nature of narrative (or qualitative) educational research. The question about the relationship between language and world, between a narrative and reality leads us to the concepts 'expression' and 'evocation' which profoundly characterize human existence both ethically and aesthetically. A further issue that comes up here concerns the vicissitudes of these concepts (and to what realisations they give occasion) within the educational literature. Finally one is confronted with the question of whether the resistance encountered in the realm of literature is analogous to the resistance of an educational practice. In other words, whether this practice too, and necessarily so, escapes the 'surview' research wants to offer. Ultimately this leads to an investigation of the consequences of the fact that qualitative research can be heterogeneous and produce different (kinds of) results presented in various ways, for the nature of educational research.

Evidently, what will be offered in this paper cannot be more than a number of sketches of landscapes which were made in the course of my own journeying of how I came to see the problems qualitative research confronts us with—to paraphrase Wittgenstein (cf. Wittgenstein, 1953, p. vii). It provides, one could say, a rationale of a 'new' way of looking at educational research. There too, 'A *picture* held us captive. And we could not get outside it, for it lay in our language and language seemed to repeat it to us inexorably.' (Wittgenstein, 1953, I, §115)

## The Philosophical Framework for Qualitative Educational Research

The starting point of this research is the unity of 'language-and-the-world' as expressed by Wittgenstein in his later work through the concept of the *'form of life'*. At the basis of it one finds those fundamental presuppositions which support our speaking and acting on the epistemological, ethical, religious and metaphysical level. Language-games (which consist of particular expressions and activities) belong to a form of life. These translate as it were the context principle. Only within a language-game can one speak of justification, of evidence and proof, of errors, of good and bad reasoning, correct and wrong ways of measuring. This is the reason why we will always take the learning context into account in order to understand the meaning of a word. A radical separation between 'what is' (a state of affairs) and 'what is said about this' is not possible. Values and norms affect 'what is said by us' and refer to 'what is important for us'. Using the work of Charles Taylor (1985a and b; 1989; 1991) the Wittgensteinian third person perspective will be given shape at the level of the individual and from there the task of a social science will be elaborated.

For Charles Taylor:

> ... to be a full human agent, to be a person or self in the ordinary meaning, is to exist in a space defined by distinctions of worth. A self is a being for whom certain questions of category value have arisen, and received at least partial answers. Perhaps they have been given authoritatively by the culture more than they have been elaborated in the deliberation of the person concerned, but they are his in the sense that they are incorporated into his selfunderstanding, in some degree and fashion. (Taylor, 1985a, p. 3)

A 'naturalistic' interpretation is for him necessarily limited, as it has no eye for this interpretation of oneself and refuses, by the use of a neutral scientific language, to place the human being against the background of value distinctions. Thus an emotion such as 'shame' shows us that 'what we are ashamed of' is only conceivable within a form of life in which there is a striving for dignity, a life between others to whose respect one aspires. This is the reason why man cannot understand himself as an object between other objects: *'verstehen'* is his mode of being. In order to indicate the meaning which is present in our acting, Taylor uses the concept of 'practice': at this level there is a particular vision of the actor, a relationship towards others and society and there are furthermore implicit norms which have to be met. The task of social science is to bring clarity into these practices. A successful interpretation clarifies a meaning which is confused, fragmented, strange, puzzling, contradictory or present in a vague form and has to 'improve' that practice. But a theory of the human sciences 'only' rarely makes an actual practice explicit, in other words the understanding of those involved. A strong motive for theory construction but also for their adoption is the fact that our implicit understanding is in one way or another inadequate or mistaken. Theories enlarge, criticize and challenge our understanding. Of course, it can never just be a matter of applying these results (as in the case of the natural sciences). The practice we speak about has as its central element the understanding of those who are involved. Only in qualitative research is it possible to do justice to the subject as subject, and thus not to reduce it to an object.

The task of the social sciences as this is conceived by Taylor is analogous to Wittgenstein's understanding of the aim of philosophy. In its most general and positive form this aim is to offer an *Übersicht*, *surview* or *perspicuous representation*. This can only be achieved by a patient investigation of the way sentences and expression are 'applied' and of their rule-governed connections. Philosophy should not be involved with metaphysical propositions in order to express the essence of something; there are no new facts to be discovered, only new insights in old facts. Thus to recall the particular is THE method for every philosophical investigation: its result is also referred to as a new way of looking at things (cf. Wittgenstein, 1953, I, §401). Wittgenstein pointed out that giving reasons in philosophy can be compared with giving reasons in aesthetics. One may speak of a debate, but this does not lead to conclusions; rather, its function is to make those involved sensitive to the way something can be appreciated (cf. Moore, 1955). And where he describes his method he speaks of 'giving examples'. Such a philosophy may be written as a poetic composition (cf. Wittgenstein, 1980, p. 82). The descriptive method and the understanding Wittgenstein attributes to philosophy can also be applied to the human sciences. Besides a hypothesis which can explain a particular behaviour by indicating how different phenomena are explained by each other, one can make explicit the way one understands a particular practice. The difference lies in what one aspires to, what one is interested in. The perspicuous representation in the human sciences makes it possible to understand in the sense of 'seeing connections'. At other places he speaks of *'putting things side by side'*. What does this mean for the educational context?

What has been claimed concerning social science within this framework immediately applies to an empirical educational science. The theory will describe and challenge. It is the task of philosophy of education to make the grammar explicit: the presuppositions of the actual educational language and the contours of an educational question. Besides indicating demonstrable fallacies, mistaken arguments and inconceivable or unacceptable presuppositions, there is first of all the offering of an interpretation which can only evoke or speak to someone by making explicit the reasons which carry someone's *engagement*. But it will be clear that it is not all the same what is philosophically argued; to put this more precisely, it needs to be carried by the intersubjective level. Where it concerns empirical research within a Wittgensteinian framework, the determination of what is the case will assume precedence in order to reach an *Übersicht*. The focus of philosophy of education will be on the justification, of what is the case in a particular way but of which it is also accepted that it could have been different. Clearly, on both levels the focus is on the particular.

Thus far I have given an overview of the general framework. Discussions concerning this belong to the heart of every philosophical approach, but it is important to indicate that in the social sciences (and also within educational sciences—cf. among others Pring, 2000), these discussions have always claimed an important place (cf. Elster, 1989; 1999; Hempel, 1965; Hollis, 1994; Kincaid, 1996; Martin & McIntyre, 1994; Winch, 1958). Besides the indicated embeddedness within the Anglo-Saxon context, it needs to be underscored that the nature of research itself has also been a central concern within the continental tradition (such as within phenomenology or critical theory—see for an initial overview of the literature Levering, 2001; Masschelein, 2001; Carr & Kemnis, 1986).

Evidently, the positions concerning philosophical or empirical research within the tradition of Wittgenstein and Taylor also confront us with a number of problems.

For the time being I accept that though they cannot be separated, they can at least be distinguished. Among the most important problems are the degree to which results can be generalized and, combined with this; the nature of research itself, the possibility of distinguishing evocation and argumentation, and last but not least what is to be understood by an improvement of a particular practice. These problems can be illustrated by qualitative educational research. By way of example I have chosen narrative analysis.

## A Paradigmatic Example: Possibilities and Pressing Problems for Narrative Analysis in Educational Research

According to Polkinghorne (1995, pp. 5–7) narrative research distinguishes itself from other kinds of qualitative research by the use of diachronic data. Contrary to synchronic data this is material that is characterized by a particular evolution in time or a developmental perspective. There is a starting point in the past and a progress in time which leads to the actual state. Polkinghorne (1995) uses '*narrative inquiry*' as the broad term in which he distinguishes between an '*analysis of narratives*' and '*narrative analysis*'. In the '*analysis of narratives*' the researcher assembles stories and then looks for common themes within them. This is a paradigmatic approach because it aims to allocate the assembled cases to different categories. In order to achieve this one looks for characteristics which are common to the different cases, thus making abstraction from the particular. The degree to which one uses existing theories may be different. The aim is not only to discover and describe classes of cases, but also to indicate relations between them. Thus the reality becomes easier to survey, though this is at the cost of what makes some things unique, or by ignoring context data. In '*narrative analysis*', on the contrary, one wants to understand a particular case not by allocating it to a broader category, but by highlighting its particularity. One does not make abstraction of its uniqueness, but tries precisely to show it as a particular story. The data used here are not exclusively story-like. Information can be gathered from various sources (transcriptions of interviews, diaries, policy documents, reports of observations, notes of fieldwork, etc.). In the process of writing the report the researcher relates the events and activities to each other by presenting them as contributing to the development of a plot, i.e. the narrative structure which indicates how the different events form part of a certain outcome. During the process of writing, the researcher appeals to his expertise in the discipline. The resulting story does not only have to correspond with the data, but at the same time it has to reveal a particular kind or order and meaningfulness which as such was not clear before. This result should therefore not be seen as a report of what actually happened from an objective point of view, but instead as the result of consecutive constructions. It is thus evident that at least in principle more than one story can be written and that almost every researcher might write a different one. Thus justice is done to the multifariousness of reality, but at the same time this raises problems about the nature of research, in its most radical form phrased as whether this is really still research.

In the present context, theoretical justification (both for the use of narrative materials and for what one does with them) is often sought by referring to the writing of Paul Ricoeur. According to this author personal identity has to be understood after the model of a story. Only thus can it be guaranteed that someone remains identical. According to Ricoeur our lives are a quest for a narrative identity to be acquired by 'applying' models which are passed on to us by the culture we share. But the subject cannot autonomously give shape to her identity; the intersubjective context takes precedence. Not only does it start by means of language—which is foremost the language of the others—but the individual is also already part of the stories told (about her) by the others, which sets limits to the composition of one's narrative identity. Therefore, to tell a story becomes according to Ricoeur (1991, p. 30) a secondary process which is grafted on our being entrapped in stories. Ricoeur tries to show through his dealing with the so-called threefold mimesis that there is a necessary connection between the activity of telling a story and the temporal character of human experience. In Mimesis 1, acting is understood from our acquaintance with the conceptual network and symbolic mediation and presupposes an acknowledgement of temporal structures; here what is at stake is a kind of implicit understanding we have of human activities and their temporal character. Mimesis 2 is understood as '*mise en intrigue*' which mediates between separate events and history as a whole and which brings together divergent elements such as actors, aims, means etc. and takes care that concord conquers discord, in other words, that unexpected things are integrated in the plot. What is involved here is the process of emplotment ('*mise en intrigue*'), the stage in which the events are brought together in the composition of the story. Finally, and of the utmost relevance too for the further use of Ricoeur within the context of educational research, there is Mimesis 3: through the intersection of the world of the text and the listener the story gains the power to open the horizon of possible experience; the process of composition of the configuration does not occur within the text but within the mind of the reader. New evaluations of reality are possible through the emancipation from the ordinary. The meaning of a story is generated by the intersection of the world of the text and the world of the listener or reader. Through this a reconfiguration of life by the story becomes a possibility. Through stories in which there is necessarily a plot (cf. Mimesis 2, a subcategory of 'texts') and thus not through immediate intuition, it is for Ricoeur at least partially possible to understand human existence (including the way one understands oneself). The result is not a substantial but a narrative identity.

But again we are confronted with a crucial problem which concerns the ambiguous nature of reality. I will not deal here with Ricoeur's wrestling with the problem of reference (for instance the metaphorical in history and fiction) called '*refiguration*' in his later work; it is remarkable however that he does not want to take sides in the dichotomy between fiction and 'what is real' and because of that he cannot offer a satisfactory solution for the problem of reference. Ricoeur's enticing analysis moreover conceals an important presupposition, namely the extent to which the self can appear as transparent to herself. To put this more simply and immediately within the context of research: telling a story about oneself urges one to force the elements in the contours of a plot, compelling them in spite of everything into a whole. That our acting is intelligible, that it can be spoken of as a unity, seems to contradict, however, the fact that we sometimes do things which just don't make sense. Indeed, things sometimes appeal to us, we are moved, fascinated, do things against our better judgement, and for this there seems to be hardly any place within such a paradigm of relative transparency. Yet it seems that the kind of research we are envisaging exactly presupposes that there is such a place within a unity, that it can and even must be there. This is more important than may appear at first sight, for if our actions (perhaps our most important activities) have to be characterized in this rather passive manner, then this puts severe constraints on the possibility of using stories in order to understand what people do. Again we are confronted with the radical question of to what extent there is more than ever-renewed expression, more than just making explicit the meaning of something, and this immediately challenges the legitimacy of any research in the human sciences.

These fundamental questions are also raised where empirical educational researchers discuss the nature of *analysis of narratives* or *narrative analysis*. Thus Waite (1994) claims that choosing narrative research may be an easy way out because one simply registers the stories of those involved and reports them, accepting that they can offer an interpretation of their own world (p. 14). Connelly and Clandinin, two important writers in this field, are not at ease either. They admonish that however liberating and emancipatory 'narrative inquiry' may seem, it ought to contribute to the functioning of a particular practice and cannot just lead to a confirmation of the status quo (1992). For Goodson (1995) too, working with stories is only a starting point. Stories must be seen and judged as social constructions which enable us to localize and question the social context in which they find their place. Through such socio-philosophical analysis the focus is shifted which raises new questions. D. C. Phillips claims that in narrative research epistemology has been blown away and replaced by politics (1993, p. 4). And though he recognizes the sometimes justifiable political ambitions, this in his eyes is not an argument to dictate that a story must be accepted as credible or that it as such deserves a central place in educational research. Stories have to be epistemologically respectable. This can be seen as a different interest. Thus Connelly and Clandinin hope that narrative research will contribute to the relationship between theory and practice and that the institutional anchoring will change what they call the professional knowledge contexts. From this perspective it is understandable that they propose '*an engaging plot*' as a criterion. It is indeed imaginable that a good, moving story has a strong evocative power and because of that urges more easily to change than a sound but dull research report. But Phillips (1993) rejects criteria such as '*adequacy*', '*plausibility*' and '*an engaging plot*' because they are according to him scientifically and epistemologically irrelevant. This becomes more concrete where the consequences are discussed of the narrative approach concerning the relationship between theory and practice in the field of teacher training. A radicalisation of the idea of the personal story character of teaching may lead to a rejection of every generalization connected with education. All generalizations are then marked as distortions of 'real' stories of teachers and as collaborations with the ruling class which tries to subject the teachers. Carter (1993) warns that to over-emphasise what something means for a particular teacher may imply that these stories turn out to be relevant only for the person who wrote them, and moreover that an idolization of the 'voice of the teacher' gives these stories a kind of authenticity which is simply not justified. She shares the opinion of Elbaz (1991) who claims that teachers are not privileged authors who somehow enjoy direct access to the truth and who are the only ones who control the possibility of telling the whole story. The recognizability which naturally explains the attraction of narrative research and its possible impact on educational practice is thus confronted with some fundamental questions.

To sum up, the paradigmatic thinker searches for what is common and by doing that indisputably slights the particular. The narrative solution, on the contrary, does justice to the uniqueness of every subject. Narrative educational research, however, leads to new questions such as whether what is offered is more than just the construction of the researcher, or whether the rejection of the positivist paradigm also entails abandoning all the generally accepted criteria for scientific research. Narrative educational research gives occasion to questions which are analogous to those brought to the forefront by the framework of Wittgenstein and Taylor. Wittgenstein points at the groundlessness of that in which we are embedded through the language-games belonging to a form of life, but keeps an important place for the individual in all of this. But he is reticent about what the latter precisely implies. Where he speaks about the role of the human sciences, he 'only' refers to 'description' or to *a new way of looking at things*. He confronts us with *philosophy leaves everything as it is*, but the human being who might become different. Research too in some sense leaves everything as it is. It can offer clarity where there is vagueness, but, as Charles Taylor claims, it can also challenge us to see things differently. It can inspire us through Mimesis 3 to *a new way of looking at things* (another Wittgensteinian phrase which he sometimes uses to characterize philosophy). But is this really more than taking notice of what is happening in order to understand what is going on? And if its aim is not to have control, why is it worthwhile at all? Is its result more than just a commentary on reality which is governed by its own rules and dynamism? Taylor's notion of a 'practice' incorporates the idea of 'better', but he does not expand on what exactly this means. That the particular as it is embedded in the intersubjective plays an important role, goes without saying, but how exactly this has to be understood remains obscure. And if we accept that reality and truth is something that happens in which new things appear and others disappear and more generally if we accept *post-foundationalism*, is a theoretical reflection then more than just *Spielerei* and at the same time different from and more than *common sense*? Can something more be said than that it has to meet the requirement that it be interesting? This confronts us with the question whether and how a theoretical reflection, if it is indeed a kind of dwelling on reality, is fundamentally different from what is offered in novels and poems? These radical questions force us furthermore to think about the nature of expression and evocation. Can some further foothold be found elsewhere, and how should we address the problems at stake there?

## The Limits of our Language and the Value of Narrative

In educational research what is at stake is the understanding of a particular reality brought to the fore by language: this presupposes that this reality can be understood and moreover that its intelligibility can at least partially be made explicit. But is that really the case? The focus on language is without doubt the primordial interest of twentieth century philosophy, though the mentioned presuppositions are not accepted by everyone. In the *Tractatus* Wittgenstein tried to indicate the boundary between what can be said and what can only be shown and he held the position that the limits of my language are the limits of my world (Wittgenstein, 1922, §5.6) and that the subject does not belong to the world but forms its limit (ibid., §5.632). He accepts the idea that the world consists of states of affairs which exist independently of each other. He holds the so-called *picture theory of language*: we make images of facts and the relationship between a fact and an image is one of similarity. A revelation of its form will give us the logical structure: 'Everything that can be thought at all can be thought clearly. Everything that can be put into words can be put clearly (Wittgenstein, 1922, §4.116). According to him every object must have a sign, but only objects may have it. If we want to speak about values and meaning this has to be sought outside of the world. Thus it follows in section 7 that, 'What we cannot speak about we must pass over in silence'. Though the presuppositions of the calculus model of language of the *Tractatus* will be rejected later, Wittgenstein remains faithful to his basic assumptions: that the real problems about our life do not belong to the world, that a solution for these must be sought outside of the facts (of the world), a solution which is labelled 'the mystical'. It concerns a particular way of seeing the world which indicates that what he has in mind is something that has to do with overcoming oneself, a personal struggle which everyone must engage in to find quietness and peace in the world. It is about working on oneself. By doing philosophy Wittgenstein tried himself to deal with his demons: 'Working in philosophy ... is really more a working on oneself. On one's own interpretation. On one's way of seeing things. (And what one expects of them)' (1980, p. 16e—a remark from 1931).

Language as a possible way of signifying (by expression and evocation) myself and the other, is, as already touched upon, not only an instrument of rational inquiry. It also figures in attempts to express human existence in its non-reducible plurality—the beautiful as a sanctuary of what is not yet tied, not yet given a particular shape. Words may comfort us, may appeal to us, or make us angry, can apologize, can express regret or remorse, may insult or support; one can thank someone (at the occasion of a farewell for instance) with beautiful words and one can thank others for such beautiful words. One can express oneself by what one says, by the particular manner of saying something. Words are given and at the same time we use them—everyone gives meaning to them. 'We talk, we utter words, and only *later* get a picture of their life' (Wittgenstein, 1953, II, p. 209e) and Wittgenstein speaks about the *'feeling of meaning'*. The core of the conception of language of Wittgenstein's later work is that any attempt to say something is always partial, that it is always one-sided. No way of speaking, no doctrine whatsoever can control cultural practices and thus liberate us from the restlessness and incertitudes of the human existence, of the search for meaning in our life. He points to the fact that what we do can never be completely transparent, that it is always characterized to some extent by arbitrariness. Thus it becomes clear that in what we say we bear witness to what we long for, but also to what we are not certain of, how we try to express ourselves, try to be coherent. In an analogous way Cavell argues that we should not try to escape from the existential conditions we find ourselves in in order to look for false certainties, but urges us to be born continuously and thus to be mortal. In his *In Quest of the Ordinary: Lines of Skepticism and Romanticism* (1986) he maintains that, among other things, words in philosophy may create a distance. They allow us to start over and over again and thus generate an alliance with others who are also focused on this. Words may help us escape, but at the same time they create a home. Thus philosophy is engaged in a certain revision of the way one sees particular things and the philosopher may identify herself as someone who '*reviews her vision*', or else '*revises her reviews*', in a reflection of what one is conscious of.

The conceptualisation of social (and political) problems demands an ever-renewed rethinking of reality with similar instruments. To think again can only mean to think from a different point of view what one is trying to understand (perhaps change?). From the previous philosophical framework it will be clear that we can never be pleased with the investigation of what is already in existence. What is at stake shifts to what is at stake for someone (again for the other and for myself), where the other is recognized in her personal struggle as an emotional being— unstructured justice. Rigid approaches to social (and political) problems will have to be complemented by a more flexible ethical sensibility. Here it is no longer possible to ignore the recognition of emotions as an essential component of a comprehensive social rationality (Nussbaum, 1997): the message is to feel again. To see the other is to look for the way in which the other expresses herself, gives shape to herself in the struggle with herself. But to touch the other is also to confront the other with one's own struggle by means of the evocative instruments which are at my disposal. That we inevitably violate the other is clear enough. After all, the understanding of the other is at the same time a negation and a constitutive affirmation. We understand the other as an intentional object which we crave to understand. We want to read the story of the other, too often without recognizing the illegibility of her story. This does not necessarily imply that we would not be able or do not have to understand her. The reading of the story of the other is however at the same time a reading which is interfered with by my own story. What remains for us is to surrender to the intersection of this reading with its reader, and to what this does to us. As mentioned above, this insight has already been elaborated by Ricoeur, but the problems it gives occasion to have only partially been answered by him. It remains unclear how the other can confront us completely with her otherness.

A foothold may be found by investigating how the subject is part of the inter-subjective level. Wittgenstein's *Investigations* show the value of our freedom, of our autonomy, not as the exercise of an arbitrary choice, but as the result of the way in which nature as well as artistic products and moral responsibilities are taken seriously and even seen as necessary. He mocks those who are seduced by the promise to be able to control the cultural and who think they are able to represent our thoughts and concepts as necessary. To write is for him to surrender to certain readings (words seen as 'what is given to us') and philosophy as the result of a 'play' of reading and writing on the basis of one's own authority. Or we are able to rethink a thought that comes our way, to possess it and to judge it, or to let it go; it does not belong to us. This kind of philosophy expresses one's own life or is futile. Cavell quotes Emerson: 'The simplest words—we do not know what they mean except when we love and aspire'. To understand their meaning we have to be in a certain mood (of the heart). We find ourselves and in the answer to the way we see ourselves we find a place to begin. We have to live this antagonism: hope and despair (Emerson's *odious facts*) and thus he quotes Wittgenstein approvingly: 'It is in language that an expectation and its fulfilment make contact' (Wittgenstein, 1953, I, §445). Cavell refers to the consolations of the word; to *this* meaning for the other; as a song; as sharing in the case of food and drink, to have in some sense the 'same' experience. Here, to write becomes a means to fight the struggle with oneself (with one's own language), and poetry a means to make a bridge. In the words of Cavell:

> ... that what we are is written all over us, or branded; but here especially the other way round, that our language contains our character, that we brand the world, as for example with the concept of Fate; and then listen again to such an idea as that one's character is one's fate. Now it says openly that language is our fate. It means hence that not exactly prediction, but diction, is what puts us in bonds, that with each word we utter we emit stipulations, agreements we do no know and do not want to know we have entered, agreements we were always in, that were in effect before our participation in them. Our relation to our language—to the fact that we are subject to expression and comprehension, victims of meaning—is accordingly a key to our sense of our distance from our lives, of our sense of the alien, of ourselves as alien to ourselves, thus alienated. (Cavell, 1988, pp. 39–40)

This feeling of desolation presupposes an expression of the struggle with oneself, presupposes expression as a kind of surrendering. The written word, the poem is a weapon in this struggle. It requires no other material presence; it does not want to explain; it only suggests seeing things in a particular way. It seems a 'means' to be at home for a moment, for the lonely individual, for the subject-with-the-others.

The continuance of Wittgenstein's legacy in the work of Cavell is accompanied by a remarkable intensification of the attention on literature. This forms the foothold for an investigation in which contemporary literary theory reflects on the notion of literary language as a special kind of expression or evocation of human existence. Most pertinent in the present context is the gradually growing research concerning the relationship of literature and ethics.* One of the most prominent advocates for the recognition of literary fiction as a privileged medium for moral education in a broad sense is Martha Nussbaum. Her insights in this context are, however, not welcomed unreservedly. From a philosophical perspective she encounters a kind of criticism which bears many resemblances with what one finds concerning narrative educational research (namely the reproach that a clear and justified argumentation is given up too quickly in favour of a rather too vague, evocative 'expression' of moral problems in particular stories). But questions are also raised on the part of literary theory concerning Nussbaum's instumentalisation of literary imagination for moral aims. Such questions are a part of an already long standing renewed interest in the relationship between ethics and literature where particular attention is paid to the role of narrative (cf. Geoffrey Galt Harpham (1992) and Adam Zachary Newton (1995); also the work of Robert Eaglestone, Jill Robbins, Derek Attridge and Rei Terada; see also the recent special issue on 'Objectivity in ethics, politics and aesthetics' of the leading journal *New Literary History*, 32:4; from a more philosophical point of view the work of Richard Eldridge and for an empirical examination of Nussbaum's narrativism from the perspective of literary studies, see Hakemulder). Here the question is also raised whether the case of literature may not in fact involve something else. Perhaps literariness has to be conceived as a kind of resistance to understanding, a resistance to a 'perspicuous representation' (and thus it may perhaps not fulfil the role attributed to it by authors such as Nussbaum, i.e. to evoke sympathy). Thus attention can be given to the work of literary authors such as T.S. Eliot, Banville and Swift. Here the focus is the liberation of literature from reality, its distance and proximity, the progressing emancipation of literature and language, intensified by the impossibility to entertain an unambiguous verifiable communication with the world, finally what this says about the individual and her kind of existence.

The debate within literary theory may be investigated in order to confront its lines of force with the debate concerning the nature of educational research. This line of inquiry has not yet been pursued and is not only innovative, but extremely relevant for qualitative educational research. Incidentally, it is especially remarkable that this path has as yet not been taken given the fact that the interpretation of a literary critic of a novel or poem is to a large extent analogous to the interpretation of a particular educational practice. Granted, a careful distinction needs to be made between literary stories as instruments within a broadly understood educational context and stories as documents resulting from or about a more strictly specified educational situation. This distinction, however, does not diminish in any sense the pertinence of a critical investigation into the functioning of literary stories for the criticism of narrative educational research. This kind of research finds itself, whether it likes it or not, in a postmodern condition where stories resist the latent omnipresence of a meta-narrative in which the particular is neutralized. The research within literary theory into narrative ethics is precisely an exploration of never-ending narrative resistance within the medium of narrative intensity *par excellence*—which could be called a perverse but important and necessary detour.

## Education and Self-expression and their Relation to Educational Research

The question about the relationship between language and world, between a narrative and reality leads us to the concepts 'expression' and 'evocation' which profoundly characterize human existence both ethically and aesthetically. Thus one is confronted with the vicissitudes of these concepts (and to what realisations they give occasion to) within the educational literature. It should be possible on the basis of the outlined analysis to give these concepts a different place. A study could be made of the way 'expression' has been used in educational contexts and to what realisations this has led. Not only has the possible role of the aesthetic been contemplated in the context of bringing up children or of education (cf. among others Reid, Steiner), but also attention has been given to the experience of the child in the progressive and child-centred movement. There it has been explored what is required to enable children to express themselves, in other words what this demands of the organisation of the educational situation (cf. Rogers, Freire, Gordon and others). Subsequently, it could be investigated how this looks from the perspective of the later Wittgenstein (cf. Schulte for a psychological and Tilghman for an aesthetical angle) and integrated with the results of the previous analysis of the concepts of 'expression' and 'evocation'. And it can be worked out whether the resistance against understanding encountered in the realm of literature is akin to what is expressed by Lyotard's concept of 'event', which leads to the question whether there is an analogous resistance in an educational practice, whether it too eventually and necessarily escapes the 'surview' research wants to offer.

At first sight this resembles what is at stake where education is involved in thinking about plurality. There the starting-point is that it can no longer be held that the subject is autonomous first, after which it engages in relationships with others. The relationship with the other is, contrarily, constitutive of her own autonomy and thus takes precedence. What is questioned here is how a different relationship with others/otherness is possible if others have to be understood as (other) singularities; how the contact with others, with what is unfamiliar, can be learned, and how one can acquire the 'skill' to tolerate, endure and reshape difference, plurality, complexity and contingency; finally, how the experience of the limits of comprehensibility can be seen as an enrichment and not as a threat.

Thinking about the nature of a story may be a way to express this. On the one hand a story can be conceived as what joins people together, on the other hand as what can only 'show'. And if that is so, does education ultimately have to be conceived as an initiation into what is 'groundless'? And in that case can an educator and a student of this area do more than give expression to her story, and appeal to the *educandus* by what she holds to be constructive? If educational research can be heterogeneous and produce different (kinds of) results and moreover can be presented in various ways, if different stories can be told, will this eventually lead to the classical insight that in essence education is a matter of instilling a good disposition? Finally one is confronted with the question whether consequently educational research has to be conceived as another way to express this 'showing', as a mode of the will to join in this kind of speaking and doing: a conception which can be related to Taylor's stance concerning social sciences and enable us to characterize in a new way the nature of educational research.

Many educational researchers have been lying awake thinking about the world in order to find information that is 'useful'. Their dedication cannot be doubted. The dream of the labourer, to interpret 'what is the case' and by this knowledge to grasp 'what is predictable, what can be influenced' is, however, based upon a kind of thinking which is in need of reconsideration. '*The story* before bedtime' may offer a way out for the 'labouring sleepwalker'. Once it has been recognized that not everything can be understood, the human being can only be touched by the transcendent. One cannot *not* initiate the child. One cannot but initiate the child into one's own story. Woven into a growing network of stories, everyone articulates what she is (expression), everyone touches the other and is touched by her (evocation). That which touches is the other, with whom I am joined in an intersubjective manner, who expresses herself by what evocation is capable of. The one who says 'I' is only thanks to the other joined in what we are touched by, what cannot be said anymore, but only shown, that what is for us. And the story of the researcher— it may touch us as any other story, may invite us to tell a new, perhaps (partly) different tale, in which the thread is taken up again, the existence articulated and challenged.

## Acknowledgement

*I am indebted to Ortwin De Graef of the Faculty of Arts, KULeuven for discussions I had with him concerning the relevance of literary theory for qualitative research in general and for numerous suggestions of particular works.

## References

Attridge, D. (1999) Innovation, Literature, Ethics: Relating to the Other, *PMLA*, 114:1, pp. 20–31.

Bridges, D. & McNamee, M. (eds) (2001) The Ethics of Educational Research [Special issue], *Journal of Philosophy of Education*, 35:3.

Carr, W. & Kemnis, S. (1986) *Becoming Critical. Education, knowledge and action research* (London, The Falmer Press).

Carter, K. (1993) The Place of Story in the Study of Teaching and Teacher Education, *Educational Researcher*, 22, pp. 5–12, 18.

Cavell, S. (1988) *In Quest of the Ordinary* (Chicago, University of Chicago Press).

Cavell, S. (1990) *Conditions Handsome and Unhandsome* (Chicago, University of Chicago Press).

Cavell, S. (1994) *A Pitch of Philosophy* (Cambridge, MA, Harvard University Press).

Cavell, S. (1995) *Philosophical Passages: Wittgenstein, Emerson, Austin, Derrida* (Oxford, Blackwell).

Connelly, F. M. & Clandinin, D. J. (1992) *Asking Questions About Telling Teaching Stories.* Paper presented at the Annual Meeting of the American Educational Research Association.

Connelly, F. M. & Clandinin, D. J. (1997) Narrative Inquiry, in: J. P. Keeves (ed.), *Educational Research, Methodology, and Measurement: An international handbook* (Oxford, Pergamon) (pp. 81–86).

Eaglestone, R. (1997) *Ethical Criticism: Reading after Levinas* (Edinburgh, Edinburgh University Press).

Elbaz, F. (1991) Research on Teacher's Knowledge: The evolution of a discourse, *Journal of Curriculum Studies*, 23, pp. 1–19.

Eldridge, R. (1997) *Leading a Human Life. Wittgenstein, intentionality, and romanticism* (Chicago, University of Chicago Press).

Elster, J. (1989) *Nuts and Bolts for the Social Sciences* (Cambridge, Cambridge University Press).

Elster, J. (1999) *Alchemies of the Mind. Rationality and the emotions* (Cambridge, Cambridge University Press).

Freire, P. (1972) *Pedagogy of the Oppressed* (Harmondsworth, Penguin).

Goodson, I. F. (1995) The Story So Far: Personal knowledge and the political, *International Journal of Qualitative Studies in Education*, 8:1, pp. 89–98.

Gordon, T. (1975) *Parent Effectiveness Training: The tested new way to raise responsible children* (New York, Wyden).

Hakemulder, J. (2000) *The Moral Laboratory: Experiments examining the effects of reading literature on social perception and moral self-concept* (Amsterdam, John Benjamins).

Harpham, G. (1992) *Getting it Right: Language, literature and ethics* (Chicago, University of Chicago Press).

Hempel, C. (1965) *Aspects of Scientific Explanation* (New York, Free Press).

Hollis, M. (1994) *Philosophy of Social Science* (Cambridge, Cambridge University Press).

Kincaid, H. (1996) *Philosophical Foundations of the Social Sciences. Analyzing controversies in social research* (Cambridge, Cambridge University Press).

Levering, B. (2001) Van Fenomenologie naar Hemeneutiek, in: P. Smeyers en B. Levering (eds), *Grondslagen van de Wetenschappelijke Pedagogiek. Modern en postmodern* (Amsterdam, Boom) pp. 73–92.

Lyotard, J.-F. (1998) A propos du Différend. Entretien avec Jean-François Lyotard, *Les Cahiers de Philosophie*, 5.

Lyotard, J.-F. (1988) *The Inhuman: Reflections on time* (G. Bennington and R. Bowlby, trans.) (Cambridge, Polity).

Lyotard, J.-F. (1991) *Lectures d' Enfance* (Paris, Galilée).

Martin, M., & McIntyre, L. (eds) (1994) *Readings in the Philosophy of Social Science* (Cambridge, MA, MIT Press).

Masschelein, J. (2001) Kritische Theorie en Kritische Pedagogiek, in: P. Smeyers en B. Levering (eds), *Grondslagen van de Wetenschappelijke Pedagogiek. Modern en postmodern* (Amsterdam, Boom), pp. 93–111.

Moore, G. E. (1955) Wittgenstein's Lectures on Ethics, *Mind*, 64, pp. 1–27.

Newton, A. Z. (1995) *Narrative Ethics* (Cambridge, Harvard University Press).

Nussbaum, M. (1997) *Cultivating Humanity. A classical defense of reform in liberal education* (Cambridge, Harvard University Press).

Phillips, D. C. (1993) Gone with the Wind? Evidence, rigor and warrants in educational research, in: J. Tooley (ed.), *Papers of the Annual Conference of the Philosophy of Education Society of Great Britain* (Oxford, PESGB), pp. 4–11.

Phillips, D. C. (1997) Telling the Truth about Stories, *Teacher and Teacher Education*, 13, pp. 101–109.

Pring, R. (2000) The 'False Dualism' of Educational Research, *Journal of Philosophy of Education*, 34, pp. 247–260.

Polkinghorne, D. (1995) Narrative Configuration in Qualitative Analysis, *International Journal of Qualitative Studies in Education*, 8:1, pp. 5–23.

Ricoeur, P. (1991) Life in Quest of Narrative, in: D. Wood (ed.), *On Paul Ricoeur. Narrative and interpretation* (London, Routledge), pp. 20–33.

Ricoeur, P. (1991) Narrative Identity, in: D. Wood (ed.), *On Paul Ricoeur. Narrative and interpretation* (London, Routledge), pp. 188–199.

Robbins, J. (1999) *Altered Reading: Levinas and literature* (Chicago, University of Chicago Press).

Rogers, C. (1969) *Freedom to Learn. A view of what education might become* (Columbus, OH, Merrill).

Rhees R. (ed.) (1984) *Recollections of Wittgenstein* (Oxford, Oxford University Press).

Schulte, J. (1993) *Experience and Expression. Wittgenstein's philosophy of psychology* (Oxford, Clarendon Press).

Taylor, C. (1985) *Philosophical Papers. Vol. 1. Human agency and language* (Cambridge, Cambridge University Press).

Taylor, C. (1985) *Philosophical Papers: Vol. 2. Philosophy and the human sciences* (Cambridge, Cambridge University Press).

Taylor, C. (1989) *Sources of the Self. The making of the modern identity* (Cambridge MA, Harvard University Press).

Taylor, C. (1991) *The Ethics of Authenticity* (Cambridge MA, Harvard University Press).

Terada, R. (2001) *Feeling in Theory: Emotion after the 'Death of the Subject'* (Cambridge MA, Harvard University Press).

Tilghman, B. R. (1991) *Wittgenstein, Ethics and Aesthetics: The view from eternity* (Basingstoke, Macmillan).

Waite, D. (1994) Ethnography's Demise: What's next for narrative? Paper presented at the Annual Meeting of the American Educational Research Association, New Orleans.

Wittgenstein, L. (1922) *Tractatus Logico-Philosophicus* (D. Pears & B. F. McGuinness, trans.) (London, Routledge).

Wittgenstein, L. (1953) *Philosophical Investigations/Philosophische Untersuchungen* (G. E. M. Anscombe, trans.) (Oxford, Basil Blackwell).

Wittgenstein, L. (1979) Remarks on Frazer's Golden Bough, in: C. Luckhardt (ed.), *Wittgenstein: Sources and perspectives* (Hassocks, Sussex, The Harvester Press), pp. 61–81.

Wittgenstein, L. (1980) *Culture and Value/Vermischte Bemerkungen* (G. H. von Wright, ed.; P. Winch, trans.) (Oxford, Basil Blackwell).

Winch, P. (1958) *The Idea of a Social Science* (London, Routledge and Kegan Paul).

# 11

# 'What it Makes Sense to Say': Wittgenstein, rule-following and the nature of education: Jim Marshall on Wittgenstein's Contributions to Educational Philosophy

NICHOLAS C. BURBULES & RICHARD SMITH

It is one of Jim Marshall's many achievements in the philosophy of education that he has encouraged us—that is, the philosophy of education community in general—to re-examine the significance of the work of the later Ludwig Wittgenstein for education. That significance has not always been appreciated (Burbules & Peters, 2001). Not a few established philosophers for instance have managed to discuss the potential impact of philosophy for education (Brown, 1975) without any mention of Wittgenstein at all; references to him are few and cursory in seminal texts such as Richard Peters' *The Philosophy of Education* (1973). It is true that Wittgensteinian ideas were used during the 1970s to underpin theories of the curriculum, for instance in the later work of Paul Hirst (1974) and by Allen Brent (1978), but this seemed a misappropriation of anti-foundationalist ideas to argue for curriculum foundations (cp. Smith, 1981). Jim Marshall's work on Wittgenstein over many years serves therefore as a welcome reminder that the *Philosophical Investigations* and other texts that have proved so influential on, among other areas, the philosophy of religion, philosophy of language, and philosophy of psychology and social science, have not yet been adequately considered by the philosophy of education community at large (Peters & Marshall, 1999; Smeyers & Marshall, 1995).

Moreover, Jim Marshall's perspective on Wittgenstein, filtered through his appreciation of Foucault and other poststructuralist thinkers, emphasizes a dimension of Wittgenstein that is underappreciated generally: the Wittgenstein who is a theorist of sociocultural practices, and practices constituted within systems of discursive power. For more conventional analytical appropriations of Wittgenstein, whether in philosophy of education or 'straight' philosophy, this view is mildly scandalous—which not only does not deter Jim, but (we suspect) delights him. His view of Wittgenstein emphasizes for example the multiplicity of language games, the deconstruction of 'certainty', and the ways in which discursive systems play out within contexts of power—ideas similar to those that shaped the work of Lyotard, who also draws from Wittgenstein (Burbules, 2000). This reading of Wittgenstein as in tune with many of the concerns of writers often labeled as 'postmodern' can be seen as a more or less direct influence on the work of Michael Peters, Paul Smeyers, Nicholas Burbules, and others writing on Wittgenstein in the field of education today.

In the brief space available here we will discuss one general and one more specific way in which Wittgenstein's thinking has been insufficiently explored by philosophers of education. The broad dimension relates to Wittgenstein's insistence that human activity is rule-governed. The idea of rule-following is one of Wittgenstein's themes that can be traced across a number of important insights: in his interest in how young people learn and are initiated into social practices and 'forms of life'; in the analogy he draws between these human practices and 'games' with both overt and implicit rules; in conceptualizing the learning of such rules not through rote and repetition, but through the intriguing idea of 'learning how to go on'; in emphasizing that rules can be followed in more than one 'correct' way, so that judgments about the *meaning* of human actions frequently require a degree of interpretation about *what* rules are at work and *how* they are being followed; and finally in showing that the knowledge of how to follow a rule is frequently *tacit*, deeper than our ability—or the capacities of language—to articulate. These are truly radical ideas, full of import for education, and while some of these ideas have entered educational discourse indirectly (through the ideas of others borrowing from Wittgenstein), their full import for rethinking education has, in our view, yet to be appreciated. Jim Marshall's work continues to press these kinds of themes.

Against the tendency, vigorous in Wittgenstein's time and still pronounced in ours, to suppose that we need to learn more about 'children's minds'—as if new psychological facts or insights born of profound empathy were required—the notion of rule-governedness directs us to look at the ordinary world, in a sense already known and familiar, more carefully and in a new light (*Philosophical Investigations*, I. 144). When we are puzzled by young people's behaviour, especially, our problem may dissolve when we come to see what the behaviour *means*. To take a contemporary example, many parents of a teenage skateboarder are initially baffled by this activity, apparently anti-social and designed to achieve self-harm. Those who have the patience and the tact to attend properly to the sociocultural practices of skateboarding, however, will find that it is a highly developed sport, distinctively non-competitive, and woven in complex ways into the fabric of young people's social and emotional lives. There are facts to learn here, but the crucial move consists *in achieving a new way of looking at things* (*Philosophical Investigations*, I. 401): that is, in conceiving and framing the social phenomenon in a way that presumes its meaningfulness and coherence to its practitioners—at least 'from the inside'. This is a fundamental shift from many traditional social science approaches that are quick to attribute irrationality or deviance to non-conformative behaviors, seeking to describe and explain them through the application of concepts imposed from the outside, with the authority of the discipline—social psychology, for instance—involved. Jim Marshall wants us to understand such moves as exercises of *power*.

The way in which Peter Winch drew on Wittgenstein's work on rules in *The Idea of a Social Science* has been particularly helpful here, and his insights are still fruitful for researchers in the social sciences, including education. Following Wittgenstein, Winch would have us see that the kind of understanding we seek through social research does not always lead to generalisations, on the model of the types of explanations offered by the natural sciences (generalisations of the sort, 'All skateboarders are reacting against parents who have put pressure on them to succeed in conventional ways'). The world comes to us through language that always forms the limits of our world, and while empirical research clearly has its place the interesting move in the social domain is often to explore 'What it makes sense to say' (Winch, 1958, p. 72).

It is worth spelling out with some examples what this means for the domain of educational research. Consider, for instance, whether it makes sense to think of self-esteem as an unalloyed good (cp. Smith, 2002). We can choose to think of self-esteem as one of the chief ends of education, but the enterprise risks collapsing into incoherence at the point where educators attempt to engineer children's self-esteem without regard to achievements on their part that might justify it. Or consider whether the benefits of education can be sensibly expressed in terms of 'outcomes'. This seems to imply that what education attempts to achieve can be specified in advance, so that education cannot be thought of as significantly a shared and to some extent risky process of exploration. A particularly good example, and one which recurs constantly in both undergraduate and postgraduate dissertations, is the aspiration to discover whether this or that approach to reading 'improves children's reading skills'. Here the crucial question seems to be whether it really makes sense to think of reading as exhaustively or even essentially a set of *skills*— a question which is of course philosophical, and cannot be answered empirically.

For Wittgenstein, and for those following him here, it is not that exploration of these and similar questions merely tidies the conceptual ground on which useful empirical research can then take place (the so-called Lockean or under-labourer conception of philosophy). The point is rather that investigating what it does and does not make sense to say *itself* often supplies the insights that constitute progress, as in the examples above. This point is particularly important since it is so widely assumed that worthwhile research, in education as elsewhere, comes down to finding practical solutions to practical problems or, as a popular phrase has it, to discovering *what works*. This is of a piece with the supposition that educational research should be principally or perhaps even exclusively empirical. Teaching becomes seen as a technology which needs to be evidence-based, on the analogy of medicine. From this it follows that educational researchers should exercise themselves to establish a determinate body of knowledge: 'an agreed knowledge-base for teachers', 'evidence of what works in what circumstances' (Hargreaves, 1996, p. 2). And from here it is only a short step to the idea that there exist research methods that virtually any aspiring researcher can pick up with relative ease, regardless of the specific context and of his or her general intellectual prowess and powers of judgement. Such simplemindedness flies in the face of the Wittgensteinian notion of rule-governedness and its consequences for achieving a useful knowledge of human affairs; and in the context of state policy, the connection that Jim Marshall has always urged us to note with issues of *power* could not be more clear.

One very specific case where Wittgenstein helps us to understand education in a distinctive way concerns the advances in neuroscience which have led some to suppose that knowledge of the 'hard wiring' of the brain will eventually tell us what we want to know about human learning. For instance, it seems to be assumed in some quarters that a brain scan can tell us when a student has learned (or knows, or understands) something (for examples of this tendency, and a clear philosophical critique of the assumptions behind them, see Davis, 2004). What is odd about such notions can perhaps be glimpsed by considering whether an electrochemical re-configuration of the brain could constitute learning the meaning of, to take a relatively simple case, 'Stalin' (as if learning such *meanings* could be identified with something like having a mental image of the dictator). As noted before, meaning is a matter of rule-following, which is why Wittgenstein argued the impossibility of any language being private. Someone who talks of her boss as 'a proper Stalin' but simply means that he has a similarly bushy moustache does not know the *meaning* of the word she is using. And of course, meanings change: at one time 'Stalin' suggested the great ally of the west against fascism; more recently, it has come to be used to connote cruel and paranoid dictatorship. This only reinforces the point, and does not diminish it, that learning a language is essentially a matter of learning to share rules with other people in a particular community.

It is essential here to grasp that even understanding the meaning of 'Stalin' is no straightforward matter, as if we could first identify that and then discover what interventions, via chemicals or electrodes, brought it about. But it would be patently nonsensical to imagine that anyone could come to understand more complex areas of knowledge, such as calculus, or the causes of the Second World War, or *King Lear*, as a result of such intervention. Here, understanding even a piece of the subject would require understanding a great many other things. To understand such complex matters is to re-orient one's self to the world. If the meaning of the term 'Stalin' is to be discovered via an encyclopedia, rather than via a dictionary, then the meaning of *King Lear* or the Second World War would require an entire library and a great deal of personal experience of the world.

There is a revealing comparison to be made here with the way it is sometimes naively supposed that sociobiology will one day replace social science, telling us whether crime, or aggression, or sexual orientation is really 'all in the genes'. Again it is not that we have a firm, existing understanding of what crime is, so that—secure in that understanding—the important task for us now becomes to correlate it with certain brain-states (so that it might be more objectively studied, with an eye toward preventing or changing it, for example). Clearly what counts as crime changes over time and from place to place: the terrorist becomes the freedom-fighter, the criminalized homosexual becomes the gay neighbour whom we like and ask to baby-sit. Crime, or aggression, or sexual orientation, are not 'natural kinds'; they are not even just one thing, uncontroversially identifiable, like red hair or a tendency to stoop. In some countries smoking cannabis will get you expelled from school at the very least, while in other countries you can drop into a café and enjoy a joint with your friends as you discuss your homework.

What is at issue here becomes particularly evident when we shift perspective from our (natural) role as social scientists examining the behaviour of others and recall the times when others have sought to understand *us*. One of the writers of this paper has a colleague who reports giving a paper mildly critical of certain notions of citizenship education to an audience that, it transpired, consisted largely of teachers of citizenship education. Their response was to question her motives, in an atmosphere of hostility: was she an agent of subject-centred traditionalism, an elitist opposed to social inclusion, committed to undermining their interdisciplinary work with the marginalized and the oppressed? It was clear that they did not understand the rule-governed activity that consists of 'giving an academic paper', nor the context (the 'form of life') that gives it legitimacy and meaning. What the academic sees in one set of terms, essentially social ones—responding to an invitation, exploring a literature, criticising entrenched assumptions—the audience here saw as a question of personal motives, of what was 'in the head' of the giver of the paper. This is not to say, of course, that there might not be particular personal motives at play here, even ones perhaps that the academic did not understand herself. But before approaching this level of explanation we have to do justice to the kind of activity that, so to speak, lies before us on the surface. It is in this sense, Wittgenstein reminds us, that the mind is essentially public, not essentially private: 'nothing is hidden' (*Philosophical Investigations*, I. 126).

In examples such as these, we see the complex picture of social practices Wittgenstein put before us. For writers like Winch, the constraints of understanding a foreign 'form of life' lead in the direction of incommensurability, or at the very least deep uncertainty. For Lyotard (1993, p. 20), the incommensurability of 'islands of language' is a virtue to be valued and preserved. For John Austin, on the other hand, the rules of various language games could be analysed and laid out with precision. All of these writers, and others, take their insights from the *Philosophical Investigations* and other texts of Wittgenstein's later career. But for educators especially, these insights about how a form of life is constituted; about the role of learning the appropriate uses of language; about language games and rule-following as constitutive of the distinct character of a form of life; and about the complex and indeterminate task of initiating the young (and other novices) into that form of life, all together present a mosaic of questions—puzzles really—that challenge the simple-minded models of socialization often given to us by the social sciences. Further, they challenge us to rethink easy generalizations about the superiority of some forms of life over others, and to interrogate the course of prescriptions about what is 'normal' and what is 'deviant'. Such disciplining practices and rationalizations, Jim Marshall would have us bear in mind, are manifested particularly strongly in our notions about learning and the character of young people. It is no accident that his book title with Paul Smeyers highlights 'Wittgenstein's Challenge'—for Wittgenstein is a highly unconventional figure, and thinker, whose ideas pose a radical challenge to our educational categories and practices. Re-examining and questioning such assumptions, Jim Marshall reminds us, remains a challenge to be taken up seriously: one on which philosophers of education, it sometimes seems, have barely begun.

# References

Brent, A. (1978) *Philosophical Foundations for the Curriculum* (London, George Allen & Unwin)
Brown, S. C. (ed.) (1974) *Philosophers Discuss Education* (London, Macmillan).
Burbules, N. C. (2000) Lyotard on Wittgenstein: The differend, language games, and education, in: P. Standish and P. Dhillon (eds), *Lyotard: Just Education* (New York, Routledge) pp. 36–53.
Burbules, N. C. and Peters, M. (2001) Ludwig Wittgenstein, in: J. Palmer (ed.), *Fifty Modern Thinkers on Education* (London, Routledge) pp. 15–23.
Davis, A. (2004) The Credentials of Brain-based Learning, *Journal of Philosophy of Education*, 38:1, pp. 21–35.
Hargreaves, D. (1996) *Teaching as a Research-based Profession* (London, Teacher Training Agency).
Hirst, P. (1974) *Knowledge and the Curriculum* (London, Routledge & Kegan Paul).
Lyotard, J.-F. (1993) Wittgenstein 'After', in: W. Readings and K. P. Geiman (eds), *Jean-François Lyotard: Political writings* (Minneapolis, University of Minnesota Press).
Peters, M. and Marshall, J. D. (1999) *Wittgenstein: Philosophy, postmodernism, pedagogy* (Westport, Conn., Bergin & Garvey).
Smeyers, P. and Marshall, J. D. (eds) (1995) *Philosophy and Education: Accepting Wittgenstein's challenge* (Dordrecht, Kluwer Academic Publishers).
Smith, R. (2002) Self-esteem: The kindly apocalypse, *Journal of Philosophy of Education*, 36:1, pp. 87–100.
Smith, R. (1981) Hirst's Unruly Theory: Forms of knowledge, truth and meaning, *Educational Studies*, 7:1, pp. 17–25.
Winch, P. (1958) *The Idea of a Social Science* (London, Routledge).
Wittgenstein, L. (1968) *Philosophical Investigations* (G.E.M. Anscombe, trans.) (Oxford, Blackwell).

## 12

# Lightning and Frenzy: Music education, adolescence, and the anxiety of influence

Paul Standish
*University of Sheffield*

... to influence a person is to give him one's own soul. He does not think his natural thoughts, or burn with his natural passions. His virtues are not real to him. His sins, if there are such things as sins, are borrowed. He becomes an echo of someone else's music, an actor of a part that has not been written for him.

—Lord Wotton to Dorian, in Oscar Wilde's *The Picture of Dorian Gray*

His health and greatness consist in his being the channel through which heaven flows to earth ... Are there not moments in the history of heaven when the human race was not counted by individuals, but was only the Influenced, was God in distribution, God rushing into multiform benefit? It is sublime to receive, sublime to love, but this lust is imparting as from *us*, this desire to be loved, the wish to be recognized as individuals,—is finite, comes of a lower strain.

—Ralph Waldo Emerson, *Self-Reliance*

Let's call him Simon. He was about seventeen at the time, and this was the day of the oral exam for his English language qualification. There were about twelve other students in the somewhat drab classroom, looking on listlessly but with some apprehension for they would all—this was the requirement—eventually take their turn at speaking on a subject of their choosing for five minutes, with five minutes for questions. Simon was to talk about his electric guitar, which he had brought with him for the occasion. Nervous and awkward, he stood up and began to speak. The guitar was a shiny, if slightly battered Fender, which he had picked up second-hand and which he was plainly proud of. He had been playing for about six months. He began by explaining why he had been attracted to the guitar, how he had picked up his first chords, how he had learned to read some music (though really all you needed to know was the name of the appropriate chord for each bar of a song), and how much he practised. He faltered at times and became flustered, but as the closing stages came into view his confidence grew, and when he told us of the songs he was just starting to write himself, his words became self-consciously lyrical, even bombastic: 'I see my main influences', he said finally, 'as Jimi Hendrix and Eric Clapton'.

Simon's talk was not that good, and at the time there did not seem to be anything about it that marked it out from many of the others. But for some reason it stayed with me. It left me with a degree of discomfort mixed with a kind of perverse fascination—the squirming self-consciousness, the gaucherie and pretentiousness. What, I have continued to wonder, are we to make of Simon's musical education and of the struggling for identity that it seemed to involve? Simon was anxious to claim his influences, to appropriate these names, and to identify himself through them. But he spoke in the clichéd terms of the *New Musical Express* or of a radio DJ specialising in 'serious' pop music. What anxiety of influence was there?

In what follows I want to begin by picking up aspects of an argument advanced in a chapter from *Nietzsche's Legacy for Education*, edited by Michael Peters, James Marshall and Paul Smeyers, in which James Marshall addresses the topic 'Nietzsche's New Philosopher: The Arts and the Self'. Against this background I shall say something about the nature of influence in the arts and the kind of anxiety it induces, amplifying this in terms of broader questions of influence and self-reliance, before turning back to Simon and the particular ways in which such matters impinge on the challenge to educators concerned especially with music education and other aspects of arts education.

Marshall's account revolves around the theme of the relationship between the Apollonian, the epitome of form and order, and the Dionysian, force of energy and destruction alike, that is developed particularly in *The Birth of Tragedy*[1] but that is of profound importance throughout Nietzsche's work. The balance between these gods is taken to be critical for art, as it is for civilisation itself. For Nietzsche it is the denial of the Dionysian that is at the heart of the decline of Western civilisation, a conviction that became stronger as his writings developed and that was central to his searching for a new way of thinking and being—the 'new philosopher' who might overcome this debilitating condition in a transvaluation of all values, a *creation* of values. Indeed, as Marshall claims,

> if we are to go beyond good and evil, then the new philosopher must be more Dionysian than in the account of art in *The Birth of Tragedy*. It is no longer a question of some balance between the two but of going beyond, not of balancing old values ... but of creating new ones, not of legislating on old values but of legislating new ones. (Marshall, 2001, p. 122)

Of course, this relationship is of critical importance also to the way in which individuals are to understand themselves and live their lives, and it is this that gives Marshall the second term in his sub-title: he is concerned not only with education in the arts but with the development of the self. But the implications of this for education, in terms of both pedagogy and the curriculum, are far from easy to interpret, as Marshall's conclusion acknowledges. His final sentence, recalling the crowd's mistaking of Zarathustra for a circus performer, asks: 'How then are we to know that we are hearing a new philosopher rather than a busker?' The risk that we are urged to take up, through the images and ideas that Nietzsche presents to us, exposes us also to the possible encroachments of the impostor, and of self-deception, affectation and pretence.

Nietzsche's writings relate his theme to great art—to the plays of Aeschylus and Sophocles, the music of Wagner. There is, it would seem, a huge problem, an inevitable bathos involved, when any connection is sought with Simon's musical education, as briefly sketched at the beginning of this discussion, even though it seems reasonably clear that what is at stake for Simon is nothing other than the finding or creating of identity: he is burdened by some kind of searching for the self, and the nature of influence is crucial to this. This sense of bathos—from the heroic to the banal—is perhaps commonly felt by teachers of adolescents, especially those concerned with the arts. It is the nature of this problem and its wider implications for education that I shall try, in due course, to address.

For a while, however, let's stay with the heroic. It must have been around the time that I heard Simon speak that I had first read Harold Bloom's *The Anxiety of Influence* (Bloom, 1973). In what is itself an enormously influential book, Bloom's concern, as he makes clear, is with the work of great poets. In elaborating a theory of poetic influence he is not, as he makes equally clear, interested in the 'wearisome industry of source-hunting, of allusion-counting' (p. 31): he seeks to understand what it is that the best poets do and their relation to the influences by which they are affected. The central principle he arrives at, which is 'not more true for its outrageousness, but merely true enough', is that

> *Poetic Influence—when it involves two strong, authentic poets,—always proceeds by a misreading of the prior poet, an act of creative correction that is actually and necessarily a misinterpretation. The history of fruitful poetic influence, which is to say the main tradition of Western poetry since the Renaissance, is a history of anxiety and self-saving caricature, of distortion, of perverse, wilful revisionism without which modern poetry as such could not exist* (p. 30, italics in original).

Ben Jonson, the playwright, Bloom tells us, had spoken favourably of *imitation*, where influence is health, and of the diligent work required to achieve this: 'to be able to convert the substance or riches of another poet to his own use. To make choice of one excellent man above the rest, and so to follow him till he grow very he, or so like him as the copy may be mistaken for the original' (p. 27). But with the Enlightenment's passion for genius, originality, and authenticity, Jonson's faith in the artistic value of diligent work could not be fully sustained. Bloom contrasts this with the way that Edward Young laments the great precursors: 'They *engross* our attention, and so prevent a due inspection of ourselves; they *prejudice* our judgement in favor of their abilities, and so lessen the sense of our own; and they *intimidate* us with the splendor of their renown' (ibid.). Bloom relates the breaking away from imitation, and the revisionism it implies for the practice of criticism, to heresy. But whereas heresy tended to have its effects on received doctrine by an alteration of balances, the orientation of modern thought, as his principle indicates, is towards a kind of creative correction. On the strength of this, Bloom proposes a new approach to practical criticism that is based upon giving up the 'failed enterprise of trying to "understand" any single poem as an entity in itself' in favour of the 'quest of learning to read ... in terms of its poet's deliberate misinterpretation, *as a poet*, of a precursor poem or of poetry in general' (Bloom, 1972, p. 43). As Bloom later expresses the matter, 'Influence, as I conceive it, means that there are *no* texts, but only relationships *between* texts' (Bloom, 1975, p. 3). Although he identifies a number of forms that such deliberate misinterpretation can take, the guiding notion is that of the swerve (or *clinamen*)—what Coleridge had called the '*lene clinamen*, the gentle bias'.[2]

Bloom's demanding and puzzling, 'outrageous' principle applies to great poets, we have heard, yet matters do not perhaps stop there: as his own epigraph, from Wallace Stevens, intimates, 'the theory/Of poetry is the theory of life'. And, as if underlying the breadth of significance of what is at issue here, Bloom relates the 'perversity of the spirit' that is poetic influence to romantic love, citing Kierkegaard's provocative remark: 'When two people fall in love and begin to feel that they are made for one another, then it is time for them to break off, for by going on they have everything to lose and nothing to gain' (p. 31).

It is not insignificant for present purposes that a section of Marshall's article ponders the influence on Nietzsche of Schopenhauer, the article itself finding its path between the readings of Gilles Deleuze (Nietzsche has 'hardly any predecessors' (Marshall, 2001, p. 109)), Julian Young ('Nietzsche *breathed* Schopenhauer and cannot be understood without him' (ibid.)), and others. Nor is it immaterial that the account of the relationship between the Apollonian and the Dionysian comes to be understood less as a new balancing of these terms—akin, say, to a stabilising of influences—than as a new dynamic. Dionysian forces erupt in the artist. The will is movement. The new philosopher goes beyond good and evil.

Elsewhere Bloom has identified Emerson as one of the supreme writers on poetic influence. 'Insist on yourself: never imitate', Emerson writes in 1841 in his essay 'Self-Reliance'. The promise of the New World, which is Emerson's context and in part his theme, brings with it the expectation of a new literature, a new way of thinking and living, freed from the burden of influence that is its European past. And, as this quotation suggests, the significance of this will extend beyond the realms of the highbrow in art to the living of ordinary lives. The point is pressed further by Henry Thoreau, Emerson's disciple, who attempts to demonstrate in *Walden* that the heroic and the ordinary are to be seen in close proximity—to be, it might be said, allegories of one another.[3] What Emerson intends by this formulation is never easily expounded, for it is clear that he wishes to sustain conflicting impulses (from the individual and from influence). It is worth noting in passing that, if this were expressed in terms that were simply to be applied, the reader would be saved from precisely the effort of reading that a healthy engagement with influence demands.

Bloom is too tidy when he illustrates the relation between individual and influence in terms of Nietzsche's paired gods:

> We might follow Nietzsche, Emerson's admirer, and note that as Apollo apparently represents each new poet's individuation, so Dionysus ought to be emblematic of each poet's return to his subsuming precursors.

Some such realization informed Emerson's dilemma, for he believed that poetry came only from Dionysian influx, yet he preached an Apollonian Self-Reliance, while fearing the very individuation it would bring. (Bloom, 1975, p. 166)

This does indeed provide us with a way of considering the tensions in Emerson's position, regarding both his conception of poetic influence and originality, and its broader ethical implications, but it appropriates to the Apollonian the idea of self-reliance, and aligns influence with Dionysian influx, in a way that prejudges the issue. Regarding influence, a distinction needs to be drawn between the acceptance of influence as a kind of imitation, on the one hand, and a sensitivity or receptiveness to influx, on the other. For Emerson, the conformism that may be implied by the former is to be resisted, though this is in no way to suggest that there may be any easy avoidance of enculturation. Conversely, to resist influx, for Emerson and Nietzsche, would be a symptom of the *weakness* of the isolated, assertive ego, of an overly cerebral bourgeois individualism. What Emerson means by self-reliance *incorporates* a relation to influence. Indeed, as Bloom goes on to acknowledge, there is a sense in which it incorporates a yearning, not for a kind of abstracted independence and individuality but for the influence of an Over-Soul. (Bloom refers to this as the 'Central Man who is yet to come' (p. 166), and elsewhere Emerson speaks in terms of Genius.) Moreover, given Emerson's sustained emphasis on the practice of reading, his treatment of which defies classification as either literal or metaphorical, it becomes apparent that the relationship between the Over-Soul and the cultural inheritance is not one of denial but of reading in a new way. Influence then becomes influx. With regard to both Nietzsche and his precursor, Marshall's reckoning of the gods is apt: 'It is no longer a question of some balance between the two but of going beyond ...'.

Stanley Cavell has done much to illustrate the ways in which Nietzsche's early thought is itself in the sway of Emerson. In a recent article, 'Old and New in Emerson and Nietzsche', he takes up a theme that is of particular relevance to the 'going beyond' that is at issue here. He begins by drawing attention to the characterisation, in *Beyond Good and Evil*, of the (new) philosopher as 'a man of tomorrow and the day after tomorrow':

> What struck me ... was that the phrase 'tomorrow and the day after tomorrow,' translating the german *Morgen und Übermorgen*, puts in play the prefix *Über-*, so characteristic a site for Nietzschean inflection, marking a distinction homologous to that between *Mensch* and *Übermensch*. To what end? Take *Morgen* in its sense of morning, as well as of tomorrow, and we may discern in *Übermorgen* an idea of an after-, or over-, or super-morning. (Cavell, 2003, p. 224)

The thought that is entertained in the phrase, Cavell claims, is of a dawn or new light, a morning, even a rebirth, that is still to be claimed and still, that is, to be realised. This is a thought that recurs in Emerson and that, in the 'infinite expectation of the dawn', is an obsessive motif for Thoreau's *Walden*. Contemplating an ancient Chinese inscription, Thoreau remarks: ' "Renew thyself completely each day; do it again, and again, and forever again." I can understand that. Morning brings back the heroic ages ...'; he recognises this as carrying a suggestion that he has it in him to wake up to his condition: 'Morning is when I am awake and there is dawn in me ...'; and he acknowledges our constant failure fully to do this, and hence the obligation on us to continue to live with a kind of dissatisfaction with ourselves: 'I have never yet met a man who was quite awake. How could I have looked him in the face?' (Thoreau, 1986, pp. 133–134).

In Nietzsche, the phrase—*Morgen und Übermorgen*—occurs again in the Preface to *Human, All Too Human*, the eight paragraphs of which plainly bear Emerson's influence. Subtitled *A Book for Free Spirits*, this text appeals to such spirits, casting them, as it were, as imagined readers, and claiming at once that they do not exist but that

> There *could* someday be such free spirits, that our Europe will have such lively, daring fellows among its sons of tomorrow, real and palpable and not merely, as in my case, phantoms and a hermit's shadow play: I am the last person to want to doubt that. I already see them coming, slowly, slowly; and perhaps I am doing something to hasten their coming when I describe before the fact the fateful conditions that I *see* giving rise to them, the paths on which I *see* them coming? (Nietzsche, 1886, §2)

The thinking that is enjoined here, as Cavell shows, involves a kind of turning, an aversion from conformity, which is something other than the denial of influence. Amidst the multiple connections of these words with Emerson's, Cavell notes the imagery of light that is evident in this text, but he does not expand on this in this essay other than to register its convergence with the desire, in 'Self-Reliance', 'to detect and watch that gleam of light which flashes across his mind from within' (Cavell, 2003, p. 229).[4]

It is precisely this imagery, however, that is evident in Marshall's account. Marshall quotes Zarathustra: 'Where is the lightning to lick you with its tongue? Where is the frenzy with which you should be inoculated? Behold I teach you the Overman: he is this lightning, he is this frenzy' (Nietzsche, *Thus Spake Zarathustra*, Part I, §3); and later: 'I tell you: one must still have the chaos in one, to give birth to a dancing star. I tell you: ye still have chaos in you' (Part I, §5). In *Beyond Good and Evil*, Marshall shows us Nietzsche's new philosopher struck by 'lightning bolts' (§292).

In the Preface to *Human, All Too Human*, Nietzsche speaks of the way that, in order to 'ripen to sweet perfection', a 'free spirit' stands in need of a '*great separation*', emphasising a term that names what amounts to a signal theme in *Walden*. Nietzsche writes: 'An urge, a pressure, governs it, mastering the soul like a command: the will and wish awaken to go away, anywhere, at any cost: a violent, dangerous curiosity for an undiscovered world flames up and flickers in all the senses', bringing with it 'a lightning flash of contempt toward that which was its "obligation" ', and giving way to an 'excess that gives the free spirit the dangerous privilege of being permitted to live *experimentally*' and to 'the sudden illuminations of a still turbulent, still changeable state of health' (§§3, 4, 6). Nietzsche's Dionysian imagery of light and of darkness, of a chaos that can give birth to a dancing star, is aligned with processes of becoming that are depicted in terms of sickness and health, where sickness waits upon separation. What is presented here is not a linear trajectory of development but rather a continual demand, an embrace of sickness as a condition of health. So too, separation is to be understood not as a unique rupture in one's life but as something for which one must always be ready. This at least would be the essence of the Thoreauvian idea that Nietzsche appears to take up.

If this is so, the particular traumas that afflict adolescence, which Simon's talk illustrates in some degree, can be seen in terms of this struggle with 'sickness' and separation. But, are we really to imagine that we might find the gleam of light in the glitter of Simon's guitar? Once again, the sense of bathos disinclines us to go further with this thought. To reiterate the point, however, it is not the case that adolescence is here being idealised as the unique or supreme occasion of separation. It is rather that it is a time when the encounter with separation (say, from childhood, parents, certainties) is faced in a new, disturbing, and typically highly visible way. Without hasty assumptions to the effect that the profundity of the Nietzschean position is simply to be transposed to this classroom context, or that the heroic burden of poetic influence in Bloom has resonance here, let us nevertheless retrace some of the key elements that have emerged so far to see if they can help us to think more fruitfully about the experience of Simon. Simon is after all a real adolescent person, and the nature of his experience and of the influences on this is of consequence for anyone concerned with his education, especially his education in the arts.

Of course, Simon's talk of influence is clichéd, but might it not also reflect some intimation on his part that there is something important at stake here? Is it possible that in enlisting the vocabulary of influence he is voicing a sense that there must somewhere be powerful forces at work, even if he is not sure quite what these forces are, and even if he does not truly feel them yet himself? If this is so, the vocabulary of 'influence' would act as a way of leading him towards the possibilities of those deeper currents, just as, for the young child especially, the vocabulary of prayer may precede, and be a means to, the gaining of religious belief. We are, to be sure, close to pretentiousness here, just as the child who says the words of the prayer is close to superstition, and it may be that Simon will never really escape this. In part this will depend upon the quality of the works of art to which he is exposed and on how his attention is directed towards them (including the kinds of language and other practices in which all this takes place). The objection to pretentiousness is its falseness. One aspect of this—the one that is most pertinent to present, educational concerns—is that, if he is pretentious, Simon is forfeiting the possibility of a real engagement with things, that he is involved in self-deception, and that, in Rousseau's terms, he subsides into a kind of inflamed *amour-propre* in which, in being dependent upon the approval of others, he is subordinated to their will. (Of course, there can be forms of pretentiousness that do not involve self-deception but that are instead aimed at the deception of others, and it may be that in his desire to impress there is an element of this in Simon's case. But let us assume that this is not the substance of his problem and that it is not primarily in these terms that it impacts on him.) If, as we have seen, the risk that Nietzsche's thought urges us to take up exposes us also to the possible encroachments of self-deception, affectation and pretence, it may be that Simon's attraction to these ways of speaking, his closeness to pretentiousness, is a manifestation of a necessary struggle with sickness.

On the view developed here then, what Simon says may be evidence of his sense that there is something in the music of his heroes and in the vocabulary of influence that has more to do with influx—his faltering speech registering energies he imagines to be passing through this music and to be celebrated in these words. Or, to try a different way of addressing this, it may be that his gauche affirmation of his 'main influences' constitutes a kind of play-acting that lays the way for a mature receptiveness to such energies. There are limits here to the analogy with prayer. Just as the language of prayer is a kind of discipline experienced by the young child against a background of relative innocence, so too the discipline of music practice is perhaps experienced by the young musician as relatively meaningless: in both cases the practice may precede an understanding of its value and purpose. While the former can be the prelude to religious belief, it is indeed true that the latter, even where it is resentfully undertaken, may eventually be the spark of the gleam of light within (say, of an authentic love of music). But, in contrast to the context of the child's praying, Simon's venturing of these words occurs against a background of turbulence in which chaotic energies are already underway. In terms of Simon's aesthetic education, his words would constitute a playing with the idea of influence in contrast to a more diligent though submissive application to the work (to the discipline of regular practice). While no substitute for diligent work, and while they are unlikely to make him an accomplished musician, they might still reflect a gleam of light within.

We have said that a danger in Simon's pretentiousness leaves him bound to the opinions and responses of others. We can imagine young people who do not succumb to pretentiousness, even if they remain bound in more stubborn ways. Think, for example, of the diligent, submissive student whose music education is successful in technical terms but whose engagement is primarily imitative—say, the young violinist who successfully passes all her 'grade' examinations and plays well in the local youth orchestra. And in contrast, think of the person who enjoys listening to music in a relatively light-hearted and unreflective way, and who may enjoy strumming a guitar, but who would find talk of 'influences' embarrassingly highbrow. There may in both cases be a kind of conformism that shields the individual from the very uncertainty, the sickness, to which Simon is exposed. His struggle with pretentiousness is a manifestation of that sickness. Hence, although Simon's talk of influences is the very palest reflection of Bloom's reflections on poetic influence, it is not as if there is no connection here, nor that the kind of malady with which the great artist must grapple regarding influence is entirely divorced from whatever it is that attracts and confuses Simon, a confusion that positions him somewhere between a the possibility of a musical education and self-conscious reflection or narcissism. Our discomfort with these matters may incline us to be dismissive of Simon's responses. There will be false dawns, to be sure, but at least Simon's behaviour intimates some expectation of the dawn.

In fact, there are connections between these problems of influence and some of the most obstinate questions that education raises. To what extent should the schooling of young people be concerned with initiating them into worthwhile modes of thought and traditions of enquiry, with a kind of enculturation; and to what extent with the unfolding of the child from within, in a process of learning through experience? To what extent is the former to be rejected as purely imitative, and the latter to be condemned as involving a kind of deprivation for the young person of the very vocabularies and ways of thought that would enable them to develop creatively and authentically. While these questions and doubts are familiar enough in respect of education as a whole, they become particularly acute when the concern is with education in the arts, where the gaps between high art and popular art, between the virtuoso and the beginner, between imitative skill and creative originality, and between conformity and experimentation all raise critical questions for the curriculum and for learning.

One can imagine Simon in later years recoiling at his memories of himself on this occasion. Who does not recoil from what they did as an adolescent? Such recoil might lead to a search for better influences or come about as a result of finding them, and it might also engender a healthy caution regarding how one speaks about these things. But one can imagine also that this healthy caution might itself decline into a kind of playing-safe in what we say, with the result that in the end such thoughts are never entertained. One can imagine forms of intimidation that might hasten this. This would be a lapse into sanitised conformity, an immunisation against the sickness that we need.

For the teacher and the learner, the anxiety of influence is not simply to be dispelled; rather it needs to be channelled, relieving excessive concern over originality while avoiding falling into an imitative conformism. Lord Wotton's advice to Dorian, quoted in the epigraph to this discussion, may capture a widely held fear about the ways that influence can stifle natural passions, undermining creativity, spontaneity, and originality. But any examination of influence that is attuned to Nietzschean thought must retain a sense of influence as Dionysian influx—perhaps, in Marshall's words, 'of necessities welling up inside the artist', as of 'forces in the earth which erupt', of the light that is born of a darkness within (Marshall, 2001, p. 122). If this is undertaken, it becomes possible to understand influence less in terms of relations between individuals and more as the flow of energy—of thought and feeling, and of their realisation in the material products of our art and culture—for which the poet and his precursor, or the student and her teacher, are conduits. 'His health and greatness', Emerson writes, 'consist in his being the channel through which heaven flows to earth ...' The Overman is lightning, is frenzy. The teacher must aspire to be a conductor of that intensity, and the learner in her turn.[5]

## Notes

1. Nietzsche's subtitle for the book is 'Out of the Spirit of Music'.
2. Bloom explains that he had originally thought that this use of the term was his own (Bloom, 1975, p. 200).

3. In Thoreau's 'experiment in living' at Walden Pond, his battle with the weeds that attack his bean-field is described in terms of the Trojan War (Thoreau, 1986, p. 207).
4. For a detailed discussion of the gleam of light, which relates Emersonian moral perfectionism to education, see Naoko Saito, 2004.
5. For further discussion of teaching as the conducting of intensity, see the essays by Gordon Bearne and James Williams in Dhillon and Standish, 2000, and the chapter entitled 'Apollo and Dionysus' in Blake *et al.* (2000).

## Reference

Blake, N., Smeyers, P., Smith, R., & Standish, P. (2000) *Education in an Age of Nihilism* (London, Routledge Falmer).

Bloom, H. (1973) *The Anxiety of Influence: A Theory of Poetry* (Oxford, Oxford University Press).

Bloom, H. (1973) *A Map of Misreading* (Oxford, Oxford University Press).

Cavell, S. (2003) *Emerson's Transcendental Etudes* (Stanford, CA, Stanford University Press).

Dhillon, P., & Standish, P. (eds) (2000) *Lyotard: Just education* (London, Routledge).

Marshall, J. (2001) Nietzsche's New Philosopher: The Arts and the Self, in: M. Peters, J. Marshall, and P. Smeyers, P. (eds) (2001), *Nietzsche's Legacy for Education: Past and present values* (Westport CN and London, Bergin & Garvey).

Nietzsche, F. (1886) *Human, All Too Human*, trans. H. Zimmern. Online at: http://www.publicappeal.org/library/nietzsche/Nietzsche_human_all_too_human/ (accessed: 10/04/2004).

Nietzsche, F. [1883] (1969) *Thus Spoke Zarathustra: A book for everyone and no one.* Trans. with an introduction by R. J. Hollingdale (Baltimore, MD, Penguin Books).

Peters, M., Marshall, J., & Smeyers, P. (eds) (2001) *Nietzsche's Legacy for Education: Past and present values* (Westport CN and London, Bergin & Garvey).

Saito, N. (2004) *The Gleam of Light* (New York, Fordham University Press, forthcoming).

Thoreau, H. D. (1986) *Walden* and *Civil Disobedience* (Harmondsworth, Penguin).

## 13

# Break with Tradition: Marshall's contribution to a Foucauldian philosophy of education

LYNDA STONE
*University of North Carolina at Chapel Hill*

An 'essay in honor of' does not usually begin with a critique of the honoree and his work. This one does, as frame, as writing against tradition. The critique, by John Drummond, appears in the *Journal of Philosophy of Education* as a review essay of James Marshall's book, *Michel Foucault: Personal Autonomy and Education.*[1] Today, this text is singularly important as an explication of Foucault's writings for education. The book and others of Marshall's publications make a significant contribution to an emerging body of interdisciplinary Foucault studies that among spheres concerns education. The work further demonstrates a break with tradition and serves as a prime exemplar for a Foucauldian philosophy of education.

### Frame

Working from Marshall's preface, Drummond takes up his task and then offers a basis for critique:

> Marshall ... has set himself two major and ... specific tasks. First the book is to serve as an introductory text on Foucault and his relevance to education. ... Second, and combined with this, Marshall also seeks to offer a Foucauldian critique of ... the autonomous individual. At first blush, we may take the view that these two tasks do not sit easily together.[2]

Lamenting that the order of purposes is not 'straightforward', he continues,

> I found myself puzzled and often a little irritated at the way the book jumps around. ... [This is] a consequence of the fact that there does not seem to be any discernable logical flow between ... diverse chapters and, in particular, what I often found to be diverse sections within chapters.[3]

While Drummond does acknowledge that Marshall's text is 'full of good exegetical nuggets on Foucault' and that it is a useful introduction, his overall judgment is negative because the text is not 'logically coherent'.[4] In what follows an implicit case is made that Drummond's assessment is itself seriously flawed: this is because he does not recognize that Marshall offers a 'different' logical structure. Different logics result from different conceptions of philosophy and 'philosophies' of concepts. Marshall's logic is a break with tradition in philosophy of education and arises precisely from his understanding and treatment of Foucault.

## Inspiration

Marshall not only introduces Foucault for an education audience, he is inspired by him in his own philosophical approach. He asserts that 'an introduction, on its own, cannot show ... relevance to education. Unless ... [Foucault's] ideas are put to work, unless they are *used* as opposed to *mentioned* in some sphere or area of education, then they may be of little relevance'.[5] Use takes three forms in Foucault's *oeuvre*, archaeology, genealogy, and ethics or problematization. Building from an archaeological base, genealogy analyzes relations among discursive and non-discursive forces that indicate exercises, of strategies of power, manifest in diagram. Because Marshall works with Foucault's *Discipline and Punish*, itself a genealogy, his use is genealogical. Two aspects are pertinent. One is attention to 'structural breaks in presentation ... [that represent] the method of genealogy'.[6] The other, with roots in archaeology, is treatment of concepts particular to realms of study.

Across methodologies initially, there is a central relationship in Foucauldian thought of history and philosophy. In a now famous statement in *The History of Sexuality*, Volume 2, Foucault asserts that in utilizing historical references his studies are not the work of a 'historian'.[7] He explains, '[Each investigation is] ... the record of a long and tentative exercise that needed to be revised and corrected again and again. It was a philosophical exercise. The object was to learn to what extent the effort to think one's own history can free thought from what it silently thinks, and so enable it to think differently'.[8]

Traversing history and philosophy Foucault positions his work against a dominant tradition in the doing of social history in France, particularly the Annales School. He also writes against philosophy that is humanist, formalist, phenomenological, hermeneutical, and existentialist. He is neither greatly Marxist nor Freudian while acknowledging their general influences; he connects his work especially to that of Nietzsche and to Heidegger. Further, he is post-structuralist as one understands the presence of structuralist elements. He wants to write differently; he wants to offer ruptures; he wants to intervene and disrupt a dominant western view of rationality and intellectual processes of its representation. Foucault's various investigations into how reason 'functions' reveal that any one formulation 'is only *one* possible form among others'. Here is a paraphrased summing statement: 'In this abundance of branchings, ramifications, breaks, and ruptures ... [there was any one] important event or episode; it has considerable consequences, but it was not a *unique* phenomenon'.[9]

## Breaks

As a basis both for 'break', and for 'concept', Foucault credits particular influence on his thought that is not well-known outside of France. This is from a tradition in philosophy of science and mathematics, from Gaston Bachelard and especially Foucault's teacher who followed Bachelard as professor at the Sorbonne, Georges Canguilhem.

According to Foucault, in the middle decades of the twentieth century, French philosophy exhibits a 'cleavage' that has earlier roots. On one side is philosophy of experience, of meaning, of the subject, and on the other side philosophy of knowledge, of rationality, and of the concept. He places Sartre and Merleau-Ponty squarely in the first, and himself along with Jean Cavailles, Alexander Koyré, Bachelard and Canguilhem in the second. Earlier Bergson, Poincaré, and Comte are included in Foucault's lineage—and Michel Serres continues this tradition today.[10]

In the venue of this brief essay, a detailed explication of what commentator Gary Gutting terms Foucault's relationship to the Bachelard-Canguilhem network is not possible.[11] To begin, significant Bachelard writings remain untranslated into English—and, indeed, they are somewhat outdated, reflecting a previous age in philosophy of science. In general Gutting writes, 'Foucault was ... [not] a mere disciple of Bachelard and Canguilhem. ... [He] extends, adapts, and transforms their idea and methods'.[12] Indeed key ideas can be traced to Bachelard; these are the centrality of reason in knowledge and in philosophy and the appearance of breaks in their histories. For Bachelard, reason is manifest in specific scientific events, themselves in larger 'regions of rationality'. Each regional history is characterized by relations; successive regions exhibit novelty and change even as science is progressive. One reads particular forecasts of Foucault's project in Bachelard. Here are two examples. First, '[concepts] and methods alike depend on empirical results. A new experiment may lead to a fundamental change in scientific thinking ... [that] entails a change of logic'.[13] Second, '[there] are no simple phenomena; every phenomenon is a fabric of relations. There is no such thing as a simple *nature*, a simple substance; a substance is a web of attributes'.[14] With a resulting diversity and complexity in science, there is correspondingly no monolithic, universal rationality.

Bachelard's influence on Foucault's stance toward rationality is even more direct in the idea of epistemological breaks. Based in Gutting's excellent explanation, Bachelard poses two conceptions of breaks, related to obstacles, acts and profiles.[15] A first form of break is the splitting off and even contradiction of scientific knowledge from commonsense experiences and beliefs. A second describes the relationship of scientific conceptualizations or theories at variance with each other. Their differences may entail views of nature, operations of method, overall in Bachelard's idiom, 'a new scientific spirit'. A significant feature of the new spirit is change in concepts.

Foucault links himself to Bachelard and Canguilhem in several places, most notably in the introduction to *The Archaeology of Knowledge* and in an essay, 'Life: Experience and Science,' the English language introduction of the latter's book, *The Normal and the Pathological*. Early on, Canguilhem establishes his own link in a review of Foucault's *The Order of Things*. Following from Gutting above, in *Archaeology*, Foucault takes up Bachelard in this acknowledgement:

> Interruptions ... [in histories have] status and nature ... [that] vary considerably. There are the *epistemological acts* and *thresholds* described by Bachelard: they suspend the continuous accumulation of knowledge, interrupt its slow development, and force it to enter a new time, cut off from its empirical origin and its original motivations.[16]

Canguilhem's review of Foucault's *Order* focuses in part on a turning of Bachelardian breaks to *episteme*. Here is the schema: A cultural code orders human experience in a given era; it is linguistic, perceptual, and practical, theorized in a science or philosophy. Named by Foucault *episteme*, further it 'is what is required for us even to imagine the possibility' of a science or philosophy.[17] *Episteme* are recognized from inside and outside of themselves, by diving 'deep down from our own epistemic shores ... [to reach] a submerged *episteme*'.[18]

A summary is now in order. Via Bachelard and Canguihlem (Cavailles and others), Foucault's adapts a central historic, epistemological conception in his archaeological work that continues into his genealogies. *Episteme* break from each other, between what come to be constituted as different eras. Within an era, different traditions surely function as each can have a unique relationship to the *episteme*. Also found within *episteme* are changing concepts, related to historic events and located, for Foucault, in statements. This 'philosophy of the concept' is itself a break from previous philosophy.

## Concepts

Adding Marshall to the Bachelard-Canguilhem-Foucault network, as surely is his intention, posits a break with tradition in doing philosophy of education and necessitates a different logic.[19] That logic recognizes at the least distinct sub-traditions within a larger cultural/intellectual *episteme* and potentially a new era inspired by Foucault. In his text, a logic of juxtaposition operates between Foucault and analytical philosophy of education—with Foucault's work as premise. In the final chapter the two sub-traditions are related to a third that offers insight into their relationship: this is from Wittgenstein.[20] Throughout, his logic is generally one of structural breaks pinpointed in places by different concepts and concept treatments. Contra Drummond's critique, Marshall's text exhibits a logic appropriate to 'using' Foucault and to 'doing' Foucauldian philosophy of education.

While Marshall does not offer methodological detail, traditional treatment is analytical; a break with tradition is Foucauldian. For the first, he suggests the centrality of 'meaning' in the tradition that relies largely on the writings of Richard Peters, a founder of British Analytical Philosophy of Education. Peters writes in the seventies, 'In the past decade, the philosophy of education has been steadily establishing itself in Britain as a branch of philosophy'.[21] Its education source is C. D. Hardie's text *Truth and Fallacy in Educational Theory* from the forties; Hardie's roots are the Cambridge analytical school of G. E. Moore and C. D. Broad. Devolving in lineages from Peters and Paul Hirst in Britain, Israel Scheffler in the USA, James Gribble in Australia, and Ivan Snook in New Zealand among others, a family resemblance of treatment of concepts evolves. Resemblance concerns determination of meaning in/of practice based in the understanding of concepts. From British-trained Robin Barrow, the aim of attention to concepts is 'to clarify ... in order to assess them' in terms of 'how well formulated or articulated ... [they are]'.[22] For him unless there is conceptual coherence and specificity, there can be no understanding. Further, he distinguishes words from concepts, the latter as a kind of 'ideal'; others do not posit such an ideal form.

From above, in the Canguihem introduction Foucault discusses 'the concept' whose basis is the theme of 'discontinuity'. Specifically, he writes, 'Canguilhem stresses the fact that for him identifying discontinuities does not have to do with postulates or results; it is more a 'way of proceeding' ... integral with the history of the sciences'.[23] Discontinuity in concepts points to a 'fact of life'; this is that 'error is the root of what produces human thought and its history'.[24] In the thematic, error, contingent occurrence, disturbance, mistake comes to be disease, deficiency, 'or' monstrosity. More directly the scientific/philosophical project is 'to determine the situation of the *concept in life*' (emphasis in original).[25] Continuing, here is Foucault: [The] concept ... is one of the modes of ... information which every living being takes from its environment and by which conversely it structures its environment. ... Forming concepts is a way of living and not a way of killing life; it is a way to live in a relative mobility'.[26]

In *Archaeology*, Foucault transforms Canguilhem's concept from the domain of science to discourses in general. In this programmatic text, the analysis focuses on discursive formations, their elements and relations. With assistance again from Gutting, Foucault's attention is on levels of systems of thought (rather than who speaks or writes): book, *oeuvre*, period, tradition and their means of transmission.[27] These levels are 'recorded' in actual monuments of discourse, the latter a reconceptualization of historical 'events' or 'empirical' elements. Sets of statements circulate and traverse levels. First, most significantly, statements are not units of traditional grammar or logic: they are better understood perhaps as utterances. Within statement units are four components: objects, enunciative modalites, concepts, and themes. Objects, what statements are about, entail objectivity, the interplay of rules that make possible their appearance at a given time.[28] Enunciative modalities, the cognitive status of statements, entail rules of interaction, division and dependence among them. Concepts, the terms of their formulation, entail rules, in Foucault's words, 'not in the coherence of concepts, but in their simultaneous or successive emergence, in the distance that separates them and even in their incompatibility'.[29] Themes, theoretical viewpoints, entail rules prior to theory-choice, of possible dispersion of choices and of strategic possibilities.[30] Gutting writes that overall, '[the] same discursive formation will be a vehicle for discourse about different systems of objects, categories in terms of different conceptual frameworks, and its statements will have variety of enunciative modalities and may develop very diverse theoretical viewpoints'.[31] Most pertinent, in their relations with discursive formations, Foucault describes specific rules of concept formation as forms of succession and coexistence and procedures of intervention. The first two relate concepts to enunciative modalities and the last to statements.[32]

## Contribution

Utilizing a logic of structural breaks, James Marshall demonstrates a contrast between the treatment of concepts in analytical philosophy of education and a Foucauldian philosophy. All too simply, in the first there is emphasis on pinning down meaning through a primary logic of reference to objects as well as among linguistic entities. In the second the purpose is not to pin down but to demonstrate how concepts circulate and relate to each other within and across language structures; herein a basic openness is valued, a conception of difference rather than sameness.

In conclusion, Marshall breaks with tradition in philosophy of education to signal a new 'relation to the episteme' in the field. Using Foucault from his own recognition of the influences of Bachelard and Canguilhem, he puts to work a textual structure of discontinuity—of juxaposition. Further, he offers original concepts, 'busnocratic rationality' and 'busno-power' through a Foucaldian methodology.[33] Then at the close he turns to a logic of the third in comparing the concept of 'punishment' between the two sub-traditions and that of Wittgenstein. In this he substantiates what is arguably Foucault's most important point, that within a western history of reason' there are no unique phenomenom'. In demonstrating the fluidity of 'punishment,' as in the text overall, Marshall makes a singular contribution to the field of philosophy of education.[34]

## Notes

1. Drummond, J. (2000) Foucault for Students of Education, *Journal of Philosophy of Education*, 34:4, pp. 709–719; J. D. Marshall (1996) *Michel Foucault: Personal autonomy and education* (Dordrecht, Kluwer).
2. Drummond, Foucault for Students, p. 709.
3. Ibid., pp. 709–710.
4. Ibid., p. 718.
5. Marshall, J. (1996) *Michel Foucault: Personal autonomy and education* (Dordrecht, Kluwer). p. 1.
6. Ibid., p. 16.
7. Foucault, M. (1984/1990) *The Use of Pleasure, The history of sexuality, Volume 2* (New York, Vintage), see p. 9. In multiple language publications, the first date is French and the second is English.
8. Foucault, *Use of Pleasure*, p. 9.
9. Foucault, M. [1983] (1994/1998) Structuralism and Post-Structuralism, in: *Michel Foucault, Aesthetics, Method and Epistemology, Essential works of Foucault, 1954–1984, Volume 2* (G. Raulet, Interviewer; J. Harding, trans.; P. Rabinow, ed.) (New York, The New Press), pp. 441, 442.
10. See M. Foucault [1985] (1994/1989, 1998) Life: Experience and science, in: *Michel Foucault, Aesthetics, Method and Epistemology, Essential Works of Foucault, 1954–1984, Volume 2* (R. Hurley, trans.; P. Rabinow, ed.) (New York, The New Press), p. 466.
11. Foucault did meet and correspond with Bachelard; Canguilhem was his teacher and friend. See D. Eribon (1989/1991) *Michel Foucault* (B. Wing, trans.) (Cambridge, Mass, Harvard University Press). Foucault did meet and correspond with Bachelard; Canguilhem was his teacher and friend. See Didier Eribon's biography, *Michel Foucault* on these relationships and Foucault's debt to Canguihem in 'The Discourse on Language,' p. 235.
12. G. Gutting, *Michel Foucault's Archaeology of Scientific Reason* (Cambridge: Cambridge University Press, 1989), p. 54. Gutting, p. 54.
13. G. Bachelard (1934/1984) *The New Scientific Spirit* (A. Goldhammer, trans.) (Boston, Beacon Press), pp. 136, 137.
14. Bachelard, *New Scientific Spirit*, pp. 147–148.
15. Gutting, *Archaeology of Scientific Reason*, pp. 16–19.
16. M. Foucault (1969/1972) *The Archaeology of Knowledge* (A. Smith, Trans.) (New York: Pantheon), p. 4.

17. G. Canguilhem (1994) The Death of Man, of Exhaustion of the Cogito? in: G. Gutting, (ed.) *The Cambridge Companion to Foucault*, (C. Porter, trans.) (Cambridge, Cambridge University Press), p. 77. This review appears to date from the early seventies and is a first recent translation.

18. Canguilhem, The Death of Man, see pp. 81, 78.

19. See Marshall on roots in Bachelard, Canguilhem and philosophy of the concept, Ibid., pp. 5, 6, 7, 15.

20. Ibid., pp. 195–196.

21. R. S. Peters, (ed.) (1973) Introduction, *Philosophy of Education* (Oxford, Oxford University Press), p. 1.

22. R. Barrow (1988) Preface to the Second Edition, in: R. Barrow & R. Woods, *An Introduction to Philosophy of Education* (3rd edn.) (London, Routledge), p. x.

23. Foucault, *Life: Experience and Science*, p. 471.

24. P. 476.

25. P. 475.

26. Ibid.

27. Gutting, *Archaeology of Scientific Reason*, beginning, p. 231.

28. Foucault, *Archaeology of Knowledge*, see beginning, pp. 32–33 to p. 37.

29. Ibid., p. 35.

30. Ibid., p. 37.

31. Gutting, p. 232.

32. Foucault, *Archaeology*, pp. 56–59.

33. Marshall, ibid., pp. 187–193.

34. Thanks to Aaron Cooley for references and discussion and to Michael Peters and Paul Smeyers for the invitation.

# 14
# Curriculum Vitae

(Dated January 2005)

| | |
|---|---|
| **Name** | James Derek Marshall, B.A. Sp.Hons. in Philosophy, Ph.D.(Brist.) |
| **Nationality** | Dual Citizenship: New Zealand and United Kingdom |
| **Date and Place of Birth:** | 20.1.1937 at Timaru, New Zealand |
| **Marital Status** | Formerly married to Bridget Lois Marshall (now deceased) |
| | Now married to Lynda Stone (date: 16.08.2004) |
| | Three children; Peppy 40, (James) Dominique 35 and Marcus 33 years |
| **Address for Correspondence** | School of Education, |
| | The University of Auckland, |
| | Private Bag 92019, |
| | Auckland, New Zealand |

Telephone:  Work: (64) (9) 3737.599 x5304
            Home: (64) (9) 478 8626
Fax:        Work: (64)(9) 373 7455
            Home: (64)(9) 478 8179
E-mail:     <j.marshall@auckland.ac.nz>

| | |
|---|---|
| **Present Position** | Professor of Education (part time, 0.4) |
| | The University of Auckland |

## Education:

| | |
|---|---|
| 1949 | : McKenzie Villers Scholarship (open Scholarship, Canterbury Province) |
| 1950–54 | : Waitaki Boys High School, Oamaru |
| 1955–57 | : Britannia Royal Naval College, Dartmouth |
| 1959–61 | : Auckland University (Massey University) Part time |
| 1964–67 | : Bristol University, Undergraduate. Special Honours in Philosophy |
| 1967–72 | : Bristol University, PhD student, part-time; 1970–71 was fulltime |

## Qualifications:

| | |
|---|---|
| 1967 | : B.A., Special Honours in Philosophy, Bristol University |

1973            : Ph.D. in Philosophy, 'The Problem of Identity', Bristol University. Supervisor, Prof. Stephan Körner

## Occupations:

1955–63         : Naval Officer (including command of H.M. Vessel for ten months, and $2^{nd}$ navigating officer of an aircraft carrier)
1963–4          : Industry (Kelvin Hughes, London—Manufacturers of marine navigation instruments)
1964–67         : Part-time secondary teaching (Bristol (North Somerset) area)
1967–72         : Teaching, Teacher Education and for Bristol University, B.Ed., Degree
1971–72         : Part time Tutoring in Philosophy for Open University
1973–2003  : Full time University Teaching

## Teaching Positions:

1964–67         : Part time secondary teaching in Bristol area (Maths and Science)
1967–68         : Lecturer in Education, St. Mary's College, The Park, Cheltenham, U.K. (teacher education)
1969–73         : Senior Lecturer in Education, St. Mary's College
1967–73         : Recognised Teacher for B.Ed., University of Bristol
1970–71         : Post Graduate Tutor, Department of Philosophy, University of Bristol (study leave from St. Mary's College)
1971 & 72   : Tutor in Philosophy (part time), Open University
1973–74         : Lecturer in Education, The University of Auckland
1975–85         : Senior Lecturer in Education, The University of Auckland
1981            : Visiting Scholar, Stanford University
1982            : Visiting Scholar, Boston University
1986–89         : Associate Professor of Education, The University of Auckland
1986            : Visiting Colleague, University of Hawaii
1987            : Visiting Lecturer, King's College, London
1987–89         : Acting H.O.D., Department of Education, The University of Auckland
1989–91         : Professor of Education, H.O.D. Department of Education, The University of Auckland
1991            : Visiting Professor, Simon Fraser University
1991            : Visiting Professor, Katholieke Universiteit Leuven
1992–96         : Dean, Faculty of Education, The University of Auckland. (Foundation Dean of a new Faculty)
1994            : Visiting Fellow, Edith Cowan University
1995            : Visiting Scholar, University of Wisconsin-Madison
1997–98         : Visiting Research Fellow, Katholieke Universiteit Leuven, België.
1997–           : Professor of Education, The University of Auckland.
2001            : Visiting Professor University of Glasgow
2003            : Professor of Education, The University of Auckland (0.4 part time)

**On-Line Publications**
**Published**

2000 MARSHALL, J. D., 'Foucault on Governmentality', in (eds) GHIRAL-DELLI, P., PETERS, M. A., Encyclopaedia of Philosophy of Education at http://www.educacao.pro.br/.

2000 MARSHALL, J. D., Entretesta cum James Marshall

2001 MARSHALL, J. D., Bachelard Y La Filosophía de la Educación', Transl. Stella Accorinti in (eds) GHIRALDELLI, P., PETERS, M. A., Encyclopaedia of Philosophy of Education at http://www.educacao.pro.br/.

2000 MARSHALL, J. D., in (eds) GHIRALDELLI, P., PETERS, M. A., 'The Legal Model of Punishment', Encyclopaedia of Philosophy of Education at http://www.educacao.pro.br/.

2000 MARSHALL, J. D., in (eds) GHIRALDELLI, P., PETERS, M. A., 'The Justifications of Punishment', Encyclopaedia of Philosophy of Education at http://www.educacao.pro.br/.

2000 MARSHALL, J. D., in (eds) GHIRALDELLI, P., PETERS, M. A., 'Michel Foucault: Disciplinary Punishment', Encyclopaedia of Philosophy of Education at http://www.educacao.pro.br/.

2000 MARSHALL, J. D., in (eds) GHIRALDELLI, P., PETERS, M. A., 'The Punishment of Children', Encyclopaedia of Philosophy of Education at http://www.educacao.pro.br/.

2000 MARSHALL, J. D., 'Albert Camus (1912–1960)—Philosopher of the Absurd', in (eds) GHIRALDELLI, P., PETERS, M. A., Encyclopaedia of Philosophy of Education at http://www.educacao.pro.br/.

2000 MARSHALL, J. D., 'Simone de Beauvoir (1908–86)—Philosopher of the Self', in (eds) GHIRALDELLI, P., PETERS, M. A., Encyclopaedia of Philosophy of Education at http://www.educacao.pro.br/.

2000 MARSHALL, J. D., 'Thomas Hobbes (1588–1679): education and govern-mentality', in (eds) GHIRALDELLI, P., PETERS, M. A., Encyclopaedia of Philosophy of Education at http://www.educacao.pro.br/.

2000 MARSHALL, J. D., 'Bye Bye Cultures', International Editorial, Virtual Magazine, at HYPERLINK http://filosophia.pro.br/http://filosofia.pro.br/.

1999 MARSHALL, J. D., 'Gaston Bachelard' in (eds) GHIRALDELLI, P., PETERS, M. A., Encyclopedia of Philosophy of Education at http://www.educacao.pro.br/.

1999 MARSHALL, J. D., 'Georges Canguilhem. (1904–1995)' in (eds) GHIRAL-DELLI, P., PETERS, M. A., Encyclopedia of Philosophy of Education at http://www.educacao.pro.br/.

1999 MARSHALL, J. D., 'Foucault and Science' in (eds) GHIRALDELLI, P., PETERS, M. A., Encyclopedia of Philosophy of Education at http://www.educacao.pro.br/.

**Books**
**Forthcoming**

2005 MARSHALL, J. D., *Michel Foucault: a filosofia neostructuralism*, Sao Paulo: D.P.A.

**Published**

2004 MARSHALL, J. D., (ed.) *Poststructuralism, Philosophy, Pedagogy*. Dordrecht: Kluwer Academic Press.

2001 PETERS, M. A., MARSHALL, J. D., SMEYERS, P. J. (eds), *Nietzsche's Legacy for Education: Past and Present Values*, Westport, Conn.: Bergin and Garvey.

2000 MARSHALL, J. D., COXON, E., JENKINS, K., JONES, A. (eds), *Politics, Policy, Pedagogy: Education in Aotearoa/New Zealand*. Palmerston North: Dunmore Press, 219pp.

2000 MARSHALL, J. D. (Special Guest Editor), 'Indigenous Peoples and Philosophy of Education', *Educational Philosophy and Theory*, 32(1), 150pp.

2000 MARSHALL, J. D., PETERS, M. A., Special Guest Editors, 'Education, Neoliberalism and the Knowledge Economy', *Access: critical perspectives on cultural and policy studies in education*, 19(2).

1999 MARSHALL, J. D., PETERS, M. A. (eds), *Education Policy*, Cheltenham, Glos.: Edward Elgar, 872pp.

1999 PETERS, M. A., MARSHALL, J. D., *Wittgenstein: philosophy, postmodernism and pedagogy*. New York: Bergin and Garvey, 237pp.

1998 MARSHALL, J. D., SINGH, A., (Special Guest Editors), 'Information Technology and Education', *Access: critical perspectives on cultural and policy studies in education*, 17(1), 1–91 & i–x.

1997 MARSHALL, J. D., MARSHALL, D. J., *Discipline and Punishment in New Zealand Education*, Palmerston North: Dunmore Press, pp. 187.

1997 MARSHALL, J. D., PETERS, M. A., FITZSIMONS, P. (Special Guest Editors), 'Education and the Constitution of Self', *Educational Philosophy and Theory*, 29(2), 1–108 & i–xi.

1996 MARSHALL, J. D., *Michel Foucault: personal autonomy and education*, Dordrecht: Kluwer, pp. 245.

1996 PETERS, M. A., MARSHALL, J. D., *Individualism and Community: education and social policy in the postmodern condition*, London: Falmer Press, pp. 237.

1996 PETERS, M. A., MARSHALL, J. D., HOPE, W., WEBSTER. S. (eds), *Critical Theory, Post Structuralism, and the Social Context*, Palmerston North: Dunmore Press, pp. 276.

1995 SMEYERS, P. J., MARSHALL, J. D. (eds), *Wittgenstein and Education: accepting the challenge*, Dordrecht: Kluwer, 244pp.

1995 MARSHALL, J. D. (ed.), *The Economics of Education*, The Second Faculty of Education Lectures, Auckland: The Faculty of Education, University of Auckland, 125pp.

1995 JONES, A., MARSHALL, J. D., MATTHEWS, K. M., SMITH, G. H., SMITH, L. T., *Myths and Realities; schooling in New Zealand*, 2nd edition revised, Palmerston North: Dunmore Press, 237pp.

1995 SMEYERS, P., MARSHALL, J. D. (Special Guest Editors), 'Philosophy and Education: accepting Wittgenstein's challenge', *Studies in Philosophy and Education*, 14(2&3).

1994 MARSHALL, J. D. (ed.), *Revisiting the 'Reforms' in Education*. The Faculty of Education Annual Lectures, Auckland: The Faculty of Education, The University of Auckland, 99pp.

1994 COXON, E., JENKINS, K., MARSHALL, J. D., MASSEY, L. (eds), *The Politics of Learning and Teaching in Aotearoa*, New Zealand, Palmerston North: Dunmore Press (Co-ordinating and Principal Editor), 280pp.

1993 LANDER, J., BURNETT, K., MARSHALL, J. D., *The Retention of Maori in Schooling: a partially annotated bibliography*, Monograph No. 17, Auckland: Research Unit in Maori Education, The University of Auckland, 35pp.

1991 MARSHALL, J. D., *The Treaty of Waitangi, Educational Reforms and the Education of Maori*, Monograph No. 1, Auckland: Research Unit in Maori Education, The University of Auckland, 27pp.

1990 JONES, A., MCCULLOCH, G. J., MARSHALL, J. D., SMITH, G. H., SMITH, L. T., *Myths and Realities: Schooling in New Zealand*, Palmerston North: Dunmore Press, 179pp. (Co-ordinator and major contributor). Reprinted 1992, 1993, 1994.

1990 POLICY STUDIES GROUP, Department of Education, *What Makes a Good School?* Wellington: Government Printer, 48pp. (Contributor).

1988 MARSHALL, J. D., *Why Go To School?*, Palmerston North: Dunmore Press, 104pp.

1987 MARSHALL, J. D., *Pragmatism or Positivism: philosophy of education in New Zealand*, Monograph No. 2, New Zealand Association for Research in Education, 84pp.

1983 MARSHALL, J. D. (2nd Edition, revised) *What is Education? An introduction to philosophy of education*, Palmerston North: Dunmore Press, 169pp.

1981 MARSHALL, J. D., *What is Education: an introduction to philosophy of education*, Palmerston North: Dunmore Press, 155pp.

## Chapters in Books

2004 MARSHALL, J. D., 'Michel Foucault: Marxism, Liberation and Freedom', in (eds) BAKER, B. M., HEYNING, K. E., *Dangerous Coagulations? The Uses of Foucault in the study of education*, New York: Peter Lang, 265–278.

2003 MARSHALL, J. D., 'Introduction' in (ed.) MARSHALL, J. D., *Poststructuralism, Philosophy, Pedagogy*, Dordrecht: Kluwer.

2003 MARSHALL, J. D., 'French Philosophy Post WWII-1968', in (ed.) MARSHALL, J. D., *Poststructuralism, Philosophy, Pedagogy*, Dordrecht: Kluwer.

## Published

2004 PETERS, M. A., MARSHALL, J. D., 'The Politics of Curriculum: autonomous choosers and enterprise culture, in (eds) O'NEILL, A-M., CLARKE, J., OPENSHAW, R., *Reshaping Culture, Knowledge and Learning: policy and content in the New Zealand Curriculum framework*, Palmerston North: Dunmore, 109–125.

2002 MARSHALL, J. D., 'Foreword' in BESLEY, T., *Counselling Youth: Foucault, power and the ethics of subjectivity*. Westport, Conn: Bergin & Garvey, ii–iii.

2001 MARSHALL, J. D., 'Entrevesta cum James Marshall' in (ed.) Paulo Ghiraldelli, *Filosofia Edução e Politica Entrevisas*. Sao Paulo: DPA.

2001 MARSHALL, J. D., 'The Absurdity of Hope: Rorty on Dewey, Foucault and Optimism', in (eds) GHIRALDELLI, P., PETERS, M. A., *Education, Philosophy and Culture: revisiting Richard Rorty*, Boulder, Col.: Rowman and Littlefield.

2001 MARSHALL, J. D., 'Caring for the Adult Self' in ASPIN, D., CHAPMAN, J., HATTON, M., SAWANO, Y., *International Handbook on Lifelong Learning*. Dordrecht: Kluwer, 119–134.

2001 MARSHALL, J. D., 'Nietzsche's New Philosopher: The Arts and the Self' in (eds) PETERS, M. A., MARSHALL, J. D., SMEYERS, P. J., *Nietzsche's Legacy for Education: Past and Present Values*, Westport, Conn.: Bergin and Garvey, 107–123.

2001 PETERS, M. A., MARSHALL, J. D., SMEYERS, P. J., 'Traces of Nietzsche: Interpretation, Translation and the Canon', in (eds) PETERS, M. A., MARSHALL, J. D., SMEYERS, P. J., *Nietzsche's Legacy for Education: Past and Present Values*, Westport, Conn.: Bergin and Garvey, xv–xxx.

2000 MARSHALL, J. D., 'Bright Futures Technology: curriculum, Maori and the Environment', in (eds) MARSHALL, J. D., PETERS, M. A., *Access*, 19(2), 102–131.

2000 MARSHALL, J. D., 'Electronic Writing and the Wrapping of Language', in (eds) BLAKE, N., STANDISH, P., *Enquiries at the Interface: philosophical problems of online education*, Oxford; Blackwell, 135–149.

2000 MARSHALL, J. D., 'The Language of Indigenous Others: the case of Maori in New Zealand' in (ed.) CURRAN, R. A., *Philosophy of Education 1999*. Urbana-Champaign, Il.: Philosophy of Education Society.

2000 MARSHALL, J. D., 'Preface', in (eds) MARSHALL, J. D., COXON, E., JENKINS, K., JONES, A. (eds) *Politics, Policy, Pedagogy: education in Aotearoa/New Zealand*. Palmerston North: Dunmore Press, 7.

2000 MARSHALL, J. D., 'Bright Futures and the Knowledge Society', in (eds) MARSHALL, J. D., COXON, E., JONES, A., *The Politics of Educational Policy in Aotearoa/New Zealand*. Palmerston North: Dunmore Press, 187–215.

2000 MARSHALL, J. D., 'Michel Foucault: the pedagogy of caring for a self', in *Philosophy of Education Society of Great Britain*, Papers of the 34th. Annual Conference, New College Oxford, 14–16 April.

2000 MARSHALL, J. D., 'Educational Philosophy, Language and Culture in the 21st. Century', *Philosophy of Education in the New Milennium*, Vol. 2, Conference Proceedings of the 7th. Biennial Conference of the International Network of Philosophers of Education, University of Sydney, 18–21 August, 48–53.

2000 MARSHALL, J. D., PETERS, M. A., 'Foreword', *Access*, 19(2), ii.

2000 PETERS, M. A. MARSHALL, J. D., SMEYERS, P. J., IRWIN, R., FITZSIMONS, P., 'Nietzsche's Legacy for Education', *Philosophy of Education in the New Milennium*, Vol. 3, Conference Proceedings of the 7th. Biennial Conference of the International Network of Philosophers of Education, University of Sydney, 18–21 August, 38–39.

2000 PETERS, M. A., MARSHALL, J. D., FITZSIMONS, P., 'Managerialism and Educational Policy in a Global Context: Neoliberalism, Foucault and the Doctrine of Self-Management' in (eds) BURBULES, N., TORRES, C., *Globalisation and Educational Policy*, New York: Routledge, 109–132.

2000 MARSHALL, J. D., COXON, E., JENKINS, K., JONES, A., 'Politics, policy, Pedagogy; An Introduction', in (eds) MARSHALL, J. D., COXON, E., JENKINS, K., JONES, A., *The Politics of Educational Policy in Aotearoa/New Zealand*. Palmerston North: Dunmore Press, 9–23.

1999 MARSHALL, J. D., 'The Mode of Information and Education: insights on critical theory from Michel Foucault', in (ed.) POPKEWITZ, T., FENDLER, L. (1999), *Critical Theories in Education: changing terrains of knowledge and politics*. New York: Routledge, 141–163.

1999 MARSHALL, J. D., 'Technology in the New Zealand Curriculum', in (ed.) THRUPP, M., *A Decade of Reform in New Zealand Education: where to now?* Hamilton: University of Waikato and New Zealand Journal of Educational Studies, 34(2), 167–175.

1999 MARSHALL, J. D., 'Foucault's Critique of Neo-liberalism' in WOOCK, R., CLYNNE, F. (eds) *Proceedings of the Annual Conference of the Australian and New Zealand Comparative and International Education Society*, Melbourne, December, 131–141.

1999 MARSHALL, J. D., PETERS, M. A., 'Educational Policy at the End of the Milennium' in (eds) MARSHALL, J. D., PETERS, M. A. (1999) *Education Policy*, Cheltenham, Glos.: Edward Elgar, xxv–xxxv.

1999 PETERS, M. A., MARSHALL, J. D., 'Educational Policy Analysis and the Politics of Interpretation', in (eds) MARSHALL, J. D., PETERS, M. A. (1999), *Education Policy*, Cheltenham, Glos.: Edward Elgar, 67–84.

1999 MARSHALL, J. D., 'Poststructuralist Philosophy and Education', in (ed.) HIGGS, P. (1999), *Metatheories in Educational Theory and Practice*, Johannesburg: Heinemann, 251–268.

1999 SMEYERS, P. J., MARSHALL, J. D., 'A Filosofia de Educação', in (ed.) GHIRALDELLI, P., *O Que É Filosofia da Educação*, Rio de Janeiro, DP&A Editora, 89–121.

1999 PETERS, M. A., FITZSIMONS, P., MARSHALL, J. D., 'Managemerialism and Education Policy in a Global Context: Neoliberalism, Foucault and the Doctrine of Self Management', in TORRES, C., BURBULES, N., *Education and Globalisation: critical concepts*, New York: Peter Lang.

1999 PETERS, M. A., MARSHALL, J. D., FITZSIMONS, P., 'Postmodernism and the New Theology of the Curriculum', in (eds) LANKSHEAR, C., PETERS, M. A., ALBA, A., GONZALES, E., *Curriculum in the Postmodern Condition*, New York: Peter Lang.

1998 MARSHALL, J. D., 'Michel Foucault', in (ed.) PETERS, M. A. (1998), *Naming the Multiple: poststructuralism and education*, New York: Bergin Garvey, 65–83.

1998 MARSHALL, J. D., 'Technology in the New Zealand Curriculum', *Looking at the Past, Looking to the Future: educational change and comparative perspectives*. Proceedings of the 26th. Annual Conference of the Australia and New Zealand Comparative and International Education Society, Auckland, December, 120–126.

1997 MARSHALL, J. D., 'Dewey and the "New Vocationalism"', in (ed.) LAIRD, S., *Philosophy of Education 1997*. Urbana, Il.: Philosophy of Education Society, 163–171.

1997 MARSHALL, J. D., 'Post analytic and post-empiricist philosophy of education: insights from Foucault and Wittgenstein', in (ed.) ASPIN, D. (1997), *Logical Empiricism and Post Empiricism in Educational Discourse*, Johannesburg: Heinemann.

1997 MARSHALL, J. D., 'Michel Foucault: personal autonomy as an aim of education', in (ed.) O'FARRELL, C., *Foucault: the legacy. Brisbane*: Queensland University of Technology, 592–602.

1997 MARSHALL, J. D., 'The New Vocationalism', in (eds) MATTHEWS, K. M., OLSSEN, M., *Educational Policy in New Zealand in the 1990s: and beyond*. Palmerson North: Dunmore Press, 304–326.

1997 MARSHALL, J. D., 'Friendship and the Other: Simone de Beauvoir on silence'. *Papers of the 31st Annual Conference. Philosophy of Education Society of Great Britain*, 156–165.

1997 MARSHALL, J. D., PETERS, M. A., 'Postmodernism and Education', *International Encyclopedia of Sociology of Education*. Oxford: Pergammon Press.

1996 MARSHALL, J. D., 'Liberal Education and Governmentality' in (eds) PETERS, M. A., MARSHALL, J. D., HOPE, W., Webster, S., *Critical Theory, Post-Strucuralism and the Social Context*, Palmerston North: Dunmore Press, 106–126.

1996 MARSHALL, J. D., 'Education in The Mode of Information: some philosophical issues', in (ed.) Margonis, F. (1996) *Philosophy of Education 1996*, Illinois: Philosophy of Education Society, 268–276.

1996 MARSHALL, J. D., 'Information on "Information": recent curriculum reform', *Conflict and Consensus: educational, moral and political dimensions*. Proceedings of the 5th. Biennial Conferences of the International Network of Philosophers of Education, Rand Africans University, August, 197–205.

1996 PETERS, M. A., MARSHALL, J. D., 'Education and Empowerment: postmodernism and the critique of humanism' in (ed.) MCCLAREN, P., *Postmodernism, Postcolonialism and Pedagogy*, Albert Park, Vic.: James Nicholas, 205–225.

1995 MARSHALL, J. D., 'Skills, Information and Quality for the Autonomous Chooser' in (eds) OLSSEN, M., MATTHEWS, K. M., *Education, Democracy and Reforms*, Auckland: NZARE Monograph, 45–60.

1995 MARSHALL, J. D., 'On What We May Hope: Rorty on Dewey and Foucault' in (ed.) GARRISON, J., *The New Scholarship on Dewey*, Dordrecht: Kluwer, 139–155.

1995 MARSHALL, J. D., 'Wittgenstein and Foucault: resolving philosophical puzzles', in (eds) SMEYERS, P. J., MARSHALL, J. D., *Wittgenstein and Education: accepting the challenge*, Dordrecht: Kluwer, 205–220.

1995 MARSHALL, J. D., 'Pedagogy and Apedagogy: Lyotard and Foucault at Vincennes', in (ed.) PETERS, M. A., *Education and the Postmodern Condition*, New York: Bergin and Garvey, 167–192.

1995 MARSHALL, J. D., 'Foucault and Neo-Liberalism: biopower and busnopower', in (ed.) NEIMAN, A., *Philosophy of Education 1995*, Proceedings of The Philosophy of Education Society, Illinois: Philosophy of Education Society, 320–329.

1995 MARSHALL, J. D., 'Needs, Interests, Growth and Personal Autonomy: Foucault on power', in (ed.) KOHLI, W., *Critical Conversations in Philosophy of Education: from theory to practice and back*, New York: Routledge, Chapman Hall, 364–378.

1995 MARSHALL, J. D., 'Preface' and 'Introduction' in (ed.) MARSHALL, J. D. (1995), *The Economics of Education*, Auckland, The Faculty of Education, the University of Auckland, i and 1–4.

1995 SMEYERS, P. J., MARSHALL, J. D., 'The Wittgensteinian Frame of Reference and Philosophy of Education at the End of the Twentieth Century' in (eds) SMEYERS, P. J., MARSHALL, J. D., *Philosophy and Education: accepting Wittgenstein's challenge*, Dordrecht: Kluwer, 3–35.

1995 SMEYERS, P. J., MARSHALL, J. D., 'Epilogue' in SMEYERS, P. J., MARSHALL, J. D. (eds) *Philosophy and Education: accepting Wittgenstein's challenge*, Dordrecht: Kluwer, 221–224.

1994 MARSHALL, J. D., 'Governmentalidade e Educaço Liberal' in (ed.) SILVA, T. T., *O Sujeito da Educaçao: estudos Foucaultianas*, Petrópolis: Vozes, 21–34.

1994 MARSHALL, J. D., 'The Autonomous Chooser and "Reforms" in Education' in (ed.) SMEYERS, P. J. (1994), *Identity, Culture and Education*, Proceedings of the Fourth Conference of the International Network of Philosophers of Education, Leuven, August 1994.

1994 MARSHALL, J. D., 'Preface' and 'Introduction' in (ed.) MARSHALL, J. D. (1994), *Revisiting the Reforms in Education*, Auckland: Faculty of Education, The University of Auckland, i and 1–5.

1994 MARSHALL, J. D., PETERS, M. A., 'Post-Modernism and Education', *International Encyclopedia of Education*, (2nd Edition), Vol. 8, Oxford: Pergammon Press, 4639–4634.

1994 COXON, E., MASSEY, L., MARSHALL, J. D., 'Introduction' in (eds) COXON, E., JENKINS, K., MARSHALL, J. D., MASSEY, L., *The Politics of Learning and Teaching in Aotearoa-New Zealand*, Palmerston North: Dunmore Press, 9–33.

1994 HOLLAND, B., MARSHALL, J. D., 'The "Reforms" in Education: a partially annotated bibliography', in (ed.) MARSHALL, J. D. (1994) *Revisiting the Reforms in Education*, Auckland: The Faculty of Education, The University of Auckland, 61–97.

1994 PETERS, M. A., MARSHALL, J. D., 'Educational Policy Analysis and the Politics of Interpretation', reprinted in (ed.) RIST, R. C., *Policy Evaluation*, Cheltenham: Edward Elgar Publishing.

1994 PETERS, M. A., MARSHALL, J. D., MASSEY, L., 'Recent Educational Reforms in New Zealand' in (eds) COXON, E., JENKINS, K., MARSHALL, J. D., MASSEY, L., *The Politics of Learning and Teaching in Aotearoa/New Zealand*, Palmerston North: Dunmore, 251–272.

1993 MARSHALL, J. D., 'Foucault y la Investigación Educativa' in (ed.) BALL, S., *Foucault y la Educación*, Madrid: Marata, 11–28.

1993 MARSHALL, J. D., 'Quality Control in New Zealand Universities: account-ability and autonomy' in (ed.) CHAN, J. F. L., *Quality and Its Applications*, Pro-ceedings of the First Newcastle Conference on Quality and Its Applications, September 1993, Cleadon: Penshaw Press, 283–288.

1992 MARSHALL, J. D., 'Principles and the National Curriculum: centralised development', *Teacher Education: an investment in New Zealand's future'*, Proceedings of the New Zealand Council for Teacher Education Conference, Auckland, June, 1–12.

1991 MARSHALL, J. D., PETERS, M. A., SMITH, G. H., 'The Business Round Table and the Privatisation of Education: individualism and the attack on Maori' in (eds) GORDON, L., CODD, J. A., *Education Policy and the Changing Role of the State*, Delta Studies in Education 1. Proceedings of the N.Z.A.R.E. Seminar on Education Policy, Massey University, July 1990. Palmerston North: Massey University.

1990 MARSHALL, J. D., 'Foucault and Educational Research' in (ed.) BALL, S., *Foucault and Education: discipline and knowledge*, London and New York: Routledge, 11–28.

1990 MARSHALL, J. D., PETERS, M. A., 'Community and Empowerment: theory and practice in Tai Tokerau' in (eds) CODD, J. A., RICHARD HARKER, R., NASH, R., *Political Issues in New Zealand Education*, Palmerston North: Dunmore Press, 198–214.

1988 PETERS, M. A., MARSHALL, J. D., 'Social Policy and the Move to Community', *Future Directions: Report of The Royal Commission on Social Policy*, Vol. III. Wellington: Royal Commission on Social Policy, 655–676.

1988 PETERS, M. A., MARSHALL, J. D., 'Social Policy and the Move to Com-munity: practical implications for Service Delivery', *Future Directions: Report of the Royal Commission on Social Policy*, Vol. III. Wellington: Royal Commission on Social Policy, 677–702.

1988 PETERS, M. A., MARSHALL, J. D., 'Te Reo O Te Tai Tokerau: community evaluation, empowerment and opportunities of oral Maori language reproduction', *Future Directions: Report of the Royal Commission on Social Policy*, Vol. III. Wellington: Royal Commission on Social Policy, 703–744.

1988 PETERS, M. A., MARSHALL, J. D., 'Empowerment and the Ideal Learning Community' in (ed.) WYLIE, K., *Proceedings of the First Research into Educational Policy Conference*, Wellington: N.Z.C.E.R., 24pp.

1982 MARSHALL, J. D., 'Against the Necessity of Punishment', in (eds) CRIT-TENDEN, B. J., *Philosophical Issues in Education*, Vol. 2, Philosophy of Education Society of Australasia, 137–156.

1982 MARSHALL, J. D., 'Meaning, Meaningfulness and Education' in (ed.) KERR, D. B., *Philosophy of Education 1982*, Proceedings of the Thirty Eighth Annual Meeting of the Philosophy of Education Society (USA), 210–213.

## Journal Articles
## Forthcoming

2005 MARSHALL, J. D., 'Entravesta cum James Marshall' by interviewer Ghiraldelli, P., reprinted with major amendments in (eds) PETERS, M. A., SMEYERS, P. J. (2005) 'Festschrift for James Marshall'. *Educational Philosophy and Theory*, 37:3.

2005 MARSHALL, J. D., 'Interview with James Marshall' by Michael A., Peters in (eds) PETERS, M. A., SMEYERS, P. J. (2005) 'James Marshall', *Educational Philosophy and Theory*, 37.

2005 MARSHALL, J. D., 'Revisiting the Task/Achievement Analysis of Teaching in Neo-Liberal Times', *Educational Philosophy and Theory*, 37.

## Published

2004 MARSHALL, J. D., 'Two Forms of Philosophical Argument or Critique', *Educational Philosophy and Theory*, 36(4).

2004 MARSHALL, J. D., 'Access, Vols. 1–20: a partially annotated bibliography, *Access*, 20(2).

2003 MARSHALL, J. D., PETERS, M. A., IRWIN, R. J., 'From Colonialism to Globalisation: performativity in New Zealand education', in (eds) S MEYERS, P. J., DEPAEPE, M., 'Beyond Empiricism: On Criteria for Educational Research', *Studia Pedagogica*, 34, 65–77.

2002 MARSHALL, J. D., 'Michel Foucault: liberation, freedom', education, *Educational Philosophy and Theory*, 34(4), 413–418.

2002 MARSHALL, J. D., 'Philosophy of Educational Research and What Works', *Educational Philosophy and Theory*, 34(3),

2002 PETERS, M. A., MARSHALL, J. D., 'Reading Wittgenstein: The Rehearsal of Prejudice. A Response to McCarty, *Studies in Philosophy and Education*, 21(3), 263–271.

2001 MARSHALL, J. D., 'Varieties of Neo-liberalism: a Foucaultian perspective', *Educational Philosophy and Theory*, 33(3&4), 293–304.

2001 MARSHALL, J. D., 'A Critical Theory of the Self: Nietzsche, Wittgenstein, Foucault', *Studies in Philosophy and Education*, 20(1), 75–91.

2001 PETERS, M. A., MARSHALL, J. D., 'Introduction: New Zealand, Neo-liberalism and the Knowledge Economy, *Access: Critical Perspectiveness on Cultural and Policy Studies in Education*, 19(2), 1–8.

2000 MARSHALL, J. D., 'Thinking Again: modern or postmodern?', I 31(3), 331–334, 2000.

2000 MARSHALL, J. D., 'Electronic Writing and the Wrapping of Language', in *Journal of Philosophy of Education*, 34 (Special Issue, April), 135–149.

2000 MARSHALL, J. D., 'Technology and Indigenous People: the case of Maori'. *Educational Philosophy and Theory*, 31(1), 119–131.

2000 MARSHALL, J. D., 'Reforming a Liberal State Education System: the case of New Zealand', *Ciência Geográphica* (Brasil).

2000 MARSHALL, J. D. (with MARTIN, B.), 'Introduction: The Boundaries of Belief: territories of encounter between indigenous peoples and western philosophies', *Educational Philosophy and Theory*, 31(1), 15–24.

2000 MARSHALL, J. D., 'Education and the Postmodern World: rethinking some educational stories', *Educational Theory*, 50(1), 117–126.

2000 MARSHALL, J. D., 'Bright Futures Technology: curriculum, Maori and the environment', *Access: critical perspectives on cultural and policy studies in education*, 19(2), 102–131.

2000 MARSHALL, J. D., PETERS, M. A., 'Foreword', *Access*, 19(2), ii.

2000 PETERS, M. A., MARSHALL, J. D., 'Foreword', *Access*, 19(1), i.

2000 PETERS, M. A., MARSHALL, J. D., 'Introduction', *Access* 19(2), 1–8.

1999 MARSHALL, J. D., 'Performativity: Lyotard and Foucault through Searle and Austin', *Studies in Philosophy and Education*, 18(5), 309–317.

1999 MARSHALL, J. D., 'I am LW: Wittgenstein on the Self', *Educational Philosophy and Theory*, 31(2), 113–121.

1999 MARSHALL, J. D., 'Technology in the New Zealand Curriculum', *New Zealand Journal of Educational Studies*, 34(2), 167–175.

1999 PETERS, M. A., MARSHALL, J. D., FITZSIMONS, P., 'Poststructuralism and Curriculum Theory: neo-liberalism, the information economy and cultural authority', *Journal of Curriculum Theorising*, 15(2), 111–130.

1999 MARSHALL, J. D., 'Foreword to "Universities in the 20ᵗʰ Century"', *Access*, 18(2), i.

1998 MARSHALL, J. D., 'Simone de Beauvoir: the self in the metaphysical novels'. *Philosophical Studies in Education 1997*, 90–101.

1998 MARSHALL, J. D., 'Information on Information: recent curriculum reform', *Studies in Philosophy and Education* 17(4), 313–321.

1998 MARSHALL, J. D., 'Kenneth Wain on Foucault and Postmodernism: a reply', *Studies in Philosophy and Education*, 17(2–3), 177–183.

1998 MARSHALL, J. D., 'The Punishment of Children' *Pedagogisch Tijdschrift*, 23(4), 369–386.

1988 MARSHALL, J. D., 'Forward', *Access: critical perspectives on cultural and policy studies in education*, 17(1), iii–vi.

1998 MARSHALL, J. D., 'A Wittgensteinian Approach to Communication in the Mode of Information', *Access: critical perspectives on cultural and policy studies in education*, 17(1), 42–52.

1997 MARSHALL, J. D., 'Problematising the Individual and Constituting "the" Self'. *Educational Philosophy and Theory*, 29(1), 32–49.

1997 MARSHALL, J. D., PETERS, M. A., FITZSIMONS, P., 'Education and the Philosophy of the Subject (or constitution of the self)'. *Educational Philosophy and Theory*, 29(1), v–xi.

1996 MARSHALL, J. D., 'The Autonomous Chooser and "Reforms" in Education', *Studies in Philosophy and Education*, 15(1), 89–96.

1996 PETERS, M. A., MARSHALL, J. D., 'The Politics of Curriculum: busnocratic rationality and enterprise culture' in (ed.) O'NEIL, M., *Delta: policy and practice in education*, 48(1), 33–46.

1995 MARSHALL, J. D., 'Wittgenstein and Foucault: resolving philosophical puzzles', *Studies in Philosophy and Education*, 14(2–3), 329–344.

1995 MARSHALL, J. D., 'Michel Foucault: governmentality and liberal education', *Studies in Philosophy and Education*, 14(1), 23–34.

1995 MARSHALL, J. D., 'Constructivism Without Epistemology', *Access*, 13(2), 64–70.

1995 MARSHALL, J. D., PETERS, M. A., 'The Governance of Educational Research', *The Australian Educational Researcher*, 22(2), 107–120.

1995 PETERS, M. A., MARSHALL, J. D., 'After the Philosophy of the Subject: a response to McKenzie', *Educational Philosophy and Theory*, 27(1), 41–54.

1995 PETERS, M. A., MARSHALL, J. D., 'An Interview with Mark Poster', *New Zealand Journal of Media Studies*, 2(1), 45–53.

1995 SMEYERS, P. J., MARSHALL, J. D., 'The Wittgensteinian Frame of Reference and Philosophy of Education at the End of the Twentieth Century', *Studies in Philosophy and Education*, 14(2–3), 127–159.

1995 SMEYERS, P. J., MARSHALL, J. D., 'Philosophy and Education: Accepting Wittgenstein's challenge. Epilogue,' *Studies in Philosophy and Education*, 14(2–3), 345–348.

1994/95 MARSHALL, J. D., 'On What We May Hope: Rorty on Dewey and Foucault', *Studies in Philosophy and Education*, 13(4), 307–323.

1993 PETERS, M. A. MARSHALL, J. D., PARR, B., 'The Marketisation of Tertiary Education in New Zealand', *Australian Universities Review*, 36(2), 34–39.

1993 PETERS, M. A., MARSHALL, J. D., 'Beyond the Philosophy of the Subject: liberalism, education and the critique of individualism', *Educational Philosophy and Theory*, 25(1), 19–39.

1993 PETERS, M. A., MARSHALL, J. D., 'Educational Policy Analysis and the Politics of Interpretation: the search for a well defined problem', *Evaluation Review*, 17(3),310–330.

1992 MARSHALL, J. D., 'Questions Filosòfiques de l'Educaió, *Temps d'Educació* 7, 167–184.

1992 PETERS, M. A., MARSHALL, J. D., 'Doing it the Right Way: Devolution in New Zealand', *Principal Matters*, April, 16–17.

1992 MARSHALL, J. D., Review of Pierre Bourdieu In Other Words: essays towards a reflexive sociology, Stanford, C.A.: Stanford University Press. In *International Journal of Qualitative Studies in Education*, 5(3), 269–271.

1991 MARSHALL, J. D., PETERS, M. A., 'Educational 'Reforms and New Right Thinking: an example from New Zealand', *Educational Philosophy and Theory*, 23(2), 46–57.

1991 PETERS, M. A., MARSHALL, J. D., 'Education and Empowerment: postmodernism and the critique of humanism', *Education and Society*, 9(1–2), 123–134.

1990 MARSHALL, J. D., 'Asking Philosophical Questions about Education: Foucault on Punishment'. *Educational Philosophy and Theory*, 22(2), 81–92.

1990 MARSHALL, J. D., PETERS, M. A., 'The Insertion of New Right Thinking into Education: an example from New Zealand', *Journal of Education Policy*, 5(2), 143–156.

1990 PETERS, M. A., MARSHALL, J. D., 'Institutionalised Racism and the 'Retention' of Maori Students in Northland', *New Zealand Sociology*, 5(1), 44–66.

1990 PETERS, M. A., MARSHALL, J. D., 'Children of Rogernomics: the New Right, individualism and the culture of narcissism', *Sites*, 21, 174–191.

1990 PETERS, M. A., MARSHALL, J. D., 'Education, the New Right and the Crisis of the Welfare State in New Zealand', *Discourse*, 11(1), 77–90.

1990 MARSHALL, J. D., PETERS, M. A., 'Empowering Teachers', *Unicorn*, 16(3), 163–168.

1989 MARSHALL, J. D., 'Foucault and Education', *Australian Journal of Education*, 33(2), 97–111.

1989 MARSHALL, J. D., 'The Incompatibility of Punishment and Moral Education: a reply to Peter Hobson', *Journal of Moral Education*, 18(2), 130–3.

1989 MARSHALL, J. D., PETERS, M. A., 'Te Reo O Te Tai Tokerau: the assessment of oral Maori', *Journal of Multilingual and Multicultural Development*, 10(6), 499–514.

1989 MARSHALL, J. D., PETERS, M. A., 'Te Reo O Te Tai Tokerau: a community approach to the assessment and promotion of oral Maori', *Pacific Education*, 1(3), 70–89.

1989 PETERS, M. A., PARA, D., MARSHALL, J. D., 'Te Reo O Te Tai Tokerau: language evaluation and empowerment', *New Zealand Journal of Educational Studies*, 24(1), 141–158.

1989 PETERS, M. A., PARA, D., MARSHALL, J. D., 'Te Reo O Te Tai Tokerau: the need for consolidation and national implementation', *Access*, 8(1), 10–25.

1988 PETERS, M. A., MARSHALL, J. D., The Politics of "Choice" and "Community", *Access*, 7, 84–106.

1988 MARSHALL, J. D., LANKSHEAR, C. J., 'Foreword', *Access: contemporary themes in educational enquiry*, 7, ii–iii.

1987 MARSHALL, J. D., 'An Anti-Foundational Approach to Authority and Discipline', *Discourse: the Australian journal of education*, 7(2), 1–20.

1987 MARSHALL, J. D., LANKSHEAR, C. J., 'Editors' Foreword', *Access: contemporary themes in educational enquiry*, 6(2), ii.

1986 MARSHALL, J. D., LANKSHEAR, C. J., 'Editors' Foreword', *Access: contemporary themes in educational enquiry*, 5(2), i.

1986 PETERS, M. A., MARSHALL, J. D., SHAW, R., 'The Development and Trials of a Decision Making Model', *Evaluation Review*, 10(1), 15–27.

1986 MARSHALL, J. D., PETERS, M. A., 'Evaluation and Education: practical problems and theoretical perspectives', *New Zealand Journal of Educational Studies*, 21(1), 29–41.

1986 MARSHALL, J. D., PETERS, M. A., 'New Perspectives on Piaget's Philosophy', *Educational Theory*, 36(2), 125–136.

1986 MARSHALL, J. D., PETERS, M. A., 'Administrative Discretionary Justice: a report on the development of a model of decision-making', *Public Administration: Journal of the Royal Institute of Administration*, 64, 453–459.

1985 MARSHALL, J. D., PETERS, M. A., 'Evaluation and Education: the ideal learning community', *Policy Sciences*, 18(3), 263–288.

1985 MARSHALL, J. D., 'Implications for the Conduct of Educational Research of Adopting Dewey's Theory of Inquiry', *Discourse: the Australian journal of education*, 5(2), 54–66.

1985 MARSHALL, J. D., 'Wittgenstein on Rules: implications for authority and discipline in education', *Journal of Philosophy of Education*, 19(1), 3–11.

1985 MARSHALL, J. D., LANKSHEAR, C. J., 'Editors' Foreword', *Access: contemporary themes in educational enquiry*, 4(1), ii.

1985 MARSHALL, J. D., LANKSHEAR, C. J., 'Editors' Foreword', *Access: contemporary themes in educational enquiry*, 4(1), ii.

1984 MARSHALL, J. D., 'Punishment and Moral Education', *Journal of Moral Education*, 13(2), 79–85.

1984 MARSHALL, J. D., 'John Dewey and Educational Research', *Journal of Research and Development in Education*, 17(3), 66–77.

1984 MARSHALL, J. D., 'Against the Necessity of Punishment', *Education Research and Perspectives*, 11(2), 73–84.

1984 MARSHALL, J. D., 'John Wilson on the Necessity of Punishment', *Journal of Philosophy of Education*, 18(1), 97–104.

1984 MARSHALL, J. D., LANKSHEAR, C. J., 'Editors' Foreword', *Access: contemporary themes in educational enquiry*, 3(2), ii.

1984 MARSHALL, J. D., LANKSHEAR, C. J., 'Editors' Foreword', *Access: contemporary themes in educational enquiry*, 3(1), ii.

1984 MARSHALL, J. D., HOFF, A., 'Religious Indoctrination and the Integration Act', *New Zealand Journal of Educational Studies*, 19(2), 124–135.

1983 MARSHALL, J. D., 'Philosophy of Education in New Zealand', *Educational Analysis*, 4(1), 19–24.

1983 MARSHALL, J. D., LANKSHEAR, C. J., 'Editors' Foreword', *Access: contemporary themes in educational enquiry*, 2(2), ii.

1983 MARSHALL, J. D., LANKSHEAR, C. J., 'Editors' Foreword', *Access: contemporary themes in educational enquiry*, 2(1), ii.

1982 MARSHALL, J. D., 'Facts, Research Data & John Dewey', *Educational Philosophy and Theory*, 14(2), 61–72.

1982 MARSHALL, J. D., LANKSHEAR, C. J., 'Editors Foreword', *Access: contemporary themes in educational enquiry*, 1(1), ii.

1981 MARSHALL, J. D., PETERS, M. A., SHEPHEARD, M., 'Brent's Transcendental Deductions of the Forms of Knowledge', *Journal of Philosophy of Education*, 15(2), 267–277.

1981 MARSHALL, J. D., PETERS, M. A., SHEPHEARD, M., 'Self Refutation Arguments Against Young's Epistemology', *Educational Philosophy and Theory*, 13(2), 43–50.

1981 MARSHALL, J. D., 'Objectivity and Observation', *Discourse: the Australian Journal of Education*, 2(1), 63–75.

1981 MARSHALL, J. D., 'Educational Research and Scientific Method', *New Zealand Journal of Educational Studies*, 16(3), 128–137.

1981 MARSHALL, J. D., 'Review of Teacher Training at North Shore Teachers College', *HERDSA News*, July, 8–9.

1980 MARSHALL, J. D., 'Thomas Hobbes: Obligation and Education in the Commonwealth', *Journal of Philosophy of Education*, 14(2), 193–203.

1980 MARSHALL, J. D., 'Social Studies and the Disciplines', *Changes*, 3, 35–42.

1980 MARSHALL, J. D., 'Political and Economic Retrenchment in Education', *The Journal (NZPPTA)*, July, 20–21.

1980 MARSHALL, J. D., 'Education and Work', *Changes*, 3,11.

1979 MARSHALL, J. D., 'Social Science, Social Studies and Teaching Social Studies', *Changes*, 2(1), 4–7.

1978 MARSHALL, J. D., 'Implications for Teaching of a Revised Concept of Punishment', *New Zealand Teachers College Association Journal*, 15(1), 8–12.

1978 MARSHALL, J. D., 'Educational Theory and the Conceptual Framework of Common Sense', *Educational Philosophy and Theory*, 9(1), 17–31.

1977 MARSHALL, J. D., 'Is Teaching What the Philosopher Understands by it?' *British Journal of Educational Studies*, XXV(2), 186.

1977 MARSHALL, J. D., 'Has Punishment a Place in Moral Education?' *National Education*, 59(626), 108–9.

1976 MARSHALL, J. D., 'Responsibility, Health and Medical Practice', *The New Zealand Medical Journal*, Feb., 7.

1976 MARSHALL, J. D., 'Reasons, Emotions and Moral Education', *Delta*, 19, 38–45.

1976 MARSHALL, J. D., 'Philosophy and Educational Research', *New Zealand Journal of Educational Studies*, 11(1), 60–63.

1976 MARSHALL, J. D., 'What We Do To Children', *Education*, 5, 12–13.

1976 MARSHALL, J. D., 'Some Comments on Integration', *The Journal (NZPPTA)*, March, 39–42.

1975 MARSHALL, J. D., 'The Nature of Educational Theory', *Educational Philosophy and Theory*, 7(1), 15–26.

1975 MARSHALL, J. D., 'Punishment and Education', *Educational Theory*, 25(2), 148–55.

1975 MARSHALL, J. D., 'The Concept of Teaching', *Proceedings of the Philosophy of Education Society of Great Britain*, IX: 105–118, July. (Now *The Journal of Philosophy of Education*).

1972 MARSHALL, J. D., 'On Why We Don't Punish Children', *Educational Philosophy and Theory*, 4(1), 57–68.

## BOOK REVIEWS
### Published

2004 MARSHALL, J. D., Review of Kleiman, Lowell, Lewis and Stephen (1992) *Philosophy: an Introduction through Literature* (St. Pauls, Minn.: Paragon House), in *Access*, 20(2), 2001.

2004 MARSHALL, J. D., Review of Elizabeth Grierson and Janet Mansfield (2003) (eds), *The Arts in Education: critical perspectives from Aotearoa New Zealand* (Palmerston North: Dunmore Press), in *Access*, 23(2), 2004.

2001 MARSHALL, J. D., Review of David Carr (1999) Professionalism and Ethics in Teaching (London & New York: Routledge) in *Educational Philosophy and Theory*, 33(1), 118–122.

2000 MARSHALL, J. D., Review of Roger Marples (1999) The Aims of Education (London & New York: Routledge) in *Educational Philosophy and Theory*, 31(3),

2000 MARSHALL, J. D., Review of David Carr and Jan Steutel (1999) Virtue Ethics and Moral Education (London & New York: Routledge) in *Educational Philosophy and Theory*, 31(3),

2000 MARSHALL, J. D., 'Recent British Philosophy of Education', in *Access*, 19(1), 163–168.

2000 MARSHALL, J. D., Review of Peter Roberts (1999) Paulo Freire in New Zealand (Palmerston North: Dunmore Press) in *Access*, 19(2), 132–135.

1998 MARSHALL, J. D., Review of Growing Critical by John Morss, in *New Zealand Journal of Educational Studies*, 33(1), 119–121.

1983 MARSHALL, J. D., Review of John White's The Aims of Education Restated (Routledge & Kegan Paul, 1982), *New Zealand Journal of Educational Studies*, 18(2), 191–193.

### Journals

1982–8 (ed. with C. J. Lankshear), *Access*, Vols. 1–8. (co-founders, and co-editors until 1989). Co-Editor, 1996–2001. Consulting Editor 2002–.

### Technical Reports

2001 MARSHALL, J. D., 'From Colonialism to Globalisation: performativity in New Zealand education'. In (eds) SMEYERS, P. J., DEPAPE, M., *Philosophy and History of the Discipline of Education: evaluation and evolution of the criteria for educational research*, Leuven: Katholieke Universiteit Leuven, 113–116.

2001 MARSHALL, J. D. and PETERS, M. A., 'The Psychologistic Phase: testing and measurement,' in (eds) SMEYERS, P. J., DEPAPE, M., *Philosophy and History of the Discipline of Education: evaluation and evolution of the criteria for educational research*, Leuven: Katholieke Universiteit Leuven, 116–121.

2001 MARSHALL, J. D. and IRWIN, F. R., 'Post-1988: the march of performativity', in SMEYERS, P. J., DEPAPE, M., *Philosophy and History of the Discipline of Education: evaluation and evolution of the criteria for educational research*, Leuven: Katholieke Universiteit Leuven, 121–128.

2000 MARSHALL, J. D. (with PETERS, M. A., IRWIN, F. R.), 'From Pragmatism to Positivism'. Report to Research Group, *Philosophy and History of the Discipline of Education: evaluation and evolution of the criteria for educational research*, Leuven: Katholieke Universiteit Leuven.

1993 MARSHALL, J. D., He Kaupapa Whakatikatika, Report to Foundation of Research, Science and Technology, 103pp plus appendices.

1989 PETERS, M. A., MARSHALL, J. D., Nga Awangawanga Me Nga Wawato A Te Iwi O Te Tai Tokerau. (Final Report of the Project Concerning Schooling and Retention of Maori Secondary Students in Tai Tokerau), (State) Department of Education, Wellington, 156pp. plus appendices.

1987 PETERS, M. A., MARSHALL, J. D., Te Reo O Te Tai Tokerau Project for (State) Department of Education, Wellington, 252pp. (including appendices).

1986 MARSHALL, J. D., PETERS, M. A., Report on the Programme Evaluation and Policy Development Project, for State Services Commission, 182pp. (including appendices).

1984 MARSHALL, J. D., PETERS, M. A., Evaluation of the Administrative Decision Making Skills Project, for State Services Commission, 266pp. (including appendices).

1984 MARSHALL, J. D., PETERS, M. A., Evaluability Report: Administrative Decision Making Skills Project, for State Services Commission, Wellington.

1984 MARSHALL, J. D., PETERS, M. A., Assessment of the Research Report Entitled Improving the Utilisation of Information Gained Through Evaluation, for (State) Department of Education, Wellington.

1974 MARSHALL, J. D., NEWTH, A. A., WHYTE, K. A., A Review of Teacher Training at North Shore Teachers College, 160pp.

**Course Material for Advanced Studies in Teaching (Ministry of Education).**

1986 Study Guides (4)–(6), Contemporary Issues in Education, Advanced Studies for Teachers, Paper 15.13, (State) Department of Education, Wellington.

1986 Study Guide (6)—Education and Schooling, Advanced Studies for Teachers, Paper 15.12, (State) Department of Education, Wellington.

1982 Study Guide (1)–(6)—Contemporary Issues in Education, Advanced Studies for Teachers, Paper 15.13, (State) Department of Education, Wellington.

1981 Study Guides (4)–(6)—Education and Schooling, Advanced Studies for Teachers, paper 15.12, (State) Department of Education, Wellington.

## Papers Read/Presentations/Conferences/etc.

2005
(1) Invited Panelist at annual conference of South East Association of Educational Studies, Chapel Hill (NC), February.
(2) AERA Conference, Montreal, April. Symposium on Accountability nd Democratic Philosophies. Paper entitled 'Simone de Beauvoir on Accountability: self-knowledge and ethics'.
This symposium was classified as one of 5 Highlights for Division B by *Educational Researcher*, 34(2), 22.

2004
(1) Critical Pedagogy Conference, Madrid, 3 August. Michel Foucault: From Critical Theory to Critical Pedagogy'.
(2) International Network of Philosophers of Education, Madrid, 4–8 August. 'Two Forms of Philosophical Argument or Critique'.

2003
(1) AERA Chicago, April. Member of Symposium on Poststructuralist Philosophy of Education — paper entitled 'Foucault and his Forbears'.
(2) Philosophy of Education Society, University of Auckland, November — participant.

2001
(1) Auckland University Research Group's Reports to Research Project *Philosophy and History of the Discipline of Education: evaluation and evolution of the criteria for educational research*, Leuven: Katholieke Universiteit Leuven. See technical reports 2001 for details.
(2) Seminar series on Foucault and Educational Research, University of Glasgow.
(3) Varieties of Neo-Liberalism', AERA Conference, Seattle.

2000
(1) 'Michel Foucault: liberation and freedom'. Part of an invited symposium for the inaugural Foucault and Education Conference, Fairmont Hotel, 22 New Orleans April.
(2) 'Michel Foucault: the pedagogy of caring for a self'. 34th. Annual Conference of the Philosophy of Education Society of Great Britain, New College Oxford, 14–16 April.

(3) 'Educational Philosophy, Language and Culture in the 21$^{st}$. Century', 7$^{th}$. Biennial Conference of the International Network of Philosophers of Education, University of Sydney, 18–21 August.

(4) First meeting in Leuven for Research Group *Philosophy and History of the Discipline of Education: evaluation and evolution of the criteria for educational research*, Katholieke Universiteit Leuven. Report from New Zealand delivered.

1999

Baton Rouge, Louisiana State University, March: 'The Internationalisation of Curriculum Studies'.

(1) Marshall, James D. 'Martin Heidegger: Technology, Technicity and the Curriculum'.

(2) Peters, Michael, James D. Marshall and Patrick Fitzsimons. 'Poststructuralism and Curriculum Theory: neo-liberalism, the information economy and cultural authority'.

(3) American Research Association (AERA), New Orleans.

(4) University of Waikato, July: (i) 'A Decade of Reform in New Zealand Education: Where to now?'

(ii) Marshall, James D. 'Technology in the New Zealand Curriculum'.

(5) Philosophy of Education Society of Australasia, Royal Melbourne Institute of Technology, November. 'Globalisation and its Consequences for Philosophy of Education'.

Marshall, James D. 'The Globalisation of Meaning'.

(6) AAERA/NZARE, Melbourne, Nov-December. Participant.

(7) Australian and New Zealand Comparative and International Association, Melbourne, December.

Marshall, James D. 'Foucault's Critique of Neo-liberalism'.

1998

(1) Katholieke Universiteit Leuven, Jan–Feb. Seminar Series on the Self (six sessions)

(2) University of Utrecht, Feb. 'The Punishment of Children'.

(3) AERA, San Diego, March: (i) 'Performativity: Lyotard, Foucault, Austin'. (ii) Discussant for Phil.SIG Symposium organised by Tom Popkevitz.

(4) Philosophy of Education Society of Australasia Annual Conference, Auckland, November. 'Technology in the New Zealand Curriculum'. NZARE, Dunedin, December

1997

(1) AERA, Chicago, April. Organised Philosophy SIG Symposium on Poststructuralism. 'French Philosophy post-1968'.

(2) Annual Conference of Philosophy of Education Society (North America), Vancouver, April. 'John Dewey and the New Vocationalism'

(3) Philosophy of Education Society of Great Britain, Oxford, April. 'Simone de Beauvoir on the Other: silence and friendship'.

(4) Philosophy of Education Society of Australasia Annual Conference, Sydney, July. Simone de Beauvoir: the metaphysical novels.

(5) University of Auckland, Child and Family Health Seminar, September.' Discipline and Punishment in New Zealand Education'.

(6) University of Otago, July: (i) 'Simone de Beauvoir: the self in the metaphysical novels'; (ii) 'French Philosophy post WW II'.

(7) Ohio Valley Philosophy of Education Society Annual Conference, Cincinatti, October. 'Simone de Beauvoir: the self in the metaphysical novels'.

## 1996

(1) Annual Conference of Philosophy of Education Society (North America), Houston, March. 'Education in the Mode of Information' AERA, New York, April. 'Wittgenstein and Constructivism'

(2) International Network of Philosophers of Education, 5th Biennial Conference, Johannesburg, August. 'Information on information: recent curriculum reform'.

(3) Philosophy of Education Society, Brisbane. 'The New Vocationalism'.
NZARE, Nelson, December, 'Wittgenstein, Constructivism and Mathematics Education'.

## 1995

(1) Annual Conference of Philosophy of Education Society (North America), San Francisco, April. 'Foucault and Neo-Liberalism: busno-power and bio-power', and presentation, 'Philosophy of Education in New Zealand'.

(2) University of Wisconsin-Madison, Seminar, April. 'Michel Foucault'.

(3) AERA, San Francisco, April. Participant.

(4) Annual Conference of the Philosophy of Education Society of Australasia, Melbourne, 29 Novemeber–2 December. 'Educationalists in the Mode of Information'.

## 1994

(1) Foucault Legacy Conference—Surfers Paradise (Q.U.T), July. 'Personal Autonomy as an Aim of Education'.

(2) International Philosophers of Education Conference, Leuven, August. 'The Autonomous Chooser and and Reforms in Education'.

(3) NZARE Conference, Auckland, 23 July. 'Skills, Information and Quality for the Autonomous Chooser'.

(4) Auckland—Philosophy of Education Society of Australasia, November. 'Busnocratic Rationality and Busno-power'.

## 1993

(1) High Quality Schooling and the Evaluation of Maori Learning, Wellington, May. 'Doing Research in Tai Tokerau'

(2) Quality and its Applications, First Newcastle International Conference on Quality and its Applications, Newcastle, Setember. 'Quality Control; In New Zealand Universities: accountability and autonomy'.

(3) Philosophy of Education Society of Australasia, Annual Conference, Sydney, October.

(4) Monash University.

## 1992

(1) New Zealand Council For Teacher Education Conference, Auckland, June. 'Principles and the National Curriculum:centralised development'.

(2) International network for the Philosophy of Education, Second Biennial Conference, Varna, Bulgaria, August. 'Michel Foucault: governmentality and education'.

(3) Katholiek Universiteit Leuven, 3 October. 'Michel Foucault and Education'.

(4) University of Neijmegen, 5 October. 'Foucault and Wittgenstein: asking philosophical questions'.

## 1991

(1) University of London, 8 January, 'Asking Philosophical Questions about Education: Michel Foucault on Punishment'.

(2) Invited Address, Inaugural Conference on Law and Education, Monash University, 10–13 July 'The Treaty of Waitangi, Educational Reforms and the Education of Maori'.

(3) Simon Fraser University, 24 October, 'Foucault and Autonomy'.

(4) University of British Columbia, 1 November, 'New Forms of Reading and Writing for "New" Times'.

## 1990

(1) Inaugural Lecture, University of Auckland, 12 July. 'Educational Research and Higher Education'.

(2) International Network of Philosophers of Education Second Conference, University of London, 20–24 August, 'Educational Reforms and New Right Thinking: an example from New Zealand'.

(3) Invited Address, New Zealand Home Schooling Association Conference, Auckland, 22 September. 'Schooling in The New Schools'.

(4) (with Michael Peters and Graham Smith). 'The Business Round Table and the Privatisation of Education: Individualism and the Attack on Maori'. N.Z.A.R.E. Special Interest Conference, Massey University, July, 1990.

(5) Campus Radio April 23$^{rd}$, 'The B.Ed. Degree'.

## 1989

(with Michael A. Peters) 'Children of Rogernomics: The New Right, Individualism and the Children of Narcissism'. N.Z.A.R.E. Conference, Upper Hutt, December, 1989.

## 1988

(1) 'Te Reo O Te Tai Tokerau: the Need for Consolidation'. N.Z.A.R.E. Conference, Massey University, (December, 1988).

(2) 'Evaluation, Education and Empowerment: theory and practice in Tai Tokerau'. The Institute of Policy Studies, Griffith University, November, 1989.

## 1987

(1) 'Foucault and Education', Kings College, London.

(2) 'Michel Foucault', Institute of Education, London.

(3) 'Foucault and Power', Bristol University.

(4) 'Foucault and Educational Research', First Joint A.A.R.E./N.Z.A.R.E. Conference, Christchurch.

## 1986

(1) 'Evaluation as Education', University of Hawaii.

(2) 'What has Michel Foucault to Offer Education?', University of Adelaide.

(3) 'Michel Foucault', University of Melbourne.

(4) 'Evaluation as Education', Monash University.

(5) 'Programme Evaluation and Policy Analysis', University of Sydney.

## 1985

(1) 'The Evaluation of the Administrative Decision Making Project', State Services Commission, Wellington.

(2) 'Sex Education', New Zealand Society of Sexology, Auckland Technical Institute (North Shore) Auckland.

(3) 'Evaluation as Education', Auckland Institute of Educational Research.

(4) 'An Anti-Foundational Approach to Authority and Discipline', Philosophy of Education Society of Australasia Annual Conference, University of Tasmania.

(5) 'Evaluation as Education', Otago University.

(6) 'Education and Evaluation', New Zealand Association for Research in Education, Annual Conference, Auckland College of Education.

## 1984

'Power and Education', New Zealand Educational Administration Society (Auckland Branch).

## 1983

'Against the Necessity of Punishment', Philosophy of Education Society of Australasia, Annual Conference, Massey University.

## 1982

(1) 'Dewey on Facts', Institute of Education, University of London.

(2) 'Meaning, Meaningfulness and Education', Philosophy of Education Society (North America), Annual Conference, Baltimore.

## 1981

(1) 'Dewey, Facts and Research Data', California Association of Philosophy of Education.

(2) 'Justifying the Punishment of Children', Stanford University.

## 1979

'Politics and Education', Victoria University of Wellington.

## 1977

'The Punishment of Children', Institute of Education, University of London.

1976

(1) 'What has Philosophy to Offer Educational Research?', Auckland Institute of Educational Research.
(2) 'Educational Theory and the Conceptual Framework of Commonsense', Philosophy of Education Society of Australasia Annual Conference.

1975

'Reasons, Emotions and Moral Education', (State) Department of Education, Hogben House, Christchurch.

1973

'The Philosophy of Educational Research', Canterbury University.

1972

(1) 'The Punishment of Children', Open University Summer School
(2) 'The Concept of Punishment', Philosophy of Education Society of Great Britain (West Midlands Branch).

1971

'The Problem of Identity', Bristol University.

# 15
# Interview with James Marshall

PAULO GHIRALDELLI JR.

*Faculdade de Filosofia, Ciências e Letras de Ibitinga (FAIBI)*

*Paulo:* Jim, you wrote about Philosophy of Education, but you are a philosopher. Do you think that there are differences between a philosopher of education and a 'normal' academic philosopher?

*Jim:* Although born in New Zealand, where I received my initial education, including some papers at the University of Auckland, my philosophical education was undertaken between 1964 and 1973 at the University of Bristol where I completed a PhD on *Identity* with Stephan Körner. From 1967–1973 I taught philosophy and philosophy of education for Bristol University's Bachelor of Education Degree. I was also teaching philosophy part time with the Open University (1971–2). At that time I did not think that there was a marked difference but I have shifted my position over the years, and I am not sure that I would describe what I do and write now as traditional academic philosophy.

In the 1960s and the early 1970s there was tremendous enthusiasm for philosophy of education. Several prominent philosophers—for example, David Cooper, Gilbert Ryle, Glenn Langford, D. J. O'Connor, Mary Warnock (see for example, Brown, 1975)—were interested in philosophy of education and there was tremendous enthusiasm from philosophers of education for working out the analytic programme outlined by Richard Peters and Paul Hirst. But that programme lost its way in Britain, in my view.

But I had returned to the University of Auckland in 1973 with a brief to introduce the 'new' philosophy of education, as opposed to the teaching of courses on philosophical '-isms'. In doing this I became increasingly dissatisfied with the analytic paradigm, returning to philosophy of science in discussions of research methodology, and to the writings of John Dewey after intensive study of his writings whilst on sabbatical leave at Stanford University in 1981. With Colin Lankshear who had joined me at Auckland I was also teaching courses on marxism and neo-marxism with particular reference to the work of the Australian marxist philosopher of education Kevin Harris, and I was soon to turn to Wittgenstein. My earlier interest in traditional academic philosophy withered as I concentrated on the restructuring of philosophy of education at Auckland and I was, eventually, to lose interest.

Prior to becoming a fulltime student I was a naval officer and a part time teacher. I had initially become interested in philosophy in the navy where I encountered a number of major ethical issues, though I had read a little philosophy earlier. As a teacher I became interested in how people came to understand mathematics. As I worked in philosophy of education I became increasingly concerned that philosophy of education had normative and practical implications, yet I also knew that according to academic philosophers I had studied philosophy for the wrong reasons, for philosophy was said to be a neutral meta-level study of other disciplines, not a study of ethics for example, but the study of ethical language. I came to believe that this was unethical and politically naïve (especially in education), if not stupid. Hence I am mainly interested in philosophers like Dewey, Nietzsche, Wittgenstein, and Foucault. To that list I would now add Simone de Beauvoir, Jean-Paul Sartre and Albert Camus, though they may not be philosophers according to Anglo-American canons.

Also I had returned to my earlier questions about identity and the self and that philosophy should involve 'work upon the self' but, until recently, academic philosophy had not been too interested in these questions. I do not deny however that I gratefully draw upon my wide background in the history of philosophy and ideas.

*P:* You love Foucault, I know. And you wrote on Dewey. Rorty likes to see Dewey and Foucault together against the metaphysical tradition. And in your beautiful article you didn't like this. Am I right?

*J:* I am not sure that I love Foucault. Initially he was a revelation to me, standing philosophy on its head so to say, and providing a way forward for me. A colleague who knew that I had published philosophical articles on the punishment of children was to pass me a copy of Foucault's *Discipline and Punish: the birth of the prison.* I had argued earlier, analytically, that the legal model of punishment and the traditional philosophical justifications of punishment did not fit the punishment of children, for we had different aims and intentions with the young. What I was groping for analytically was what Foucault developed 'historically' as *disciplinary punishment.* Since then I have been much more attentive to historical data and genealogical forms of argument. That said I have become quite critical of him in recent writings, mainly on questions of ommissions in relation to education and the pedagogical relationships necessary to learn to care for the self.

As for loving him I have come to think of him as a rather difficult man, if not worse! As I read more French philosophy I see large spaces within the French humanist tradition where there are similarities between Foucault and for example, Beauvoir and Camus. But he is silent on their work. At best he is dismissive and does not engage philosophically with other thinkers.

In my article on Rorty and his account of the similarities between Dewey and Foucault I argued that there were a number of points on which they differed substantially (Marshall, 1994/5). I thought Rorty was too reductionist of both Dewey and Foucault. By reducing positions, which are really much more complex, to more simplistic notions he certainly did a disservice to Foucault. For example Rorty ran Dewey and Foucault together on the social sciences arguing that whilst Foucault also saw a dark side to the social sciences they did not differ methodologically. But Foucault did not see any continuity between the exact sciences and the social sciences and often saw ordinary discourse as being discontinuous and sometimes as being superior to the social sciences and permitting new forms of local 'theory'. Dewey on the other hand saw continuities here. I thought that Rorty was just wrong on those issues.

*P:* I am socialist, but I am not communist. I think that a post modern society, if it exists, puts several philosophers in this position. What of you?

*J:* I am neither a marxist nor a communist. A socialist?—probably, though I have been called a neoliberal! I was certainly a socialist until my late 30s, coming, as I did, from a lower middle class/working class background and of Scots ancestry. A scholarship boy, which provided access to a prestigious boarding school, I was a voracious reader, but I chose to enter the Navy as an officer cadet rather than burden my family (my father had died accidentlly when I was two years of age) any further. Thus I was independent, and fiercely so. And I needed to be, as I was a Colonial mixing with aristocratic officers during my training in Britain in the Royal Navy. My experiences in boarding school and in the military caused me also to be quite fiercely socialist in my early 20s. Given my position in the miltary this was mainly at a theoretical level. But this waned in my formal study of philosophy— neither Marx nor the Levellers were on my reading lists. (The distinguished British marxist philosopher, Roy Edgley, was at Bristol at the time, but he did not teach marxism). So I have retained intensely individualistic, sometimes anarchistic propensities, finding it difficult to join groups or to be tied by the decisions of others. Thus I am certainly, and in many respects like Foucault, a man of the left. But my political position is not represented in New Zealand politics and I did not vote in parliamentary elections for nine years.

You suggest that socialism is an outcome, in some sense of the word, for philosophers in a postmodern society. But you also query whether a postmodern society exists. I have grave doubts over the use of the term 'postmodern'. Even though I have written on it in collaboration with my close friend Michael Peters, in one sense I do not know what it is. I am much happier talking about poststructuralism and poststructuralist philosophers. One cannot read Foucault, Derrida or Lyotard, in my view and not be a person on the left. Here I would add Camus because of his notion of the absurdity of life. But had I lived in Victorian England, in the conditions described so vivedly by Charles Dickens, I would also have been on the left. So there may be nothing so special about modern times.

*P:* You and Paul Smeyers wrote a great article about history of philosophy of education. In Brazil, I translated it and my students loved it. But the end of the article is short, especially as it is concerned with Wittgenstein. Do you not think of writing more about Wittgenstein and philosophy of education? And if so what?

*J:* Paul Smeyers and I met at the 1992 Conference of The International Network of Philosophers of Education in London. Since then I have spent a considerable amout of time with Paul at Katholieke Universiteit Leuven, and he has visited the University of Auckland. The chapter that you translated was the introduction to our edited collection on Wittgenstein published by Kluwer Academic Press in 1995 (but publised initially in *Studies in Philosophy and Education*). We each contributed further chapters to the book but wanted the contributors to the book to speak for themselves on Wittgenstein and education, rather than us foreclose on some particular reading of Wittgenstein in the introduction. Hence the brevity. But this was, after all, the first book on Wittgenstein and education. There are, I believe, some historically important papers on Wittgenstein and education in that collection.

I had published my first major piece on Wittgenstein in 1985 (*Journal of Philosophy of Education*) as I had been concerned for some time by interpretations of Wittgenstein's philosophy by educationalists. (As I have also been on interpretations by educationalists of Dewey's version of scientific method). Wittgenstein was not to be assimilated into ordinary language philosophy for he was primarily concerned with ethics and culture. Michael Peters and I co-authored a new book on Wittgenstein in 1999 (Bergin & Garvey) in which we interpret him as a European, as a philosopher of culture, who is not to be seen in the British analytic tradition as a sort of continuation of Bertrand Russell. Not even the *Tractatus* is worthy of that interpretation. Part of my major contribution to this new book was to start from his remarks on the self in the *Tractatus* and the *Notebooks*, identify the mystical and metaphysical influences of Schopenhauer, and take his discussion forward into his later work on first person statements. Even though the self remains rather mysterious in Wittgenstein there is, I believe, a confluence with Foucault in that the self is not an *individuated subject*. Paul and I have planned another book on Wittgenstein, but it has gone on hold. I also have a lot of unfinished work on Wittgenstein, several potential papers, drafted when I was in Leuven as a Visiting Research Fellow in October 1997–February 1998.

*P:* What do you think about philosophy of education today? We are writing a book together, you, Michael Peters and myself. Do you think that the route which philosophy of education should take can be a 'plural way'? We have planned a book but it contains different points of view. Do you think that books would be better if they were written by one author, alone?

*J:* Not necessarily as I think that, philosophically, joint authorship can be healthy. When I was finishing my doctoral thesis, writing up some of the final chapters, Stephan Körner said: 'Whatever you write will be wrong—just make it consistently wrong'. At the time I thought this quite unhelpful but over the years I believe that he was correct, namely that philosophy must be catholic. But in philosophy of education not anything or everything goes. We cannot be totally catholic—certain procedures for imparting knowledge and certain activities which are not worthwhile educationally for example, are ruled out, and properly so. Within those parameters I support what might be called a catholic approach.

Nevertheless I have became quite impatient with British philosophy and in some respects I remain so. I believe that it lost its way with the collapse of the Richard Peters/Paul Hirst analytic programme and, in particular, it had ignored marxism, critical theory and the emerging poststructuralism. There was a harsh exclusion of what was thought not to be 'proper' philosophy. Nor was it particularly sympathetic to North American philosophy of education. Indeed there is little take up on the major revival of Dewey that is occurring now in North America. There, also, poststructuralism receives a better hearing. Impatient yes, but intolerant no.

I have no brief either for single authorship or for joint authorship. If one is fortunate to have an ex student, colleague and close friend with whom you enjoy writing, as in my case with Michael Peters for over twenty years, then this should be pursued. But we publish a lot of material on our own, or with others—colleagues, students, friends. ... With Michael and I it depends upon where each person is at a particular time and whether our work separately can be maximised by a joint publication. Of course we have diverged in our thinking and in our priorities but this need not detract from writing a book. But then trust is an important key.

*P:* In Brazil, several teachers read Marx as a philosopher of education. Do you think that it is usefull?

*J:* Marxist thought has been important in education, particular sociology of education. Here I am thinking of the work of Michael Young and Michael Apple in particular. The Australian marxist philosophers of education Kevin Harris and (the early) Michael Matthews, inspired by Bachelard and Althusser, made major contributions to philosophy of education, as has critical theory, for example, in the hands of Tom Popkewitz in the US. Tom Popewitz has recently published a book on critical thinking to which I have contributed but it is a book which attempts to rethink critical theory (1999).

I suspect that this is the problem with marxism. It would need to be radically rethought because of the vast changes that have occurred in social and cultural contexts both in time and across the world. Though Althusser, Sartre and Habermas for example, have attempted to reshape marxism in their various ways there are still vestiges of liberal humanist notions of the subject. Nor does it seem to me that in the way in which individualism has become so important in liberal thinking there seems little room for 'revolutions of the proletariat'—for it is not quite clear what this means in modern economic, if not neoliberal societies, where alienation as a concept has less bite in my view than Foucault's notion of governance, surveillance and subjected selves.

In my society 'marxist' has become a term of rhetorical abuse used in *ad hominem* attacks upon individuals. Thus a leading philosopher of education, Ivan Snook, was classified by a leading politician as a marxist. Ivan is a traditional liberal philosopher of education who comments very clearly and critically on what is happening in our education systems. I am not merely defending him against such a ridiculous suggestion but observing that no one in positions of political power will listen to marxist theorists. As the *ad hominem* attack on Ivan reveals they do not need to listen to marxism because it is part of neoliberal ideology in New Zealand that marxism is discredited. Perhaps it is different in Brazil!.

*P:* Michael and I are writing a book about Rorty. It will be published in the United States by Rowand & Littlefied. You are an author in this book, together with myself, Michael Peters, Peter McLaren, Nick Burbules, Paulo Margutti, Alberto Tosi Rodrigues, Jim Garrison and others. What will be your position on Rorty?

*J:* I am pleased to have been invited to contribute to this volume. Obviously I know several of the contributors and have also published with them—but not all. My earlier paper on Rorty will be the basis for my contribution as in reading his more recent work I am still unhappy with his vast sweeping generalisations, and his reduction of certain philosophical positions to more simplistic positions, from which he argues some general theses about philosophy. I welcomed his *Philosophy and the Mirror of Nature* but I do not quite see him as the 'legal' heir of John Dewey. Thus I am still thinking about it. Second, my way of working is that I do not know what I think until I see what I write. Foucault put it more strongly when he said that if he knew what he would write he would not have the courage to start writing a book. Writing also changes the person so that the author whilst writing undergoes and reacts, changing both his thoughts and his his self, but also the text. That may not be very helpful but it reflects my position to writing and to myself.

*P:* Finally: would you come to Brazil to teach if we had a invitation?.

*J:* Paulo, but of course. I know that my work has been available in South America for some years now, and particularly in Brazil because of your translations, but I would welcome the opportunity to meet and talk with people of similar interests.
Is there good jazz in Brazil … ?

## Acknowledgement

This interview appeared first in Portuguese.

## References

Brown, S. C. (ed.) (1975) *Philosophers Discuss Education* (London: MacMillan).

Marshall, J. D. (1985) Wittgenstein on Rules: implications for authority and discipline in education, *Journal of Philosophy of Education*, 19:1, pp. 3–11.

Marshall, J. D. (1994/95) On What We May Hope: Rorty on Dewey and Foucault, *Studies in Philosophy and Education*, 13:4, pp. 307–323.

Peters, M. & Marshall, J. D. (1999) *Wittgenstein: philosophy, postmodernism and pedagogy* (New York: Bergin and Garvey).

Popkewitz, T. S. & Fendler, L. (1999) *Critical Theories in Education: changing terrains of knowledge and politics* (New York & London: Routledge).

Smeyers, P. J. & Marshall, J. D. (1995) The Wittgensteinian Frame of Reference and Philosophy of Education at the End of the Twentieth Century in P. Smeyers and J. Marshall (eds) *Philosophy and Education: accepting Wittgenstein's challenge* (Dordrecht: Kluwer) pp. 3–35.

Smeyers, P. J. & Marshall, J. D. (1995) 'Epilogue' in Paul Smeyers and James Marshall (eds) *Philosophy and Education: accepting Wittgenstein's challenge* (Dordrecht: Kluwer) pp. 221–224.

# 16

# James D. Marshall: Philosopher of Education
# Interview with Michael A. Peters

MICHAEL A. PETERS
*University of Glasgow*

This interview was conducted by email while I was at the University of Auckland in New Zealand during the summer of 2003 (i.e., January–February). I issued Jim Marshall a series of questions that I wanted to ask and he responded on email. The interview was seen essentially as a second interview to the one with Paulo Ghiraldelli, also included in this issue.

—Michael A. Peters

*Peters:* As you said in your interview with Paulo [Ghiraldelli] you completed a PhD in identity theory with Stephan Körner at Bristol. A question about why a New Zealander fresh from the Navy would begin a thesis in an aspect of logical theory at that time?

*Marshall:* The PhD was about the identity of material objects, not personal identity. At the time I thought personal identity to be too problematic. Now I have been grappling with it through Wittgenstein and Foucault. In part I answered the rest of the question in the interview with Paulo. I left the Navy in 1963, spent nearly a year in industry (a prestigious marine instrument firm in London) and then 3 years at the University of Bristol on my BA Sp. Hons in Philosophy before I started an MA, which was to became a PhD. But at the end of my second year as an undergraduate I wrote a (voluntary) dissertation on the null class. There was a lot of logic and informal logic in the philosophy curriculum at Bristol and I was introduced to Russell's definition of the null class, in terms of those things not identical with themselves, by Andrew Harrison. I tried to argue in the dissertation that it was meaningless to talk of a thing, not being identical with itself, and that therefore Russell's definition of the null class was suspect. The external examiner, Bernard Williams, said that the dissertation was interesting and this suggested to me that I might pursue identity further. It is only recently that I have returned to the topic of identity, but now it is personal identity.

*Peters:* When did you begin to read social and political philosophy? I mean it is a long way from Russell's logic to Foucault's poststructuralism, Sartre' existentialism and de Beauvoir's novels. What have been the pivotal shifts for your thinking?

*Marshall:* Well we did philosophy of the social sciences, and political philosophy at Bristol in my undergraduate degree, with David Hirschman, Robert Kirkham and Keith Graham. I published on Hobbes in 1980. And I taught courses on the philosophy of science and social sciences for a decade or so. But it was really with the work that we did together from the late seventies for the (state) Department of Education and State Services Commission that changed me.

*Peters:* Let me ask you about education and teacher training. What was your first involvement and why education? (I know that this is the title of an early book you wrote).

*Marshall:* I became involved in the Bristol B.Ed. Degree which started in 1967 (as an outcome of the Robbins Report) and which was the major part of my teaching responsibilities at St. Mary's College, Cheltenham (now part of the University of Gloucestershire). I taught a paper on the methodologies of the sciences and social sciences, and papers on ethics and epistemology, all at year 1 level from 8/ 1967–1/1973. We also did a half paper on philosophy of education. I also had responsibilities for a group of twenty or so secondary physical education women. They were a marvellous group and after three years I believe that they had taught me how to teach. I still have friends there. In answer to your question I was being interviewed for jobs in education but not in philosophy, though I was applying for both. So I decided, at 35, to take the job offered at the University of Auckland.

*Peters:* Why did a philosopher take a job in an education department? What was your first job in NZ education and describe for us the state of NZ educational philosophy?

*Marshall:* At 35 I wanted a university job and this was the first permanent university position offered to me (though not the last). I didn't really want to come back to New Zealand but my (late wife) Bridget did. She was of course right!; and she was right about where to live, as I still live in the same house. I was employed to change or 'modernise' the teaching of philosophy of education within the then Department of Education at Auckland. The only advice that I was ever given by the then Head of the Department was that it was to be done BUT done amicably. As I never discussed that issue with him again I have always assumed that 'it' was done that way.

*Peters:* Does philosophy of education have a longer cycle of influence or impact than educational research? Is there anything meaningful that we can say about the different influences of positivist and post-positivist research in education and educational philosophy?

*Marshall:* Under the present political climate in Universities in New Zealand I would say 'No'. Hopefully in philosophy of education we have reached the nadir now. I have written extensively on the positivist influences on education in New Zealand[1] and more recently on research for our international research project based at Kathiolieke Universeitat Leuven.[2]

*Peters:* I know that you have been involved in both kinds of scholarship in education. Can you tell us when you started to engage in research (as opposed to philosophy of education)? Is it meaningful to make this distinction?

*Marshall:* I am not sure that I ever made this distinction, as research for me was always philosophical in its orientation. For example the research which we did for the State Services Commission on developing a model of decision making for public servants was always philosophical and the model which we developed, and which you taught for so many public servants, was always a philosophical model. That model—Administrative Discretionary Justice—disappeared of course in the neoliberal reforms of state institutions but I still have the teaching videos somewhere.

*Peters:* What then is the history of your empirical engagements in education and how have they affected your philosophical pursuits and interests?

*Marshall:* The decision making model, Administrative Discretionary Justice, and the models of policy making which we developed, also for the State Services Commission, turned me empirically towards policy and policy analysis. Then there was the research in Ngapuhi Land (Taitokerau) on the examination of oral Maori in the national school certificate examination and on retention of Maori in the schooling system. This research was mentioned in the House of Commons and also in New Zealand's Report to the United Nations on Indigenous Peoples (in 1991, I think). I learned a lot about Ngapuhi, about how research should be conducted with indigenous peoples, and about friendship. I wrote much more thoughtfully and carefully about indigenous people and of course Maori, after those experiences. In 2000 I organised the PESA Conference at the University of Auckland on Indigenous Peoples and Education, and edited the subsequent publication for *Educational Philosophy and Education*. There was much said in these papers about indigenous knowledge.

After reading Foucault's *Discipline and Punish* I saw how important for philosophy was the use of historical data. I also spent a lot of time in New Zealand National Archives, before publishing with my elder son Dominique, in 1997, *Discipline and Punishment in New Zealand Education*. This used a lot of historical data. In the files of the old Department of Education we found some nasty information and some marvellous (logically) letters and memos written by Clarence Beeby, our famous former Director General of Education. Unfortunately we do not seem to have recently 'discovered' Directors of Education (now Secretaries and that says something) who have equalled Beeby in intellectual rigour.

During the early 1990's I also spent considerable time in Paris working in four archives/libraries but mainly the Bibliothèque Nationale. (What magnificent buildings—i.e., the old and the new). I was the second person ever to read Foucault's submission to the Implementation Commission for Fouchet's education reforms in the 1960s. The first reader was Didier Eribon, Foucault's first biographer. Those who believe that Foucault attacked science in general should read the minutes of this commission. It should therefore be clear that I do not believe in the *autonomy* of philosophy, i.e. its independence from other forms of thinking such as science and history, and from social, cultural and political factors.

*Peters:* You have written a great deal on educational policy. Can I ask you to talk briefly about links between philosophy and policy and the significance of the former for the latter.

*Marshall:* I think that since the neoliberal and new right takeover of New Zealand culture, society and politics we have been individualised as self-interested autonomous choosers. But the autonomous chooser is an individualised notion of autonomy through economic 'choosing', and is certainly not that of Kant and the Enlightenment. In the writings of Simone de Beauvoir for example the Other is *necessary* for me to determine my own personal identity. The war is to change her further: 'History burst over me, and I dissolved into fragments. I woke to find myself scattered over the four quarters of the globe, linked by every nerve in me to each and every other individual' *(Force of Circumstances)*. De Beauvoir is right on this issue I believe and the neoliberals, on autonomous choosers, are wrong. I still think that evaluation should be educative and not merely *summative* as is the case in the approach of the Educational Review Office in New Zealand. What is the point of such evaluations?: is it to educate or merely to punish? We are very good at punishing in New Zealand—especially children, intellectuals and non-winning All Black coaches.

The neoliberal structural changes that have ensued in New Zealand make our notion of the ideal learning community difficult to resuscitate. It would need to be rethought for the changed social and political structures, which now exist in New Zealand.

*Peters:* Can we talk about education and curriculum in philosophy of education? What works best and what do you recommend? (I know you favour the close reading of a text).

*Marshall:* The curriculum for philosophy of education is in part determined by an international community of philosophers of education, the history(ies) of philosophy, the particular context in which the curriculum is sited, and the particular interests/expertises of teachers of philosophy. Thus when I was appointed to the University of Auckland, I was appointed to introduce the 'new' philosophy that was permeating Anglo-American philosophy and philosophy of education. The North American 'isms' philosophy of education had run its course in my university. In turn I was to move away to Marxist thought, and then to Wittgenstein, Foucault, poststructuralist thought, and French philosophy and education. But this had to be sited in the New Zealand context, in which the plight of Maori was very important.

As an undergraduate I was subjected to close textual reading of Kant's *Critique of Pure Reason, and* Hume's *Treatise*. This is, no doubt, a type of luxury, which we cannot afford now in education. But I do believe that we should demand the reading of primary texts, that students develop their own understandings of those texts, that they are able to write coherently about those texts, and that they do not just string together quotations from secondary sources. Of course they will need secondary sources to assist them but what is important is that they should come to their *own* independent positions. I once challenged an elder colleague as to why he held a certain position. He replied that it was because a certain person had said it. 'But why believe him?' I asked. 'Because he is a very good philosopher', was the answer. I was appalled, and no doubt showed it. The questions of meaning and justification must always be important as well as questions of what counts as an argument, and what counts as a good argument. But they also must be able to see what is concealed or excluded in texts by the enframing (Heidegger) of concepts and issues in certain ways. A critical nose is needed in this march of performativity. Also what is needed is a catholic nose and 'head'. What works best depends upon the students as much as the teacher. One must know where they are coming from, especially their philosophical background, how they react to questions, criticism and so on. There is no one answer to such issues, but I have great faith in students.

*Peters:* Does philosophy of education still have a role in education today? Do you still hold out hope for its revival and significance in the world of performativity?

*Marshall:* At times I become quite depressed by the march of performativity. Even more depressing in New Zealand is the inability to penetrate the forums and agendas, which support this march. An additional discouraging factor for New Zealand is the 'departures' of people like you to Glasgow, and of Mark Olssen and Roger Dale to England. Some great people were appointed to our group at Auckland but, for various reasons, many of them have gone. Others, like myself, have now retired and have not really been replaced and some have been made redundant. There have to be thinkers who are also actors to counter performativity. I see Ivan Snook as one of the 'soldiers' in this line of battle. I hope that he is not the last, for he like myself, is aging.

*Peters:* Who or what is the model for the philosopher and which philosophers have had the most influence upon you?

*Marshall:* I do not believe there is any one model for a philosopher. There are several models, which might be adopted or adapted at different times. But one model, which I try to follow, was given to me by my PhD supervisor at Bristol, Professor Stephan Körner. I had asked him some questions as I moved towards an end to my thesis. His answer was: 'Whatever you say in philosophy will be wrong—just make it consistently wrong'. In turn I became a catholic philosopher. That remark has permeated my advanced teaching. I want to know what people want to say in theses and dissertations. I will advise them on formulating their ideas, on argument, on literatures and on design, but I have tried not to tell people what to say or believe. Two philosophers have influenced me immensely—Wittgenstein and Foucault. My doctoral thesis was Wittgensteinian (as I came to realise) and I particularly like his account in the *Investigations* of philosophical problems. Foucault has influenced me also. His account of the human sciences is, I believe, very important, as is his approach to freedom and ethics; he is fiercely independent and a private person; finally, he has style.

*Peters:* Do you believe in the notion of discipleship?

*Marshall:* No I do not. I do however believe in friendship. I have been fortunate in my academic life of having three close friends with whom I could teach or write. Colin Lankshear was first, though I did not write with him. Then there was some chap called Michael Peters for whom writing seemed to be a pathological case. And finally Paul Smeyers. We were all different but we could get on, philosophically and personally. There may be a fourth person on the horizon.

*Peters:* Looking back over the course of your career what is the single most important thing you would have liked to do, but didn't get the opportunity?

*Marshall:* To have 'murdered' the person who 'engineered' my last appointment in the Navy.

*Peters:* Which single paper and single book do you consider your best work?

*Marshall:* My book on Foucault I guess, as the two books on Wittgenstein were done with others—Paul Smeyers and, of course, yourself. Papers or Chapters? There are quite a lot here, and I find it difficult to choose. My best paper, *technically*, might be said to be 'The Concept of Teaching', in what is now *The Journal of Philosophy of Education*, in 1975. This was essentially a reductio of the literature on the concept of teaching using their own analytic analysis methodology. After that I do not really know. My paper on the autonomous chooser is not good philosophically (i.e., technically) though I believe the notion is important. Perhaps my paper on Foucault and Austin is OK (looking at performative utterances).

*Peters:* Personally and professionally how would you like to be remembered?

*Marshall:* To be remembered? Heavens! As a radical democrat (Geoffrey Bertram's comment about us both), as a catholic philosopher of education who did not push his own barrow, as a loyal friend, as a serious person but with a wacky sense of humour (often directed at myself), as a person of wide interests, and as a private and family person. After boarding school and the Navy I did not want to be *owned* by others. Hence I have tended to draw a boundary between my/our life and my institutional and professional life. I still find it very difficult to stop in halls of residence when I attend conferences. Here my late wife Bridget was the anchor. I have also been known to like travel and of course claret, and clarity, though the former may not bring the latter. My friend Denis Phillips of Stanford once described me as one of the last Renaissance men. A former teacher at secondary school—(the late) Jack Herron at Waitaki Boys High in Oamaru—said much later than school days, and late at night, that I was the most competitive little b. ... r that he had ever taught. Another former teacher at Waitaki who was later also in the Navy with me, Doug Hall, said that even in the fourth form (14 years of age) I was the most demanding student that he had taught because I would badger away until I fully understood what he was saying. I needed to *understand* and not merely 'know'. There may be an element of truth in each of these comments for I had wide interests from understanding, to sport and to the arts, especially music. But at Waitaki a slightly older friend, Graeme (Rocky) Storey, turned my reading away from the school English curriculum of Milton and Shakespeare to Greene,

Hemingway, Steinbeck, Orwell and Lawrence, and eventually I found philosophy. Jack Herron who saw my intellectual problems in my last years at school got me to calibrate our Fletchers Trolley. It had been used for some years, disgracefully, as an early version of a skateboard in a very long and lovely wooden floored, and Oamaru limestone walled corridor. This experience was invaluable in my later understanding of science and my teaching of philosophy. In my participation in sport I achieved well though not quite at the highest levels. But in sport, if I was very competitive, I really only *enjoyed* beating my friends. I did not enjoy either playing against, or beating people or clubs whom I disliked or despised. This you well remember well, Michael, from the days when we *could* play squash together! When we were in the changing rooms I used to talk to you about a philosophical problem that I was allegedly thinking about, and once I had you thinking philosophically I had, at least, the first set.

## Notes

1. See Marshall, J. D. (1987) *Pragmatism or Positivism*, Monograph No.2 (Palmerston North, NZARE).
2. See e.g., Marshall, J. D., Peters, M. A., Irwin, F. C. (2003) (Leuven, Kathiolieke Universiteit Leuven Press).

# 17
# For Jim: My friend

KEVIN HARRIS
*Macquarie University*

In its earliest days, the *Philosophy of Education Society of Australasia* (PESA) took itself most seriously. As part of ensuring quality control it had a *Qualifications Committee* which closely vetted all applications for membership, and it had a *Conference Committee* which refereed all papers submitted for presentation at the Annual Conference, and then decided either thumbs up or thumbs down.

In 1974, through sheer accident of my place of employment, I was on both Committees, and in my role on the latter Committee I had the task of refereeing a paper submitted by one James Marshall, of the University of Auckland, for the 1975 Annual Conference.

It was a very good paper; in fact an excellent paper beautifully fitting the mould that shaped so much of what philosophy of education had become in that period. The problem for James Marshall, and me, was that PESA had decided to change the mould. PESA had declared that its 1975 Annual Conference would be themed 'Radical Critiques of Philosophy of Education', and had instructed its *Conference Committee* to accept papers only on that theme. I thus returned James Marshall's paper with a polite note to the effect that it did not fit in with the Conference theme.

Return correspondence swiftly flew the Tasman. Within days there appeared on my desk a large envelope from James Marshall, University of Auckland. Inside was the original paper, and stapled to it was a note which said, in somewhat large letters:

**What theme!**

And there we have it; two words which typify Jim Marshall: on the one hand a person too focused on serious issues to bother attending to or obeying a piddling little resolution passed by a society desperately seeking an identity; and on the other hand a philosopher who just wasn't going to be bound to a theme—any theme.

That was Jim in 1974; it still is Jim three decades later. While some bashed their professional life away hammering a favoured theme, Jim restlessly went his own way, and relentlessly followed every turn and exhausted every by-way. There was early work on 'punishment', until Dewey had to be dealt with, and then Wittgenstein had to be dealt with even more thoroughly. Dewey led to pragmatism, pragmatism had to face Foucault (Jim had to learn French), Foucault pointed to Lyotard and then more generally to Postmodernism, Postmodernism opened the door to literary philosophers, Simone de Beauvoir was engaged with (and Sartre, of course, in passing), the 'literarie' revealed a thread back to Nietzsche which was followed with typical vigor; while in passing there was serious engagement with Rorty, teacher professionalism, community, Hayek, Nozick and the whole of 'New Right Liberalism', among others and others and still yet others.

What theme? Matthew Arnold noted that 'We like to be suffered to lie comfortably in the old straw of our habits, especially of our intellectual habits, even though this straw may not be very clean or fine'. Jim Marshall never allowed philosophy of education that 'luxury', and the discipline is better, fresher and cleaner for it.

I sat with him recently on his Auckland balcony, and as he looked out over the sea (which is in small part in his blood) he mused about retiring and spending his days fishing. Don't bank on it; that isn't his theme either.

# 18
# Stone/Marshall Wedding Address

D. C. PHILLIPS

Friends and relatives of Lynda Stone and Jim Marshall—dearly beloved—we are gathered here today from the four corners of the Earth, from Auckland to Bristol and Glasgow and many points in between, to celebrate this very special occasion. We have letters and emails of congratulation from friends and colleagues, near and far, who have been delighted by the news; and a week or so ago the Pope released a letter on the nature of marriage that was, I suspect, inspired by the occasion (my hypothesis is that he heard about the pending nuptials while sitting next to Michael Peters at a conference in Italy—Michael knows everybody).

Valerie and I have known both the bride and groom for almost twenty-four years, and we were extremely touched when they chose our warm and toasty Clearlake, California retreat for the site of this ceremony. (But the good news is that it is dry heat!) We were even more excited when it was discovered that I could actually officiate, although the groom's fragile equanimity was shaken by the news.

As the bride and groom are both philosophers of education, it would be remiss of me not to stress at the outset what a truly unique day this is, not only for them personally, but also in the annals of our discipline. A poststructuralist and a post-modernist being joined together in a modernist, secular version of an ancient ritual by a postpositivist who has been appointed as Deputy Commissioner of Civil Marriages (for the day of August 16, 2004) by Governor Arnold Schwarzenegger and the State of California! What an age we live in!

It is customary for a Celebrant at a wedding to say something profound, to offer words of guidance as the bride and groom begin their life together, but as I am not a normative philosopher I was at a loss as to what to tell the happy couple. So I turned to some classic writings in our field.

Our beloved Nel Noddings (a guest here today) has written a major book on *Women and Evil*, but I realized rather quickly that it would be inappropriate to quote from it—Lynda would have her worst instincts reinforced and what is left of Jim's equanimity would completely vanish. So I next turned to the writings of Michael Peters (also blessedly with us today), where I found many stimulating and eminently quotable passages, but as I didn't understand any of them I decided to move on. I thought that the groom's writings might contain something prescient, but what leapt out at me as I browsed was his overly-long attempts to make clear (a forlorn endeavor) that while he was not a postmodernist he might, indeed, be a poststructuralist. I thought this esoteric matter was probably best left for the bride and groom to settle on their honeymoon. The bride's own writings seemed more promising; I was particularly struck by the potential of Lynda's essay on Julia Kristeva, that focuses upon a particularly grisly murder that is described in one of Kristeva's books (and which is recounted, with obvious relish, by our blushing bride). Clearly Jim is getting more than he bargained for! If I possessed the skills of the psychoanalyst I could make much of a passage that Lynda quotes from this particular book, and it is with a sense of duty that I draw it to Jim's attention, also for further discussion during the honeymoon:

> For the moment I'm in the process of transition, in the middle of a kind of tranvestism ... As I put on another language. ... I live in a state of trauma. Conscious of dreaming, I have no definable place. ... Immature Stephanie Delacour ... imagines she's left the womb! But no, like everyone else she needs a giantess to shelter, reassure, or ultimately swallow her. Ah, there we have it, our intrepid globe-trotter's fantasy. ...

So, with a sense of relief, I turned to Michel Foucault.

Foucault, of course, discusses discipline and punishment, and treats the relation between the sexes in terms of the exercise of repressive power; as he aptly puts it in his *The History of Sexuality*: 'Power is not something that is acquired, seized, or shared, something that one holds onto or allows to slip away; power is exercised from innumerable points, in the interplay of nonegalitarian and mobile relations. ... Power comes from below. ...' But Jim will learn about this soon enough!

So I decided to consult two of Lynda's favorite thinkers, John Dewey and Roman Ingarten. Once again the well was dry. (Or maybe just soggy.) I was tempted—briefly—to quote some words from Dewey's *Problems of Men*, but as this seemed to leave Lynda out of the picture I decided to move on. In desperation I turned to an author with Californian connections—Robert Louis Stevenson (who wrote much of *Treasure Island* while living on top of the mountain at the head of Napa Valley, the one the wedding guests drove around after leaving Calistoga on the way to Clearlake). Stevenson once wrote that 'In marriage, a man becomes slack and selfish, and undergoes a fatty degeneration of his moral being'. Valerie said that this applied to me, but she doubted whether it fitted Jim. I think the opposite.

Then, while browsing through the ancients, I came across some words of Aristotle (not the Stagirite, but Onassis) which certainly apply to Valerie but might conceivably apply to Lynda: 'If women didn't exist, all the money in the world would have no meaning'. Sensitively, I judged this as problematic given the abysmal exchange rate between the New Zealand and US dollars. Finally I consulted Scripture, and found a passage that seemed appropriate for the union of two scholars who are entering a commuting relationship; in the Book of Daniel it is written that 'Many shall rush to and fro, and knowledge shall be increased'.

At this stage I decided to abandon my search for words of wisdom, and instead requested that the bride and groom prepare something that they could share with each other, in front of us today, before exchanging their official Californian wedding vows. ...

# 19
# Fragments of Life before Foucault

COLIN LANKSHEAR

It is now 30 years (plus a bit) since Jim Marshall arrived at Auckland University from England (in 1973). His brief was to establish philosophy of education along contemporary lines as a strong presence within the Education Department's undergraduate and graduate programs, housed within the Faculty of Arts. Previously, as in many other places, philosophy of education had been taught within the Department as a content-based study of ideas and principles associated with individual philosophers, 'movements' or 'schools', from Plato to Progressivism.

Jim had been trained as an analytical philosopher within a full-fledged Philosophy department. He had strong interests in diverse fields of philosophy—notably philosophy of mind, epistemology, philosophy of science, ethics, political philosophy, and philosophy of language. More specifically and, for some time, 'relevantly', so far as doing philosophy within a university Department of Education was concerned, he was well-versed in analytical philosophy of education along the lines developed by Richard Peters and colleagues, based on a particular reading of Wittgenstein.

By 1976 (when I began at Auckland) Jim had established educational philosophy courses in the analytic mode at all levels from the first year undergraduate Foundations of Education paper—whose enrollments exceeded 500 students each year—to the Master of Arts in Education. The offerings were diverse and, relative to the powerful hegemony established on the 'ed. psych.' side of the Department, well-subscribed. They were intellectually demanding programs. While their focus was always on issues and problems grounded in the theory and practice of education, the orientation to these was unmistakably philosophical in a capital 'P' sense. As a quite typical example, an undergraduate course concerned with the nature of educational theory from the standpoint of logics of inquiry drew on competing positions within the philosophy of science, including close examination of work by people like Peter Medewar and Karl Popper. Elsewhere, students wrestled with key ideas from the philosophy of Hobbes and Locke to get a handle on the multiple ways in which questions of power and competing metaphysics enter educational inquiry and decision-making.

At this early stage Jim's trademark interests, and his defining identity as a published philosopher of education, were already strongly associated with the study of a set of political-ethical themes coalescing around the concepts of authority, punishment, and discipline. At the time these were galvanised by a theory of personhood grounded in fairly standard conceptions of reason and rationality quite firmly grounded in Enlightenment tenets.

This is the period—from 1976 until around 1982—when I worked most closely with Jim. It was an interesting and challenging time to be a philosopher of education—particularly given what was to happen to the study of Education generally, and Philosophy of Education specifically in many Australasian universities from the late 1980s. As is well known, following amalgamation with Colleges of Education, and the transformation of many university departments and schools of Education from centres of academic educational inquiry into Faculties of Teacher Education, spaces for philosophical inquiry into educational issues as a bona fide teaching and learning focus rapidly diminished. Philosophy of Education was widely consigned to playing bit parts within programs that seemed to become increasingly 'functionalist' by the day, in accordance with state and federal government policy directives.

The period prior to this, however, was rich and complex, and Jim's own work and being as an educational philosopher reflected this. On the night I arrived by motorcycle from the South Island to be a house guest at Chez Marshall until I found a place to rent, Jim and I fell into conversation around Peter Strawson's argument about the possibility or otherwise of a non-solipsistic consciousness. In his trademark manner, he gave me more than enough space to run a line of argument. (He is one of the most patient and sympathetic listeners one could expect to meet on a month's march.) The 'new recruit' to his first academic job was eager to try and make a good impression from the outset on his immediate 'boss'. It was not to be. Horribly self-conscious, and digging myself deeper and deeper into a morass of contradictions by the second, I followed the looks on Jim's face to their logical conclusion. 'I'm not doing very well, am I?', I volunteered from the depths of embarrassment. 'No', said Jim, 'you aren't. Would you like to start again?' It went a little better the second time, and it was immediately apparent that Jim would be a philosophical colleague whose interest was in working collaboratively to arrive at more cogent views and not in scoring cheap points or, indeed, in scoring points at all.

There was plenty of this kind of thing. We shared long dialogues about Bertrand Russell's philosophy of language whilst waiting for fish to bite on the baited lines we dangled over the side of his aluminum dinghy on weekends and occasional 'non teaching' days. Endless walks along the beaches at Rothesay Bay and Brown's Bay would focus on the conditions of personhood, or on whether or not it was a necessary condition for calling something 'punishment' that a rule have been breached and, if so (or not) what *kind* of rule is involved?

In a subsequent work on punishment published twenty years after those walks on the beach, Jim restates the kinds of issues that were at stake as we idled through the sand.

> [P]unishment in this model is for the breaking of a rule, but it is not obvious that this occurs in all cases of the punishment of the young for often a rule is not breached although it may nearly be breached, or the child has a number of close approximations which are accumulated and

result in a punishment. The question of socks up or down, or the colour of a jersey might fall under the first category, and an accumulation of rudeness or insubordination under the second category. These involve 'tryings on' or the testing of the waters for both students and teachers. And if a punishment ensues it may not be because the rule has been defined in practice, but because of something about the student that needs 'correction'. (Marshall & Marshall, 1997, pp. 27–28)

Then, as now, Jim saw philosophy of education as accountable ultimately to improved educational *practice*, although not in any crude functional sense. Rather, I mean that he has always and consistently addressed his philosophical analysis and critique to tangible, identifiable issues and concerns in everyday educational theory and practice (from our educational 'worlds' as teachers, parents/guardians, lay folk, researchers, etc.).

A typical example can be found in the way Jim took up the submission made by the New Zealand Employers' Federation following publication (in 1977) of the report of the ministerial committee established in 1976 to review health and social education. The Federation maintained that New Zealand schools were not sufficiently concerned with developing the kinds of skills, knowledge, understanding and attitudes that fit students for the world of work (Marshall, 1983, p. 51). The Federation claimed, among other things, that employers 'do not need nor do they seek potential employees with only the highest possible levels of academic attainment and intellectual development'. Yet 'the general orientation of both primary and secondary schools' paralleled the 'unfortunate assumption' of the ministerial committee that 'the world of work seeks greater and greater levels of intellectual development as evidenced by academic performance'. Since most school leavers will not go on to pursue academic careers, the Federation maintained that schools would need to provide 'pre-vocational training in order [for students] to enter the workforce directly from secondary school without the stigma of being regarded as a drop out' (New Zealand Employers' Federation cited ibid.).

Jim's response, in a text pitched at undergraduate Education students and members of the public seeking to develop informed views on the key educational debate of the day, harnessed logical critique to conceptual analysis with clarity and force. Thus:

Even if we accept that schools in New Zealand do have this implied narrow academic specialization, why couldn't the Federation's ... point [about the need for pre-vocational training] be met by some agency outside of the school as we know it. Particular industries for example might provide their own bridging training from school to work.

We might agree then with the Employers' Federation about bridging training but not agree with them that this should happen in schools. This position can be supported by arguments [that] stem from certain beliefs about what schools are for—schools are there to *educate* people, not to train them, not to indoctrinate them into certain beliefs or attitudes, and not to be mere child care centres. Dickens' Salem House and Dotheboys

Hall were schools but we balk at calling what went on in them …
education. (ibid., pp. 51–52)

These and similar arguments and engagements undertaken in the role of an academic seeking to contribute to debates that were not solely or, in some cases, even
primarily academic were also integral to a further endeavour that *was* inherently
academic. The subtitle to the book from which these examples have been taken—
*What is Education?*—is 'an introduction to the philosophy of education'. At this
time a growing number of Australasian philosophers of education were actively
contesting the discursive grip the members of the 'London School' held on the field
in the English speaking world outside of the US. In Australia a critical mass of
dissent was emerging around a marxist perspective, initially associated with Kevin
Harris, Jim Walker, Robert Mackie and Michael Matthews among others. While
sympathetic to many of the ideas and criticisms being advanced by these philosophers, as well as to other positions being worked out at the time (like the materi-
alist pragmatism of Jim Walker and Colin Evers), Jim had a line of his own to work
out. As always, however, his main interest was in helping to keep debates alive and
multiple. This larger interest in maximizing opportunities for dissenting positions
to be voiced put Jim in solidarity with various colleagues who held positions in
educational philosophy that nonetheless differed substantively from his own. Establishing the journal we called *Access* in the early 1980s was one direct result of this
interest and the spirit that drove it.

From 1979 onwards, Jim became increasingly convinced—and we talked about
it a lot—that the range of academic journals dedicated principally to publishing
work in philosophy of education was too narrow. Harris' book *Education and
Knowledge* (1979) documented concrete examples of difficulties facing those working to develop marxist philosophy of education to get articles published in leading
journals serving the field. Walker's trenchant critique of analytic philosophy of
education, *The Evolution of the APE*, which Jim and I both regarded very highly,
could not get itself published. In our everyday conversations we began talking
about the need for a new journal.

In part the kind of journal we thought was needed was one that would welcome
critical perspectives in philosophy of education and kindred areas of inquiry. At the
same time we wanted a journal that would be accessible to anyone who wanted to
buy it and that would not require a mortgage to get it started and to maintain it.
We wanted a journal that was independent of commercial publisher policies and
bottom lines.

The result was the journal *Access*, born in 1982 and still alive. It retailed at NZ
$5 per year for 2 issues. The opening paper in the inaugural issue was Jim Walker's
*The Evolution of the APE*. In those days *Access* resembled a 'zine' much more than
a 'carfax'. It was handmade in the full sense of the word. Carefully typed text was
photocopied back to back and collated by hand. The cover was cut from sheets of
yellow card using a guillotine. When the pages had been assembled they were
stapled between the covers and a strip of heavy duty black binding tape was
wrapped by hand across the spine and onto the front and back covers. Twice a year

anybody passing Jim's office was likely to find him during lunchtimes and before and after the working day, assembling *Access*, fixing labels to envelopes, and mailing them out to a growing list of subscribers. The philosopher was working on his praxis. And by the time he had finished doing the bulk of the production line work *Access* was ready to go up market in terms of its presentation, but still at a friendly price.

Many early career academics got a start in *Access*, just as many more got a sound start working with Jim as postgraduate students or, like myself, in their first job. Jim has always been there for those who are starting out. During the period when I worked most closely with him I was always impressed with how he consistently found ways to bring his own intellectual interests and perspectives into productive conversation with those of the colleagues he was mentoring. The kind of depth and breadth of collegiality he developed with these colleagues was exemplary. And it went both ways.

One day, not so long after the birth of *Access*, our mutual colleague Eric Braithwaite handed Jim a copy of Foucault's *Discipline and Punish*, which Eric had just received from a publisher. 'Take a look at this', said Eric. 'It looks like it is in your kind of area. You might find it interesting'.

The rest we know.

## References

Harris, K. (1979) *Education and Knowledge* (London: Routledge).

Marshall, J. (1983) *What is Education?: An introduction to the philosophy of education* 2nd edn. (Palmerston North: Dunmore Press).

Marshall, J. and Marshall, D. (1997) *Discipline and Punishment in New Zealand Education* (Palmerston North: The Dunmore Press).

# 20
# Festschrift Reply

In replying to my festschrift (*Educational Philosophy and Theory*, 37(3), 2005) I was initially uncertain as to what I should say to those friends and colleagues who have contributed, and even unsure as to whether I should reply at all. Should I respond to those 'damned lies' and set the historical and biographical record straight, whatever that might mean? Should I engage philosophically with the authors of the first part of the book (Chapter 1 to 13)? Instead I have decided to let the 'damned lies' rest (except for Kevin Harris!). As to the second section I am reluct-ant to engage with the analyses of my work and the ideas for possible extensions of it because of two main reasons. I was concerned that the combined events of retirement from full time university employment and the appearance of a festschrift might be seen as defensively heralding or confirming *retirement*. If that might have looked to be the case for two or three years it is not so now. Rather like a camel crossing a desert and reaching an oasis I am no longer using up my carried and stored water resources but drinking afresh. The second reason follows from the first. I hope, in confirming that I have not retired from writing, and not engaging with particular arguments, that it is an appropriate response to the festschrift to share the new water from the oasis with those colleagues who contributed, but who mainly had to drink from the old 'stored' resources.

Space precludes me from mentioning in detail everyone's contributions. Comments by some commentators require my attention. Others have attempted to extend my ideas (Nick Burbules and Richard Smith, Nesta Devine and Ruth Irwin, Bruce Haynes, Felicity Haynes, Chris Mayo, Paul Smeyers, Paul Standish) – good luck.

So; 'Thank you all'.

*The New Projects*

Over the last two years I have been developing and working on three new projects. For brevity I will entitle these as follows: (1) Philosophy and the French Liberal Humanists; (2) The Foucault Rewriting Project, and (3) The Autonomy of Philosophy. Projects (1) and (2) are intertwined, whereas (3) might be thought of as an outcome of the other two. There are no logical or temporal priorities in my thinking attached to the numbering. A fourth project which I have not abandoned is the ongoing critique of 'modern' western education. I will discuss each of these projects individually as to where they are stand now and possible lines of development.

I have said that projects (1) and (2) are closely intertwined. I taught a final year undergraduate paper at the University of Auckland in the late 1970's on the 1968 student/workers revolution in France. My lasting memories of this course were:

*Time's* account and explanation of the events of May '68, seemed so wrong, and that, I did not know much about French intellectual life, especially post-WW II. In 1982 my late colleague Eric Braithwaite passed me a translated copy of Foucault's *Discipline and Punish*. Reading that was a turning point in my philosophical life.

### Philosophy and the French Humanists

This project's starting point was my reading of French philosophy post WWII so that I could locate Foucault in his philosophical and cultural milieu. But no one classification of Foucault seemed to fit as did any one interpretation of his work. Reading Didier Eribon's biography of Foucault (transl. 1991) was important here as he, as a Frenchman, was able to situate Foucault into French intellectual life, in different ways from commentators writing in English.[1] According to Eribon Foucault talked of the terrorism of *Les Temps Modernes*, of which Jean-Paul Sartre, Maurice Merleau-Ponty and Simone de Beauvoir, leading liberal humanists, were directors. But, strangely to Western philosophical 'eyes', he did not seem to engage with those philosophers. I have begun to read, reread, and write more about these philosophers. But this has taken me back to Henri Bergson who had so much influence upon 20th century French philosophy. Bergson stressed the importance and priority of self-knowledge over analytic knowledge, or knowledge of the self obtained through the (analytic) human sciences. He was the earliest critic of Comptean positivism.

The book which I am planning, and much material has been written already, locates Foucault (and possibly Derrida) in opposition to these liberal humanists, yet identifies where their ideas and work intertwine or are parallel. For example there are similarities between Foucault and Beauvoir (who was influenced strongly by Bergson) on the notion of a philosophy of lived experience as being more important in philosophy than the construction of abstract general systems.[2] They do however give different accounts of experience.

A philosophy of lived experience is important educationally. When we hear so much in education about locating education more firmly in experience as opposed to applying educational theory(ies) to educational situations, then her work can be seen as educationally important. Beauvoir's philosophy of lived experience challenges abstract general theories, and her earlier work shows how this can be done.[3]

### The Foucault Rewriting Project

At present I have written an Introduction, and Chapters One and Two which may become an extended rewrite of my 1996 book, *Michel Foucault: personal autonomy and education*. At the time of writing it is under discussion with the Publishers (Kluwer, now Springer). I have taken seriously two themes from Foucault as central to my understanding and more recent writing on him. These are the positions: (1) that there was a close link between his personal life and his works, and (2), that philosophy should evolve from personal lived experience and was not to be concerned with constructing abstract philosophical systems.

This of course runs together two 'principles' which I remember from Year I philosophy, namely not to confuse the philosopher with his(sic) philosophy, and to understand particular moral dilemmas as examples of wider (and abstract) ethical systems in conflict, even though he latter also claimed not to help in the former. Foucault is clearly 'wrong'!

The chapters in my book on liberal education and autonomy are dated. Here I see ways forward in the papers by Nesta Devine and Ruth Irwin, and Mark Olssen. And something more needs to be said about persons and their autonomy in the age of technology (Bert Lambeir). The structure of the book was critiqued by Kenneth Wain, to whom I replied, and by John Drummond, to whom I did not reply because, whilst I knew what I had done, I didn't know why. It just *felt* right. Lynda Stone however has explained to us what I had done. (If she has told me what I did, it doesn't follow that she will tell me what to do in the future!).

*The Autonomy of Philosophy Project*
The title of this book will carry the term 'anti-foundational' in its title. Michael Peters talks of me in terms not merely of being anti – but of revolt. Robert Shaw recounted some of the latter. Others, Paul Smeyers for example, identify my oscillations between being an anti-foundationalist in Wittgenstein's sense, and being a Foucauldean. This is correct of course but what follows? Should I declare myself? This had become a problem for me. However after reading Foucault's account of *problematisation* (in his last interview in 1984 with Paul Rabinow) and Henri Bergson, I am convinced that what is important is a full statement of the problem (e.g., as in Foucault), and then and only then does the question of how to react philosophically arise. In other words I am suggesting a strong sense of autonomy for philosophers, in that they should not feel the necessity for constructing, or being constrained by, abstract philosophical systems.

But what of the autonomy of philosophy itself? Clearly in its relationships to other disciplines or ways of thinking I do not see philosophy as being foundational. Nor do I see it as being above (at a meta-level) or divorced from other ways of expression such as literature, drama, poetry, the performing arts etc. But I do not follow Rorty. My concern as a teacher is with the understanding of ideas (Tina Besley and Colin Lankshear identify this concern – see also the interviews). Philosophy may not be as effective, in this respect, as other art forms. For example, I saw a new production of Camus' 'Caligula' in London in May 2003. I believe that the drama 'Caligula' is at least as *effective* for grasping the evil of the use of unbridled power than formal philosophical arguments. As I indicate in the interviews I acquired my initial philosophical position and understanding of philosophical ideas through literature not normally deemed philosophical, yet I was attempting to read philosophy (including Russell's *The Problems of Philosophy*).

My writing here is progressing slowly but I have been using philosophy and literature, and the alleged divorce between them, in several recent papers. A larger paper on 'Philosophy as Literature' is under consideration.

*Project 4*
I will continue to use philosophy to critique educational policy, theories, ideas, and practices. These concerns are identified by many if not most of the contributors. In New Zealand Ivan Snook has been exemplary in these critiques, communicating

very well with teachers and lay people. My lesser contribution to these critiques has been mainly philosophical, though Robert Shaw and Michael Peters identify a very interesting and important (to me anyway) period of work in education and in my life. I am using one of those projects in a paper to be presented at PESA's 2005 Conference in Hong Kong, in November. This is a paper which uses Simone de Beauvoir's views on the self and her ethical position (vis-à-vis epistemology) to critique the notion of *accountability* which is embedded in modern (neo-liberal) western education systems.

Also I have returned to a topic first discussed in a paper published in 1975 – teaching and learning. This will appear in *Educational Philosophy and Theory*. It returns to my critique of philosophy of education's discussion of teaching and learning and the improper use of Ryle's task/achievement distinction in those distinctions. Using Ryle's distinction again, and with John Kleinig's very helpful diagrammatic exposition of my 1975 arguments, I argue that teaching is no longer a task verb and has become an achievement verb. Expressed bleakly I argue against the notion that one doesn't teach unless the student has acquired increased value.

Finally I note Denis Phillip's contribution. Denis is a magician. This I know because he confused my younger son for years. It seems that Denis has confused his paper's audience, sending instead the paper designed for the Annual Convention of the Magician's society.

JIM MARSHALL

## Notes

1. Though see James Miller, *The Passion of Michel Foucult* (1993), and David Macey, *Michel Foucault* (1993). Neither of these was available when I wrote my book on Foucault *Michel Foucault: personal autonomy and education* (Dordrecht: Kluwer, 1996). I have drawn on these two biographies in my plans to rewrite the 1996 book.
2. On Beauvoir and a philosophy of lived experience see my forthcoming paper in *Educational Theory, Simone de Beauvoir: the philosophy of lived experience*, On Foucault see his 'How an Experience-Book is Born', *Remarks on Marx* (New York: Semiotete, 1991), Chapter Two.
3. See her collection of short stories *When Things of the Spirit Come First* (1982). See forthcoming my 'Simone de Beauvoir: the philosophy of lived experience,' *Educational Theory*.

# Notes on Contributors

**Tina Besley** is a New Zealander who lectures in Educational Studies at the University of Glasgow, Scotland, UK. She has degrees in counselling and education and has been a secondary school teacher and a school counsellor. Tina's research interests include: youth issues, in particular notions of self and identity and contemporary problems; school counselling; educational policy; educational philosophy; and the work of Michel Foucault and poststructuralism.

**Nicholas Burbules** is Grayce Wicall Gauthier Professor in the Department of Educational Policy Studies at the University of Illinois, Urbana/Champaign and Editor of *Educational Theory*.

**Nesta Devine** is a senior lecturer in education at the University of Waikato, where she specializes in education policy and secondary teacher education. Nesta taught for many years in secondary schools, studied education philosophy with Jim Marshall at the University of Auckland, and completed her Ph.D. on 'Public choice theory' in 2001. She has recently published (2004) *Education and Public Choice: A critical account of the invisible hand in education* (Praeger).

**Paulo Ghiraldelli Jr.** is a Philosopher of Education at the Universidade Católica de S. Paulo and director of the Centro de Estudos em Filosofia Americana (www.cefa.org.br). He is a Scholar of the Pragmatism Archive of Oklahoma State University (www.pragmatism.org), editor of Contemporary Pragmatism (US and Europe, Rodolpi) and the author, co-author and editor of numerous works on philosophy of education.

**Kevin Harris** is Emeritus Professor of Education at Macquarie University, Australia; and a Fellow of the Philosophy of Education Society of Australasia. He has published four books and numerous articles in the field of Philosophy of Education, and remains active in the area.

**Bruce Haynes** retired from the School of Education, Edith Cowan University and now is Secretary/Treasurer of the Philosophy of Education Society of Australasia, P.O. Box 1018, Claremont, Western Australia 6910. An earlier version of this paper was presented to the International Network of Philosophers of Education Conference, Oslo, Norway in August 2002.

**Felicity Haynes** teaches in the Graduate School of Education in The University of Western Australia and is author of (1998) The Ethical School (Routledge) and co-editor (2001) of Unseen Genders (Peter Lang). Her interests lie in applied ethics, aesthetic judgement, metaphor, evolutionary epistemology, critical and creative thinking, and Philosophy for Children.

**Ruth Irwin** comes from New Zealand and is presently at the University of Glasgow. She just finished a Doctorate on Heidegger, philosophy of the environment, and philosophy of education. Her other theoretical interests include Nietzsche, Guattari, Deleuze and Gregory Bateson.

**Bert Lambeir** holds the position of post-doctoral research fellow at the centre for philosophy of education (KU Leuven, Belgium), having written a Ph.D. on 'The Educational Cyberspace Affaire: A philosophical reading of the relevance of information and communications technology for educational theory.' His work is still focused on the relationship between ICT and education, and is situated within the Wittgensteinian tradition, though it also takes up continental philosophical insights.

**Colin Lankshear** is a freelance educational researcher and writer based as a permanent resident in Mexico. He is also Professor of Literacy and New Technologies at James Cook University, Australia, and an Adjunct Professor at Central Queensland University, Australia.

**Cris Mayo** is a professor in the Department of Educational Policy Studies and the Gender and Women's Studies Program at the University of Illinois at Urbana-Champaign. Her areas of research include gender and sexuality studies, philosophy of education, and multicultural theory.

**Mark Olssen** is Professor of Political Theory and Education, in the Department of Political, International and Policy Studies, University of Surrey. He is the author of many books and articles in New Zealand. More recently (1999) he wrote *Michel Foucault: Materialism and education* (New York, Bergin and Garvey). He has published articles in Britain in the *Journal of Education Policy, Policy Futures in Education, The British Journal of Educational Studies, Educational Psychology, The British Journal of the Sociology of Education,* and *Educational Philosophy and Theory.* He is a co-editor (2003) with Michael Peters and Colin Lankshear of two collections: *Critical Theory and the Human Condition: Founders and praxis* (New York, Peter Lang), and *Futures of Critical Theory: Dreams of difference* (New York, Rowman and Littlefield). Released in 2004 was a major book (with John Codd and Anne-Marie O'Neill) from Sage, titled *Education Policy: Globalisation, citizenship, democracy,* and an edited volume *Culture and Learning: Access and opportunity in the classroom.*

**Michael A. Peters** is Professor of Education at the University of Glasgow (UK) and holds posts as Adjunct Professor of Education at the University of Auckland and Adjunct Professor of Communication Studies at the Auckland University of Technology (NZ). He is Director of the (online) Doctoral Programme in Education at the University of Glasgow. He is executive editor of Educational Philosophy and Theory (Blackwells) and co-editor of two international online-only journals, Policy Futures in Education and E-Learning (Triangle Journals). He has research interests in educational theory and policy, and in contemporary philosophy.

**D. C. Phillips** is Professor of Education and, by courtesy, Professor of Philosophy, at Stanford University, California, USA. He is the author of numerous essays and author or co-author or editor of eleven books, the most recent of which are Post-positivism and Educational Research (with N. Burbules) and The Expanded Social Scientist's Bestiary (both with Rowman and Littlefield, 2000). Currently he has been working on a series of essays on philosophical issues in educational research.

**Robert Shaw** is a senior lecturer in business ethics at the Open Polytechnic of New Zealand. For 15 years he managed research and development projects in New

Zealand's Ministry/Department of Education. His current research interests include Heidegger's concept of truth and pedagogy.

**Paul Smeyers** is Professor at K. U. Leuven (Belgium) where he teaches philosophy of education and qualitative research methods at the Faculty of Psychology and Educational Sciences. He published extensively on Wittgenstein, Anglo-Saxon philosophy of education, postmodernism and on the nature of educational research. He heads the research community Philosophy and History of the Discipline of Education: Evaluation and evolution of the criteria for scientific research, which was established by The National Fund for Scientific Research—Flanders, Belgium (Fonds voor Wetenschappelijk Onderzoek—Vlaanderen) in 1999 involving 15 centres world-wide.

**Richard Smith** is Professor of Education and Director of Combined Degrees at the University of Durham, UK, and editor of the new journal *Ethics and Education.*

**Paul Standish** is Professor of Educational Studies at the University of Sheffield, UK. His recent books, in various collaborations with Nigel Blake, Paul Smeyers and Richard Smith, include *Thinking Again: Education After Postmodernism* (1998), *Education in an Age of Nihilism* (2000) and *The Blackwell Guides to the Philosophy of Education* (2003). He is Editor of the *Journal of Philosophy of Education* and Co-Editor of the online *Encyclopaedia of Philosophy of Education.*

**Lynda Stone** is Professor, Philosophy of Education, at the University of North Carolina at Chapel Hill, USA. She is interested in educational change from a range of social theories that include particular feminisms and poststructuralist views. Her recent work attends to ethics as basic for reform of society and schooling that the more narrow focus on knowledge and achievement has not brought to fruition. She publishes and presents internationally.

# Index